TREKKING IN THE KARAKORAM

PAKISTAN: K2, SNOW LAKE, GONDOGORO LA AND NANGA PARBAT

by Bart Jordans

JUNIPER HOUSE, MURLEY MOSS,
OXENHOLME ROAD, KENDAL, CUMBRIA LA9 7RL
www.cicerone.co.uk

First edition 2024
ISBN: 978 1 78631 056 9

Printed in Singapore by KHL Printing on responsibly sourced paper.
A catalogue record for this book is available from the British Library.
All photographs are by the author unless otherwise stated.
Bird sketches reproduced with the kind permission of Z B Mirza.

Route mapping by Lovell Johns www.lovelljohns.com
Contains OpenStreetMap.org data © OpenStreetMap contributors, CC-BY-SA. NASA relief data courtesy of ESRI

To the lovely mountain people of Pakistan, to all climbers and explorers who have died amongst the great peaks of the Karakoram, in memory of my friend and writing guru Kev Reynolds, 'a man of the mountains and a mountain of a man' and finally to my own two explorers – Laura and Max – for letting me go guiding endless adventures.

Updates to this guide

While every effort is made by our authors to ensure the accuracy of guidebooks as they go to print, changes can occur during the lifetime of an edition. Any updates that we know of for this guide will be on the Cicerone website (www.cicerone.co.uk/1056/updates), so please check before planning your trip. We also advise that you check information about such things as transport, accommodation and shops locally. Even rights of way can be altered over time. We are always grateful for information about any discrepancies between a guidebook and the facts on the ground, sent by email to updates@cicerone.co.uk or by post to Cicerone, Juniper House, Murley Moss, Oxenholme Road, Kendal, LA9 7RL.

Register your book: To sign up to receive free updates, special offers and GPX files where available, create a Cicerone account and register your purchase via the 'My Account' tab at www.cicerone.co.uk.

Front cover: K2 from Concordia

CONTENTS

Map Key 6
Route summary tables 8–11
Preface 13

INTRODUCTION 15
The thrill of the Gilgit-Baltistan areas 15

Preparations and practicalities 18
Climate and trekking seasons 18
Visas 19
Access and permits 20
Trek operators 20
Cost of trekking in Pakistan 20
Getting to Pakistan 21
Getting around in Pakistan 22
The trek access points: Gilgit and Skardu 25
Accommodation 28
Food and drink 30
Equipment 31
Maps 33
Money 34
Language and dialect in the Gilgit-Baltistan areas 35
Customs 35
Safety 37
Medical considerations and emergencies 39
Insurance 42
High-altitude problems 42
Using this guide 47

All about the Karakoram 52
People and population 52
Gilgit 53
Skardu and Baltistan 54
Religion in the Gilgit-Baltistan areas 57
Culture and architecture 58
Timeline of exploring and climbing history in the Gilgit-Baltistan areas 60
Pakistani high-altitude climbers and porters 63
Other adventure activities 66

The landscape of the Karakoram . . . 66
Geology . . . 67
Glaciers . . . 69
Rivers . . . 70
Mining . . . 72
National Parks in the Gilgit-Baltistan areas . . . 72
Plantlife . . . 77
Wildlife . . . 79
Birdlife . . . 84

THE TREKS . . . 87
Getting to Askole – the starting point for the treks . . . 88
Askole – gateway to the Karakoram . . . 90

Trek 1	**Snow Lake and the Biafo and Hispar Glaciers**	94
Day 1	Askole to Namla via Kesar's Polo Ground	99
Day 2	Namla to Mango	102
Day 3	Mango to Baintha	104
Day 4	Baintha to Napina	108
Day 5	Napina to Sim Gang	112
Day 6	Sim Gang to Hispar La via Snow Lake	115
Day 7	Hispar La to Khani Basa (Baktur Baig)	118
Day 8	Khani Basa (Baktur Baig) to Jutmal	121
Day 9	Jutmal to Shikam Baris or to camp before Pumari Chhish Glacier	123
Day 10	Pumari Chhish Glacier camp to Bitenmal	127
Day 11	Bitenmal to Falalinghish	129
Day 12	To Hispar village and beyond	132

Trek 2	**K2 Base Camp Trek**	136
Day 1	Askole to Joila	140
Day 2	Joila to Paiju	145
Day 3	Paiju to Hoborse	150
Day 4	Hoborse to Urdukas	155
Day 5	Urdukas to Gore 2	158
Day 6	Gore 2 to Concordia	162
Day 7	Excursion from Concordia	169
Day 8	Concordia to Gore 1	174
Day 9	Gore 1 to Hoborse	176
Day 10	Hoborse to Paiju	178
Day 11	Paiju to Joila	180
Day 12	Joila to Askole	182

Trek 3 **Gondogoro La via Concordia** . . . 183
Day 8 Concordia to Ali Camp . . . 187
Day 9 Ali Camp crossing the Gondogoro La to Huisprung. . . . 189
Day 10 Huisprung to Dalsan . . . 194
Day 11 Dalsan to Saitcho . . . 196
Day 12 Saitcho to Hushe. . . . 198

Nanga Parbat treks . . . 202

Trek 4 **Fairy Meadows and Rakhiot Base Camp trek** . . . 210
Day 1 Tato to Fairy Meadows . . . 212
Day 2 Fairy Meadows to Beyal via Base Camp . . . 213
Day 3 Beyal to Tato and transport to Rakhiot Bridge . . . 215

Trek 5 **Trek to Diamir Face or West Face of Nanga Parbat** . . . 218

Appendix A Useful contacts. . . . 225
Appendix B Agents in Pakistan and abroad . . . 226
Appendix C English to Urdu glossary . . . 227
Appendix D Further reading. . . . 228
Acknowledgements . . . 232

Note on mapping

The route maps in this guide are derived from publicly available data, databases and crowd-sourced data. As such they have not been through the detailed checking procedures that would generally be applied to a published map from an official mapping agency. However, we have reviewed them closely in the light of local knowledge as part of the preparation of this guide.

Symbols used on route maps

route
alternative route
start point
finish point
start/finish point
route direction
glacier
woodland
urban areas
regional border
international border
disputed border
track
vehicle track
tarmac road
airport
peak
pass
viewpoint
other feature
bridge
camp
building
helipad

Relief in metres

Relief in metres
8400–8800
8000–8400
7600–8000
7200–7600
6800–7200
6400–6800
6000–6400
5600–6000
5200–5600
4800–5200
4400–4800
4000–4400
3600–4000
3200–3600
2800–3200
2400–2800
2000–2400
1600–2000
1200–1600
800–1200
400–800
0–400

SCALE: 1:100,000

0 kilometres 1 2

0 miles 1

Contour lines are drawn at 50m intervals and highlighted at 200m intervals.

GPX files for all routes can be downloaded free at www.cicerone.co.uk/1056/GPX.

Mountain safety

Every mountain walk has its dangers, and those described in this guidebook are no exception. All who walk or climb in the mountains should recognise this and take responsibility for themselves and their companions along the way. The author and publisher have made every effort to ensure that the information contained in this guide was correct when it went to press, but, except for any liability that cannot be excluded by law, they cannot accept responsibility for any loss, injury or inconvenience sustained by any person using this book.

International distress signal *(emergency only)*
Six blasts on a whistle (and flashes with a torch after dark) spaced evenly for one minute, followed by a minute's pause. Repeat until an answer is received. The response is three signals per minute followed by a minute's pause.

Helicopter rescue
The following signals are used to communicate with a helicopter:

Help needed: raise both arms above head to form a 'Y'

Help not needed: raise one arm above head, extend other arm downward

Mountain rescue can be very expensive – be adequately insured.

ROUTE SUMMARY TABLES

Note: total days excludes rest/acclimatisation days.

Snow Lake and the Biafo and Hispar Glaciers

Day	Start	Time	Distance	Ascent	Descent	Finish altitude	Sleeping altitude difference	Page
1	Askole	5–7hr	13.9km	540m	205m	3380m	+335m	99
2	Namla	4–6hr	6.6km	345m	Negligible	3725m	+345m	102
3	Mango	4–6hr	12.2km	340m	45m	4020m	+295m	104
4	Baintha	4–6hr	16km	450m	Negligible	4470m	+450m	108
5	Napina	4–5hr	7.9km	215m	Negligible	4685m	+215m	112
6	Sim Gang	3–5hr	7.4km	466m	Negligible	5151m	+466m	115
7	Hispar La	5–7hr	9.9km	Negligible	626m	4525m	-626m	118
8	Khani Basa	5–6hr	9km	Negligible	275m	4250m	-275m	121
9	Jutmal	4–5hr	12.2km	Negligible	330m	3920m	-330m	123
10	Pumari Chhish Glacier	4–5hr	7.5km	75m	185m	3810m	-110m	127
11	Bitenmal	5–6hr	6.9km	Negligible	375m	3435m	-375m	129
12	Falalinghish	3–5hr	6.3km	95m	230m	3250m	-185m	132
Total	**12 days**	**115.8km**	**2526m**	**2271m**				

K2 Base Camp Trek

Day	Start	Time	Distance	Ascent	Descent	Finish altitude	Sleeping altitude difference	Page
1	Askole*	5–6hr	17km	105m	Negligible	3150m	+105m	140
2	Joila	6–7hr	19km	525m	280m	3395m	+245m	145
3	Paiju	6–8hr	11.7km	485m	55m	3825m	+430m	150
4	Hoborse	2–3hr	5.3km	215m	Negligible	4040m	+215m	155
5	Urdukas	6–7hr	11.4km	290m	40m	4290m	+250m	158
6	Gore 2	4–6hr	11km	295m	10m	4575m	+285m	162
7	Concordia**	9–13hr	24.4km	410m	410m	4575m	0m	169
8	Concordia	8hr	15.2km	Negligible	400m	4175m	-400m	174
9	Gore 1	7–8hr	12.4km	45m	395m	3825m	-350m	176
10	Hoborse***	6–7hr	11.7km	55m	485m	3395m	-430m	178
11	Paiju****	4–6hr	19km	280m	525m	3150m	-245m	180
12	Joila	5hr	17km	Negligible	105m	3045m	-105m	182
Total (excluding visit to K2 Base Camp)			**11 days**	**150.7km**	**2295m**	**2295m**		
Total (including visit to K2 Base Camp)			**12 days**	**175.1km**	**2705m**	**2705m**		

* the first day's route might be done by jeep in the future (and the last day's too)
** optional visit to Broad Peak Base Camp (4820m) and K2 Base Camp (4965m) from Concordia
*** sometimes it is possible to walk to Bardumal on Day 10 and to continue to Askole the following day
**** Korophon Camp may be used instead of Joila

Gondogoro La via Concordia

The first seven days of this trek (or six, if starting from Joila) are the same as the K2 Base Camp Trek. See that trek for route description.

Day	Start	Time	Distance	Ascent	Descent	Finish altitude	Sleeping altitude difference	Page
1	Askole*	5–6hr	17km	105m	Negligible	3150m	+105m	140
2	Joila	6–7hr	19km	525m	280m	3395m	+245m	145
3	Paiju	6–8hr	11.7km	485m	55m	3825m	+430m	150
4	Hoborse	2–3hr	5.3km	215m	Negligible	4040m	+215m	155
5	Urdukas	6–7hr	11.4km	290m	40m	4290m	+250m	158
6	Gore 2	4–6hr	11km	295m	10m	4575m	+285m	162
7	Concordia**	9–13hr	24.4km	410m	410m	4575m	0m	169
8	Concordia	4–5hr	10.2km	395m	30m	4940m	+365m	187
9	Ali Camp	10–12hr	10km	730m	1000m	4675m	-265m	189
10	Huisprung	3–4hr	7km	Negligible	500m	4175m	-500m	194
11	Dalsan	3–4hr	8.9km	30m	810m	3395m	-780m	196
12	Saitcho	6–7hr	10.3km	35m	275m	3155m	-240m	198
Total (excluding visit to K2 Base Camp)		**11 days**	**121.8km**	**3105m**	**3000m**			
Total (including visit to K2 Base Camp)		**12 days**	**146.2km**	**3515m**	**3410m**			

* the first day's route might be done by jeep in the future

** optional visit to Broad Peak Base Camp (4820m) and K2 Base Camp (4965m) from Concordia

Fairy Meadows and Rakhiot Base Camp trek

Day	Start	Time	Distance	Ascent	Descent	Finish altitude	Sleeping altitude difference	Page
1	Tato	2–4hr	4.4km	710m	Negligible	3295m	+710m	212
2	Fairy Meadows	4½–6hr	12.4km	680m	445m	3530m	+235m	213
3	Beyal	3–4hr	7.7km	Negligible	945m	2585m	-945m	215
Total	**3 days**		**24.5km**	**1390m**	**1390m**			

Trek to Diamir Face or West Face of Nanga Parbat

Day	Start	Time	Distance	Ascent	Descent	Finish altitude	Sleeping altitude difference	Page
1	Bunar Das	3–4hr	13.5km	770m	425m	1625m	+345m	218
2	Dimroi	5–6hr	7.4km	955m	140m	2440m	+815m	221
3	Serre	5–6hr	6.4km	1110m	10m	3540m	+1100m	224
*	Kachal	8hr	14.4km	670m	670m	3540m	0m	224
4	Kachal	5hr	6.4km	10m	1110m	2440m	-1100m	224
5	Serre	6hr to Dimroi + 2hr to Bunar Das	20.9km	565m	1725m	1280m	-1160m	224
Total (excluding visit to Diamir Base Camp	**5 days**		**54.6km**	**3410m**	**3410m**			
Total (including visit to Diamir Base Camp)	**6 days**		**69km**	**4080m**	**4080m**			

* optional visit to Diamir Base Camp (4210m)

Beyond Tato towards Fairy Meadows with Nanga Parbat (Trek 4, Stage 1; photo: Jasmine Star)

PREFACE

Guiding and climbing in the Himalaya and Karakoram since 1984, and building up an enormous love for these mountain ranges, I felt a guidebook had to be written; this edition describes five treks in the Gilgit-Baltistan area of Pakistan. Since my first visit to Pakistan in 1989 I have been lucky enough to return countless times, travelling to many corners of this magical, rugged part of the world. Throughout the years, I have steadily amassed information and knowledge, with any gaps filled in by local sources, to create what I hope is an invaluable guidebook. Since I never have been a real photographer, I asked some other people to contribute photos. Inspiration for this book came not only from having read a wide range of material written about the area (please do read all the quotes), but also from meeting and travelling with famous climbers: in 1990, I guided a BBC TV team to the Diamir Face of Nanga Parbat, where climbers Chris Bonington, Jim Curran, Sigi Hupfauer and Charles Houston were to make a documentary about Nanga Parbat.

Guiding in Pakistan is not easy, as one famous climber once said to me 'if you can guide in Pakistan, then you can guide everywhere!'

Trekking, as we know it, in the mountains of Asia started in the 1860s, when British officers and their families would take a holiday in the mountains escaping the heat, enjoying the views, hunting, exploring remote areas partly for political reasons, and later climbing. In the Northern Areas endless treks can be found, easy and difficult, short and long in duration (more treks will hopefully be described in future editions of this guide). I hope this book will inspire the reader to visit places which are described in early explorer stories and more recent expedition books. Carry this book as a guide and a friend!

My dream is one day to be able to cross borders and follow old and new trails on ever more adventurous treks.

I leave you with my favourite Urdu word on trek, which means wonderful/fantastic/awesome: *zabardas!*

Bart Jordans

Winter 2023 Copenhagen

On Biafo Glacier looking east, towards Askole (Trek 1, Stage 4; photo: Jasmine Star)

INTRODUCTION

From Hispar La looking towards Snow Lake (Trek 1, Stage 6; photo: Jasmine Star)

THE THRILL OF THE GILGIT-BALTISTAN AREAS

Sky and mountains are one in Northern Pakistan, where the Himalaya, Karakoram and Hindu Kush challenge each horizon. Within a radius of 180km, there are more than 100 summits above 7000m: two of these are less than 100 metres shy of 8000m, and another 19 of them surpass 7600m. There are also four 8000m peaks within 24km of each other at the head of the Baltoro Glacier, and further to the west another 8000m peak – Nanga Parbat – can be found. In short, you are walking in an area with the highest concentration of highest peaks anywhere in the world.

> The mountains of the Central Himalaya and Nepal are beautiful, but the mountains of the Karakoram are powerful and majestic. They inspire awe, not rapture. These peaks pierce through years of formal education and association with high mountains to evoke an echo of primitive fears buried beneath centuries of civilization.
>
> *Nicholas Clinch, A Walk in The Sky, 1958 (on the way to the first climb of Gasherbrum I or Hidden Peak 8080m)*

Drained by the mighty Indus, which divides the Himalaya from the Karakoram, this is a harsh and unforgiving land, in which hardy mountain folk inhabit beautiful villages, their crops watered by complicated irrigation systems, their link with the rest of the country being along the famous (or infamous) Karakoram Highway (KKH).

Northern Pakistan is unsurpassed as a mountain region, for this is the meeting point of three major ranges: the Pakistan Himalaya, where 8126m Nanga Parbat reigns supreme; the Karakoram (with four 8000m peaks); and the Hindu Kush, whose highest summit is the 7760m, Tirich Mir. As if this were not enough, the Pamir range also presses in from the north – so spare a moment to consider the immense powers of uplift that raised such a concentration of sharply pointed summits in an area of just 180km^2. What a magical setting!

The challenge for explorers venturing into this mountain wilderness was enormous. The Northern Area, also called Gilgit–Baltistan (not including Chitral), is located on roughly the same latitude as southern Spain or Washington DC. It covers 72,971km^2, an area as big as The Netherlands and Belgium combined, or roughly Scotland (78,000km^2) or Washington State.

Travelling in the Northern Areas has never been easy, and is still difficult in the present day. Despite a silk route crossing this country, challenges were many, such as bad (or indeed no) roads, tribal hostilities towards foreigners, robberies, heavy snow fall, rock avalanches, heat, and more. With domestic flights and a road (the

Porters singing for a safe journey travelling the Baltoro Glacier (Trek 2)

A traditional though increasingly rare footbridge made of birch tree branches and weeping willow vines (Trek 2, approach)

Karakoram Highway) the area has been opened up more, but it remains a very special place.

One of the beauties of trekking in Pakistan is the cultural interaction with the incredibly friendly people of the mountains: expect some songs and dancing where participation is really appreciated. Singing and dancing is very important for the mountain people of Pakistan. Learning – and using – a few words in Urdu will be held in high regard and you might even be invited to share a Balti bread or a tea with them (but watch out for your stomach!).

Once, on a Biafo–Hispar trek, the porters were chanting and singing prayers as part of the Muharram celebration and at the same time beating their chests: their actions, combined with the overwhelming mountain scenery, was like being in a Wagner opera and it is something I have never forgotten.

Walking in the Karakoram you need good boots, good balance, strong ankles, healthy knees: the going is tough and the conditions can be gruelling. Expect to spend many hours each day walking on loose stones of all sizes, on and off trails, in hot conditions without shade. The landscape is so broken. However, the reward of walking among these awesome peaks, and the memories you take home are worth every ounce of effort and every drip of sweat. Trekking in the mountains of Pakistan is like no other place in this world.

Preparations and practicalities

Jeep in Braldu Gorge on the way to Askole (Treks 1–3)

CLIMATE AND TREKKING SEASONS

The Northern Area is influenced by the arid weather of central Asia and the semi humid subtropics of northern South Asia. The Karakoram range is located further north than the Himalaya, which explains the colder temperatures. Climate differences between K2 and Everest are also due to differing distances from the sea: K2 is located 1450km inland and Everest just 645km. The Karakoram has a typical cold steppe climate. At high altitude, the dry air still condenses into some clouds, which produce some snow, feeding the glaciers.

In the summer, the Indian continent is drenched by the monsoon rains, but the clouds are emptied by the time they reach the Karakoram, so the area generally remains unaffected. Precipitation typically occurs during the cold winter, spring and sometimes in the beginning of the summer, which means the best time to visit the mountains is from the end of spring through summer until the beginning of autumn.

Summer trekking can be extremely hot. At altitude, thin air filters less light meaning on a cloudless day there is stronger radiation, which can increase the temperature considerably. During the night, the

NATIONAL HOLIDAYS

- **5 Feb Kashmir Day:** A day where Pakistan shows support and unity with the people of Kashmir in India.
- **23 March Pakistan Day:** Celebrating the Lahore Resolution from 1940, seen as a breakthrough in the Muslim fight for an independent state.
- **1 May Labour Day**
- **July/August (shifting dates) Muharram celebrations:** During this period try to avoid arriving into or departing from Skardu, since there are days when everything is shut down: no permits are issued, no transport is possible, internet is shut down and it's impossible to hire porters.
- **14 August Independence Day:** Celebrating independence from British rule in 1947.
- **6 September Defence Day**

And there are several other holidays on shifting dates. The main one – **Eid al-Fitr** – of three days, celebrates the end of Ramadan.

temperatures drop again. A difference of 30°C can occur between day and night-time at altitude. Another factor to consider is the average drop of 0.6°C temperature for every 100 metres of climb.

High passes are clear of snow and the temperatures at altitude are just bearable in the summer.

The mountains are controlled by the wind: in wintertime the wind blows from the west, and during summer it blows from the east, blowing a very dry wind with hardly any precipitation left.

While the summer avoids most of the snow, cold and rain, there can nevertheless still be too much snow on the Gondogoro La in June and July, making it impossible to cross. I prefer September, which is less hot and less busy.

If you happen to be on trek during Ramadan, when the staff are probably fasting during the day, do try to understand and appreciate the effort they make to maintain the service level despite going without any food or drink during the day themselves.

VISAS

Pakistan has an online visa application process for most international travellers, which can be accessed via: https://visa.nadra.gov.pk. Allow yourself plenty of time to complete the application, and it will be successful. Several documents must be uploaded as part of a tourist visa application: photograph, passport, hotel booking details (and details of your trek). There is lots of helpful information on the website, clarifying requirements for each step of the visa application process.

Make sure you allow a minimum of six weeks before departure to get your visa. Stories abound of visitors not getting their visa in time and having to cancel their trip! Print out your visa and always carry it along with your passport.

Arrivals and departures at the new Islamabad airport are straightforward.

ACCESS AND PERMITS

When trekking (and climbing) in the mountains of Pakistan, permits and other paperwork are required and must be processed via a licensed Pakistani tour operator. Certain mountain areas are accessible without permits (see each trek and ask a tour operator). The areas close to the ceasefire line with India are restricted and the British Foreign Office advises against all travel within 10 miles of the Line of Control.

Trekking without a local guide is prohibited within the restricted areas. When hiring porters, it is obligatory to insure them.

The trekking permits will be arranged by the tour operators.

TREK OPERATORS

Independent travel is possible in this area, but for trekking you must go through a licensed tour operator. These tour operators organise all the logistics, domestic transport, hotels, necessary papers and permits, plus contact with helicopter rescue services.

In Pakistan, tour operators are part of PATO (Pakistan Association of Tour Operators www.pato.org.pk). The PATO website lists more than 150 members; to find the best tour operator, check out a couple and compare services and prices. Baltistan Tours www.baltistantours.com has been my choice since 1989.

For a list of European and US-based trek operators, see Appendix B.

COST OF TREKKING IN PAKISTAN

Trekking is not cheap in Pakistan and every year the prices are going up, so you will need to carefully check the pricing of the different tour operators. Trekking costs include local transport (flight, jeeps), accommodation and food; wages for the local tour operator, staff, porters, and herders of pack animals; insurance for staff; camp equipment; daily prices for using tents at campsites (Rs 1500.00 PKR for each small tent, Rs 2000.00 PKR for each big tent); a cleaning fee to be paid at every camp; and a one-time entry amount to the Central Karakoram National Park (CKNP) (£120/€140/$150).

It is impossible to publish a trek price, since it would already have changed by the time this guidebook goes to print, however as a rough

En route to Ali Camp with Concordia behind and Broad Peak and Gasherbrum IV in clouds (Trek 3, Stage 7; photo: Tom Richardson)

estimate you could anticipate paying £150/€175/$190 per day for land-only to K2, and £160/€185/$200 per day for a land-only trek to Gondogoro La (not including jeeps).

GETTING TO PAKISTAN

By air

Pakistan has several airlines flying direct or indirect routes to Karachi, Islamabad and Lahore. However, Islamabad is the easiest to get to, and has the most options for domestic flights onwards. In 2023, Skardu International Airport began receiving flights from Dubai, and more airlines may fly there in the future.

PIA, the national carrier, has some flights from Europe to Pakistan. Other airlines which should give options to connect from all over the world to Pakistan are British Airways, Emirates, Qatar Airways, Etihad Airways, Turkish Airlines, Gulf Air, Thai Airways and Air China; however, always double check since flight schedules change frequently.

Islamabad airport is relatively new (2018) with some good facilities. It is located some distance from Islamabad city and Rawalpindi, making it an expensive taxi ride into town. An air-conditioned metrobus line offering cheap transport connects the airport with the two cities (though not at night).

On departure allow at least one extra hour to get into the airport.

By road

There is an interesting website for information on border crossings and other travel related details, especially for more unknown places in the area of the Silk Road www.caravanistan.com – check it out. To encounter fewer border problems, it is best to have a visa organised from home.

Pakistan can be accessed by road from:

- **India:** via the main border crossing at Wagah, between Amritsar and Lahore. This border crossing should be open for foreigners, but due to political relations between India and Pakistan it can be closed at any time.
- **China:** along the China National Highway 314 and Karakoram Highway via the Khunjerab Pass (4714m), one of the more beautiful passes in the world. A daily bus service operates between Kashgar in Xinjiang and Gilgit.

There are eight formal border crossings from **Afghanistan**, with a Pakistani plan to construct more. Best known is the Khyber Pass, west from Peshawar, an historically important pass. There are also crossing points from **Iran**; however, tourists have been kidnapped and killed here in the past. Many western Foreign Offices currently advise against all travel to Afghanistan and Iran.

GETTING AROUND IN PAKISTAN

By plane

Pakistan has several domestic flight routes. The most important for trekkers are the flights towards the northern areas at Skardu, Gilgit and Chitral. They are serviced by the national

On the Baltoro Glacier, looking back towards Paiju (Trek 2, Stage 3)

carrier PIA and Air Blue (2023). There are several daily scheduled flights to Skardu from a number of towns inside Pakistan, and extra flights are deployed during busy periods (and since 2023, international flights operate to Skardu).

Domestic flights are not cheap; part of the money paid by tourists is used to subsidise locals to make their flights cheaper. (Domestic flights into the mountains are getting more and more popular for the general Pakistani population, mainly to escape the heat in the cities or as honeymoon trips.)

Domestic flights into the mountains of Pakistan are subject to weather conditions and visibility. However, plans are in motion to ensure that all flights will run in any weather conditions. Skardu airport has developed enormously over the last couple of years into an international and 'all-weather' airport.

If you do fly, it is an exceptional experience, with grand views to Nanga Parbat (8126m). Try to ensure window seats on the right side (F) when flying in to Skardu and left (A) on the way back to Islamabad. Batteries should be in your hand luggage on domestic flights.

On arrival at Skardu airport, you can make the most of time waiting for your luggage to go to the foreigner's registration desk, where your passport and visa papers are checked. Once out of the airport, you will be met by your tour agent and/or local guide. You can hand over your passport to them so they can immediately start the time-consuming process of obtaining your trekking permit.

By helicopter

Helicopter safari flights (from Skardu) are available but are not cheap, mainly for the following two reasons: one, when flying they always fly in a pair and, two, the flight from Skardu to K2 Base Camp is 2hr–2hr 30min long, including 20–30min to refill at Paiju.

To check for updated prices and guidelines on how to charter a helicopter go to https://askariaviation.com.

By bus

Instead of a flight, or if the domestic flight does not run, you can investigate a kind of mini-adventure to get to Gilgit or Skardu.

The Karakoram Highway (KKH) – or Pakistan–China Friendship Highway – took 20 years to build and was opened in 1978. Some 15,000 Pakistani and 20,000 Chinese people worked on the road. Landslides, rockfall, severe winters, hot summers, and accidents resulted in a death toll of 450 to 500 road builders on the Pakistani side. The 1300km-long road, finishing in Pakistan, reaches its highest point at the Khunjerab Pass at 4714m. There are more than 100 bridges along the road, built by the Chinese. The KKH needs non-stop maintenance. The last major roadworks finished in 2020.

Local bus in Pakistan

From Islamabad to Gilgit normally takes 8–10 hours in a private bus or vehicle arranged by the tour operator. From Islamabad to Skardu it is normally around 12–13 hours' drive. The last 170km towards Skardu are not on the KKH but a side road of the KKH. Travelling by public bus takes longer, and would need to be arranged independently.

Armed tourist police will accompany any transport if needed/requested.

Metro-bus in Islamabad/Rawalpindi

This air-conditioned, cheap rapid bus system connects a large area from the two cities Islamabad and Rawalpindi to the Islamabad airport (it does not operate at night).

By taxi

In the cities taxis are available everywhere, however meters are not so ubiquitous. It is an expensive way to get to and from the international airport.

By minibus

Minibuses are available in Skardu and Gilgit, and you can hop on and off if you happen to know and understand the destination names. They are quite cheap.

On horseback

No longer used, except in cases of emergency (£60 per day on K2 trek).

By bike

In Gilgit and Skardu mountain bikes are available to hire.

THE TREK ACCESS POINTS: GILGIT AND SKARDU

Getting to Gilgit

Besides a domestic flight of just over one hour from Islamabad with PIA, Gilgit can be accessed in numerous ways. By road, you can drive the Karakoram Highway from the south along the Indus River, approach from the west along the Chitral road crossing the Shandur Pass (10–12 hours from Islamabad) or enter Pakistan from the north from Xinjiang province in China, following the KKH. Public or private vehicles are both options and can be organised by your tour operator. Car rental is available in Pakistan, but it is strongly recommended to request that a driver is included also, since driving here can be dangerous.

Gilgit airport is located somehow in the centre of town. A helipad is next to it. When flying to or from Gilgit make sure to look out for 8126m Nanga Parbat appearing rather close to the plane.

Driving the Karakoram Highway, visiting Gilgit, Hunza, all the way to the border with China (over the Khunjerab Pass) and onwards, is one of the more dramatic road journeys of the world, with several 7000m peaks to admire. Mountain biking the KKH is very popular. The road has improved enormously over the years; although this makes it wider and easier to bike, it also means increased and faster traffic. Caution is advised.

Visiting Gilgit

Before going on trek, spend some time in and around Gilgit, where you can visit the bazaar, watch a game of polo, and stock up on the delicious local apricots.

There is a good choice of hotels and guesthouses in all price classes. Shops selling provisions and adventure gear can be found in Gilgit. The city has several hospitals, medical centres, and doctors.

Karakorum International University, established in Gilgit in 2002, formed a satellite campus in Skardu in 2011, which was upgraded in 2017 to become the University of Baltistan. In 2016, the Hunza KIU and Women Campus was founded: www.kiu.edu.pk.

GILGIT'S APRICOTS

Growing up to an altitude of 3000m there are many different apricots species available in these northern areas, which, it is said, help local people stay young! Every bit of the apricot is used: the fruit to eat, the shell for fuel, the kernel for oil and an almond drink, and the pulp as animal feed. Sometimes an alcoholic apricot-based brew can be found, but keep quiet about that!

Walk around in the two-kilometre-long bazaar and enjoy the mixture of cultures meeting here for centuries. Or visit a game of polo.

Outings from Gilgit

From Gilgit there are several excursions to be made. One of the more interesting hikes is visiting the three-metre-tall Kargah Buddha rock carving, located six kilometres west of Gilgit. Another destination (by vehicle) from Gilgit is the Shandur Pass (3734m) leading to Chitral, known for its annual polo match.

Getting to Skardu

By air

With a modernised airport and extended landing strip in a big valley, Skardu International Airport is ideal for a 'bigger' plane like the Boeing 737–300 to land and take off. Possible flight problems could be that it is too overcast for a landing or too warm for a take-off in the thinner air of 2230m altitude.

After many years guiding in the Karakoram with Skardu as a starting point, I have come to appreciate actually reaching Skardu – for this can be far from certain. A flight booked to Skardu does not always equal a flight made. This is a fair-weather flight only and not flying means a long drive overland, which I have done 18 times. However, Skardu Airport becoming an International Airport means that the flights use radar beacons these days. Up until recently, the road was in bad condition and a journey

Arriving at Skardu International Airport

could take 24 hours or more. A flight: around 50 minutes. The tension and excitement at (old) Rawalpindi airport in the early hours waiting for news as to whether the flight would take off was enormous. The relief was even greater when the plane touched down in Skardu: instead of a long bus journey with a good chance of most of the group getting stomach problems and a day lost from the programme, everything could now go according to schedule.

By road

From Islamabad to Skardu it is 635km by road via Babusar Pass (12–16 hours), and 300km by air. The route follows the Karakoram Highway up until 28km south of Gilgit, where it leaves the KKH and follows the amazing 170km road built in the cliffs of the Indus River gorge, only emerging at the large sandy plain at Skardu. The road has been recently improved.

Visiting Skardu

Skardu township has grown enormously over the last few decades. Before it was a dusty one-street bazaar, but now you can easily get lost, which is an adventure all of its own. (Remember to take a visiting card from your hotel to help get you back home.) The town is a centre for a big area attracting many visitors for many reasons, including buying goods and services, visiting hospitals, resolving administrative issues, attending university. Skardu has several shops with outdoor gear, produced in Pakistan or leftover from expeditions. Skardu is also a place to stock up on any requirements for the upcoming adventure, such as food and medical items, cooking utensils, local kerosene cookers, gear for porters.

Enjoy the Purana, Naya and Chashma bazaars. Look for some local woven textiles, gemstones (around 25 different types of minerals and precious gemstones), carpets, rugs, Balti hats, Hunza hats, leather goods (footballs), apricots, embroidered and appliquéd textiles and carved woodwork. You can also visit the Skardu Fort and a polo game.

On the opposite side of the Indus River, the new campus of the University of Baltistan can be seen.

Other places to visit include:

- **Balti Museum:** Housing a nice collection of Balti related items
- **Baltistan Heritage Shop & Museum:** Museum about the history and culture of the Baltistan region
- **Manthal Buddha Rock**
- **K2 Museum:** If you aren't able to stay at the PTDC K2 Motel, go there anyway to see the motel hallways decorated with years of signed expedition postcards, photos, stickers and the Karakoram Museum situated in the beautiful garden, where you can enjoy the views with a cup of tea. Further information is in the Accommodation section. Although at the time of

publication the PTDC K2 motel is closed (looking for a new owner), a caretaker of the museum can be phoned, who will come to open the gate for you (ask or look for the number at your hotel reception). Opening times 9am–4.30pm.

Outings from Skardu

One of the more popular places to visit from Skardu are the Satpara Lakes, about eight kilometres north of the town. Another popular outing is walk to the Buddha Carving from the 8th or 9th century, three kilometres from Skardu across Sadpara Nullah on Skardu–Sadpara Road, with the meditating Maitreya Buddha in the centre framed by Bodhisattvas. Longer trips could include visiting Khapalu Fort and old Mosque, or the Deosai Plateau, or rafting the Indus River.

ACCOMMODATION

Throughout the country **hotels** can be found in all price classes. There are hundreds of hotels and guesthouses in the Skardu and Baltistan region. Further up in the Gilgit-Baltistan areas places like Gilgit, Skardu and Khaplu offer some good hotels, but once beyond those places expect simpler conditions (with exception of the Serena Hotel in Shigar, the Shigar Fort Hotel and, in Khaplu, the Serena Khaplu Palace Hotel). The Karakoram Lodge in Khaplu is a good alternative for a slimmer budget.

Skardu has around 80 hotels. In Hushe there is a refuge. For accommodation in cities and towns check out websites, general guidebooks and ask for advice from local tour operators.

There are several **youth hostels** in Pakistan; visit their website for further information www.pyhahostels.com. Some of the youth hostels in major cities run on a **B&B** basis, but in places like Gilgit many are accommodation only.

The only official **campsites** are in Islamabad and Peshawar. Otherwise, small hotels and guesthouses permit you to use their gardens for camping and make use of their facilities. Wild camping is not advised in tribal areas with local people being very curious and, in some areas, even hostile.

Visiting the Gilgit-Baltistan areas is getting more and more popular for Pakistanis from all over the country escaping the summer heat, particularly as more domestic flights are now operating to Skardu. Be aware that this can add pressure on accommodation in these regions.

Accommodation on trek

On trek there are no guesthouses, except at Nanga Parbat Fairy Meadows. There you can find three or four resorts/cottages which can be booked.

The local tour operators provide sleeping, dining, kitchen and toilet tents, and everything else needed for camping, often manufactured in

Urdukas camp (Trek 2, Stage 3)

Pakistan. Some campsites have simple facilities, like toilets and shower cabins (cold water), running water, shelter for staff and room for storage.

Skardu – K2 Motel

A place which is close to my heart and therefore needs a special mention in this book is the historic K2 Motel in Skardu. Although currently closed, it provides a wonderful insight into various climbers and trekkers over the years. A basic hotel, one of the first in Skardu and run by PTDC (Pakistan Tourism Development Corporation; owned by the Government), it has a top location with views over the Indus River and mountains in the distance, which can be enjoyed while relaxing and sipping a tea in a beautiful garden. The motel has been used by many expeditions, as well as honeymooners and couples enjoying the beautiful gardens, thus garnering the nickname of 'The Lovers' Adventures Nest'.

Two hallways are decorated with billboards, one for every year since 1985, plastered with postcards, photos, and stickers from expeditions that have passed through. A museum of sorts. Besides these impressive hallways, an actual museum is located in the garden, in a big triangle-shaped, white building housing a very interesting exhibition regarding several aspects on the Karakoram. The museum was set up by the Italians in 2004 to commemorate the golden jubilee of the first ascent of K2.

FOOD AND DRINK

Pakistani cooking is really something to look forward to. Often, in hotels, a buffet is served for all three meals, but à la carte is often available as well. Throughout the country there are plenty of exiting restaurants to choose from. In Islamabad there are several options for eating out, such as 'Loafology Breaking Bread' in the Blue (business) Area; the Marriott Hotel; the Serena Hotel. The Monal restaurant in the Marghalla Hills or in Rawalpindi is also to be recommended. Kabul Restaurant in Islamabad is another good choice.

Alcohol consumption is illegal; however, in a few international hotels you might find a bar serving alcohol. A special permit allows non-Muslims to buy alcohol. In the Northern Areas sometimes Chinese beer can be found, or Hunza 'water'.

On trek, food is just as good as in the restaurants in town. Quite often, the cook and kitchen crew on trek will work the off-season in the city restaurants. So, they are well trained to make some good food, to keep trekkers going throughout the day.

Supplies are carried for the whole trek since there are no villages along most trek routes where shopping could be possible. A kitchen crew normally uses a big kitchen tent. They are very particular in keeping it all as clean as possible – knowing that if they do not, guests might get an upset tummy.

If you should take the overland trip using the Karakoram Highway, try to enjoy the milky tea which the truck drivers drink: strong tea boiled in buffalo milk and with plenty of sugar and sometimes additionally flavoured with cardamon and pepper (chai).

Working hard from 4.00am till 9.00pm with a smile and full of service, the kitchen team at Concordia

Food on trek

- **Breakfast:** a selection of cereals, porridge, toast, eggs, cheese spread, marmalade, tea, coffee.
- **Lunch:** while on trek this will be a packed lunch with all kinds of items. If the day is short enough (a warm) lunch can be served in camp.
- **Dinner:** soup, main dish, dessert, and tea/coffee/hot chocolate.
- **Water on trek:** normally at dinner time the staff collect the empty water bottles and bags in order to fill them up with boiled water. At lunch time there is not always water available – so bring along enough when a long day is on the programme.
- **Snacks:** some Pakistani companies provide snacks, otherwise bring your own, your favourite!

EQUIPMENT

Publishing a kit list is often not needed any more since most people have their own lists based on their experience. Here are some items worth mentioning:

- suitcase to leave behind at hotel in Islamabad with a set of clean travel clothes (this is quite usual, but obviously no valuables should be left)
- duffle bag with lock – pack in big plastic bags to keep it dry
- trekking boots and camping shoes
- river crossing shoes
- easy fitting trekking clothes
- sun hat and sunglasses
- sleeping bag (-10 to -15°C as it can be cold sleeping on ice) and mattress (if not provided by tour operator)
- rucksack and waterproof cover
- umbrella against the sun
- long-sleeved shirt to protect from sun
- snacks, including sweets in case of a dry throat and altitude cough
- two or three litre water hydration bag, and a water bottle in case the bag punctures; a Steripen can be useful when the water is clear
- baby wipes
- ear plugs for sleeping at camp
- big sturdy bag to put around your duffle bag to protect it from dust and dirt while being transported on mules
- micro-spikes for the K2 trek.

When crossing the Hispar Pass and Gondogoro La, the following extra items should be on your list:

- crampons (boots should be stiff enough to wear crampons)
- climbing harness
- ice axe
- helmet
- extra warm gloves/mittens
- gaiters
- glacier sunglasses
- extra gear to keep warm.

In Skardu, there are several outdoor shops. They are often stocked with used and unused expedition gear. In Islamabad there are one or two shops selling trekking equipment.

Eroded ridges on the south side of Biafo Glacier (Trek 1, Stage 4; photo: Jasmine Star)

AN HISTORICAL KIT LIST

Some detail on gear from the 1909 Italian, Duke of the Abruzzi expedition to K2 at Urdukas 4050m:

'We also left our camp-beds, and from now on spread our sleeping-bags on the floor of the tent. Few people know it is warmer to lie directly on the waterproof bottom of the tent, when it is set up on snow or ice, than on a camp bedstead which leaves a perpetually chilly void between you and the ground.

Our sleeping-bags, ... consisted of four bags, which could be used separately or one inside the other. One was of light soft camel's hair, of eider-down, one of thick goatskin with a woollen covering, and one of waterproof canvas, to be put outside the other three'.

MAPS

Over the decades many maps have been produced for this interesting area. Some are mentioned below. Besides these maps there are also maps to be found in books and both have been used in writing this guidebook. Several guidebooks include some good maps. See Appendix D. The main goal of early expeditions was not only to explore new areas but – equally important – also to map them and produce papers, books, and reliable maps. As a result, there are some excellent older charts which are often the base for the later maps. The historical maps can be found in old books. Some of the later maps are listed here:

- **Trekking map Karakoram – K2, Gasherbrum, Broad Peak, Hispar Trek, Hunza** by Terra Quest (1:175,000) 2016 – laminated map with routes and camps indicated
- **K2 and Baltoro Glacier in the Karakorum** – Satellite Image Map (1:80,000) 2004, 2013 – a detailed

satellite map with an enormous amount of name and height data on it, printed in Poland
- **Nanga Parbat** – Alpenvereinskarte (1:50,000) Nr.0/7 Deutsche Himalaya-Expedition 1934, first print 1936, reprint 1980 – excellent map

MONEY

Money – Pakistani Rupees – is needed for shopping, drinks, and tipping. To be on the safe side bring (bigger notes) cash in UK pounds, US dollars or Euros. The notes should be without markings or tears. Convert some of them on arrival at the airport or in town. It is best to change your money at the stopover airports such as Doha, Istanbul, etc.

At the airport in Islamabad there are some banks which might be open. It is best to change money there as it is less easy to do this in town. Sometimes it is not possible at all to change money at your hotel, or if it is possible, it will be at a very unfavourable rate. There are ATM machines at the airport and in the cities, but most of them don't work (normally Standard Charter Bank/ATM accept all cards). There is a good choice of money exchangers in the Blue Sector in Islamabad.

When leaving Pakistan, it should be possible to exchange Pakistani Rupees into other currencies at the airport or you can leave left-over cash in designated charity collections at the airport.

Wages for staff

Porters are paid for each stage they walk up and receive half pay for each stage they walk back again, even if they leave the trek early. They are also paid on rest days. As well as porters, more and more pack animals are being used these days. Try to employ porters rather than pack animals since the porters are more efficient.

A K2 trek, one-way, is typically a seven-day or nine-stage trek (stages are also called haltages in local English, or *pyee* in Balti). Some trekking days cover two stages. Beyond Urdukas camp, porter wages can be a bit higher.

Wages in 2023 for porters would be Rs 1500.00 PKR per stage (plus a daily ration of sugar, rice, flour, salt and tea). Sometimes the kitchen crew will cook some dishes for the porters.

Tips

Tips are expected in hotels. Tip housekeeping staff when you leave, bellboys, door guards, kitchen staff and in any restaurants.

- bell boy Rs 300.00 PKR
- door guard Rs 200.00 PKR
- housekeeping staff Rs 500.00 PKR (in 2023)

Tips are expected on treks as well and depend on the number of days and stages. To give a rough indication, for recent a K2 trek, each client was asked to reserve £120 or €140 as a tip for the whole staff.

Besides a monetary tip at the end of a trek, consider donating any

Camp at Broad Peak Base Camp, looking south towards Concordia and the black Mitre Peak (Trek 2, Stage 7)

ROUGH WAGES FOR STAFF PER DAY (AS OF 2023)

- assistant cook Rs 3000.00 PKR
- cook Rs 3500-4000.00 PKR
- guide Rs 5000.00 PKR

Crossing the Gondogoro La, porters earn extra. A mule handler can earn up to Rs 300,000.00 PKR per year and a mule can cost Rs 100,000–150,000.00 PKR.

still-usable outdoor equipment to the trekking staff.

LANGUAGE AND DIALECT IN THE GILGIT-BALTISTAN AREAS

In Pakistan, Urdu is the national language and English the official language, which is widely understood. Throughout the country there are more than 70 dialects.

In the Gilgit-Baltistan area there are two main languages/dialects: Balti, which is an archaic dialect of Tibetan influenced by Urdu, Burushaski and Turkish; and the Indo-Aryan language Shina, used more in the Gilgit area.

CUSTOMS

Pakistan is an Islamic country which is constantly modernising in all facets of life.

Being conscious of local customs and traditions is important when travelling through Pakistan. There are some 'rules' which should be adopted.

Dress code

It is not easy to cover up when it is hot, especially if you come from a culture where many are used to wearing hardly any clothes in extremely hot weather. However, in general, try to dress conservatively: find a balance between being comfortable and being respectful. Pakistan is quite tolerant regarding dress code. However, an incident from the 1980s – where a woman wearing very short shorts had stones thrown at her and was chased back to her hotel in Skardu – is a reminder not to overstep the boundaries.

Except when on trek, women should be covered up as much as possible, with their heads, legs and shoulders covered in public, wearing long pants/skirts and (oversized) T-shirts or shirts. On trek, longer shorts are okay.

Men should not wear shorts in public although it is becoming increasingly accepted, but – again – on trek, when away from villages, it's no problem. Long pants are expected while visiting a mosque, during religious festivals, or at the buffet in the Serena hotel!

If you want to go local, which is appreciated, wear a *shalwar kameez* for men and a *kurta* or *shalwar kameez* for women. Both items could be mixed with some western-style clothes. A *shalwar kameez* covers everything needed and the material can be light and keep you cool (taking the waist rope out of the pants makes them suddenly look twice or more your waist size!).

Visiting a mosque

According to Islamic law, legs and shoulders should be covered and women should wear a head scarf.

Chaqchan Mosque in Khaplu, on the way to Hushe (photo: Muhammad Ashar)

Shoes should be taken off. Don't raise your voice. Don't eat or drink inside the mosque. During prayers and festivals keep to the background, or even better, just don't visit the mosque at all during this time.

Women are only allowed in certain sections of a mosque. Photography is sometimes allowed but should be done with care.

In the northern areas most people are followers of the Shia line. Women cover their heads in these areas. Please behave accordingly.

Alcohol and drugs

Drinking alcohol is forbidden in public for everybody. Only in some five-star hotels is alcohol permitted to be served for non-Muslims. However, Pakistan does have its own brewery, called the Murree Brewery, established in 1860 by the British. All kinds of drinks are brewed there and it sells officially to non-Muslim Pakistanis.

Drugs are prohibited: if you are caught using or in possession there will likely be a punishment, such as stick beatings or worse.

Hand shaking / hand holding

In general, it's a no-go for a man to shake hands with a woman.

In Pakistan it is normal to see men holding hands while walking on the street. This is sign of friendship and has nothing to do with homosexuality. As a western couple, it is best not to hold hands when out and about. Avoid public displays of affection.

Photography

Do not take pictures of women or military objects. In the northern areas people are more reluctant to have their picture taken, but times are changing – ask permission and exercise restraint. Taking a picture of somebody created by God is seen sometimes as blasphemy. After being on trek for a few days, porters might let you take their picture.

Washing in streams

Try to not mix up the soap with the water. Make sure that you wash far away from locals who could get offended.

SAFETY

To a certain extent, safety is in each traveller's own hands. As in any other big city be street wise: don't go around after dark on your own, don't make any ostentatious show of possible wealth, and dress accordingly (see Customs).

Visiting places of worship is okay but double check with your local guide what to do and what not to do. In general, don't get mixed up in with any religious and/or political gathering.

Check Foreign Office websites to get the latest updates regarding terrorism and sectarian violence. The Northern Areas (towards the east) are not normally on the restricted areas list.

Advice for female travellers

Travelling with a man: no problem at all. Travelling on your own or with a female companion: be aware. Even experienced travellers should exercise caution. Take the necessary precautions and act accordingly with respect to the cultural rules. Wear loose fitting clothes that cover just about everything, including your hair.

In Pakistan many people are not used to women going around by themselves. Check out the following blog by Alex (Alexandra) Reynolds for useful information travelling as a woman in Pakistan (and other places) www.lostwithpurpose.com/safe-women-travel-pakistan.

Advice for LGBTQ travellers

Same-sex relationships are forbidden in Pakistan, with strict laws in place against homosexuality. Stay quiet about it and enjoy the trekking.

Glacier travel

In Pakistan most treks include glacier trekking. This means staying alert for possible crevasses, glacier water streams, and slippery steps. The K2 trek is in general a simple walk on the glacier with maybe one or two passages that need extra care, as well as possibly wading the outlet of a glacier (bring micro spikes). The Gondogoro La and Biafo–Hispar La treks need more care. On Nanga Parbat the main routes are fine, but the more you venture beyond the indicated routes, the more care needs to be taken.

Great Trango Castle and Uli Biaho Tower on the left (Trek 2, Stage 2)

It is a notable advantage if you have used climbing gear before and know how to trek roped-up. A guide joining the more technical trips should explain what to do.

MEDICAL CONSIDERATIONS AND EMERGENCIES

Before venturing into remote areas, you should:

- work on your physical fitness
- have a dental check-up (Islamabad has some fine clinics if needed)
- consult a doctor (in good time) about immunisations and medication to take with you (let them see your itinerary)
- make up your own medical kit and read up on first aid in remote areas – see *Pocket First Aid and Wilderness Medicine* (Cicerone, 2022)
- pack adequate sun block – for every 30 metres of elevation gain, UV radiation increases by about three per cent.

Being well prepared lowers the risk of an accident but cannot eliminate the possibility that something could go wrong.

Most travellers are journeying with a local and/or foreign tour operator, who should assist in emergencies. An embassy should also be able to help, but can be far away from the mountains.

Accidents and medical crises create anxiety and tension. In the mountains you may be far from help with few resources, and basic first aid knowledge is a must.

There is a military helicopter rescue service in the northern areas of Pakistan (see 'Helicopter evacuation'). There are some hospitals in Skardu and Gilgit (and basic ones in

GETTING LOST

Getting lost in cities

Bring along a visiting card of your hotel and show it to any taxi, this should bring you back to your hotel.

Getting lost on trek

Always make sure you can see somebody ahead of you or behind you; wear a bright-coloured item. If nature calls, and you have to go off the trail, tell somebody in the party of your whereabouts. If you really get lost, try to backtrack until you meet other people or come to a trail with lots of footprints, then follow that trail until you meet people. The mountains in Pakistan are barren so there is a good chance that people spot each other quickly.

Khaplu and Shigar), but more complicated cases must be transferred to Islamabad or abroad.

Food and water hygiene

Water and food are the most common sources of disease – for example typhoid fever, shigellosis, cholera and hepatitis A. Food and drinking water become contaminated directly by faecal bugs, or flies that eat excrement. Drink only pure water, eat clean fresh food and dispose of sewage efficiently. Wash your hands more frequently than at home and keep your nails short and clean.

Consider all water, even in hotels and restaurants, unsafe to drink unless boiled; kitchens are probably only as clean as the toilets. Bottled mountain spring water is not available on trek, the kitchen crew will supply boiled water. If more drinking water is needed, carry water purification and neutraliser tablets or a filter. Be aware that the water in the Northern Areas can contain mountain sediment, giving it a brownish colour. It is very common for several trekkers in a group to get mild to severe stomach problems. Water at Concordia and Korophon is particularly bad.

Diarrhoea

This causes more trouble than all other medical hazards encountered abroad. Diarrhoea may either arise from toxins, waste products of certain

Near Hoborse camp with Trango Castle looming over the trekkers (Trek 2, Stage 3)

bacteria that grow on food (travellers' diarrhoea = food poisoning), or from infection by disease-causing bacteria carried in water and food (bacterial diarrhoea = dysentery). Wise doctors recommend preventative hygiene before treating travellers' diarrhoea with drugs. Use antibiotics with discretion. Keep your fluid levels up.

Medical kit

Besides personal medication it is always smart to bring some basic medical supplies. Often a local medical kit is carried along on trek.

A basic medical kit could contain safety pins, band aids, duct tape, closures (Steristrips 6mm), gauze squares, sterile non-stick dressings, alcohol swabs, needle to punch blisters, blister 'skin', sterile cloth and/or cotton buds, tweezers, scissors, adhesive tape bandage, protective gloves.

Medication suggestions: to combat allergies, inflammation, altitude sickness, constipation, diarrhoea, haemorrhoids, indigestion, eye and ear infections, nausea and vomiting. Also consider antibiotics, painkillers, ORS rehydration solution, throat lozenges and tiger balm.

Two of the better pharmacies are Shaheen and Watson, both located in the Blue Area in Islamabad (they also offer a wide selection of snacks).

Other sources of advice

See www.fitfortravel.nhs.uk/destinations/asia-central/pakistan.

Helicopter evacuation

Pakistan has some military helicopters that are used for emergency evacuations. To be best prepared for a helicopter rescue a prepaid service is advisable. This involves some paperwork. Normally the more established tour operators have this service organised at the beginning of each season.

The helicopter service works if the weather is okay. The Pakistan Association of Tour Operators has issued a document detailing regulations, info and guidelines regarding the helicopter services. In summary, it says that a Pakistani tour operator (active member of PATO) should pay a yearly deposit, refundable when not used, and another amount should be deposited by the tour operator at PATO before each climbing/trekking team arrives. Be aware that these amounts are not the final bill for a rescue. Make sure that you are well insured before travelling in the remote Karakoram region. There are plenty of stories of people in need of a rescue who have lost valuable time waiting for a payment to clear, because it had not been dealt with properly in advance. Normally, booking a trip through a Pakistani PATO company in connection with a company abroad should be okay. A helicopter rescue can easily cost $4000 (£3170/€3700) per hour, an amount which should be doubled since – for safety reasons – single-engine helicopters fly in pairs over glaciated and snow-bound areas. Night flying is prohibited. The better tour operators will pay a rescue deposit of $10,000 to ensure that there will be no delay due to money matters. The deposit will be refunded at the end of the season.

INSURANCE

Check the travel advice issued by your home country's Foreign Office. If there is advice against travelling, insurance companies might be reluctant to underwrite a policy. Do some research, clearly explain your travel plans, and you will most probably find an insurance company willing to issue cover.

Now and again, there are some zones within the northern areas of Pakistan that are labelled as 'no-go zones', for example along the Karakoram Highway. If you don't fly to Gilgit or Skardu and you have to drive, there is a route bypassing certain problem areas, via Babusar Pass (4175m; 326km from Islamabad and 180km from Gilgit).

It's important that your insurance covers all travel and rescue in the northern area. If you book through a western/local tour operator, they often offer an insurance solution (double check when booking).

Refer to the previous section on Medical considerations and emergencies for further information on emergency helicopter evacuation in the mountains.

HIGH-ALTITUDE PROBLEMS

Acclimatisation is the physiological process that allows humans to adapt so they can live and work in the oxygen-thin atmosphere of high altitudes. Low oxygen pressure in the atmosphere, and hence in the lungs and blood, increases the rate and depth of breathing. Initially the heart beats faster and more strongly, increasing the flow of blood to the lungs, and breathing deepens and quickens; this soon settles back to normal.

Altitude	Oxygen in atmosphere	Relative oxygen rate
0m	20.9%	= 100%
2000m	16.3%	= 88% (left over from 100% oxygen level)
3000m	14.3%	= 68%
4000m	12.7%	= 61%
5000m	11.2%	= 54%
6000m	9.6%	= 46%
7000m	8.7%	= 41%
8000m	7.6%	= 36%
9000m	6.6%	= 32%

Ali Camp (Trek 3, Stage 7; photo: Tom Richardson)

Mild Acute Mountain Sickness (AMS) is common, but it can easily evolve into severe AMS, which can be fatal, so trekkers need to be on the alert for the warning signs.

Predicting AMS

No one can predict who will suffer from AMS, whether it will be mild or severe, or when it will strike. Trekkers who have performed well at altitude will probably do so each time they go high. Those who have suffered AMS before may suffer again and at a similar altitude. Fitness and training guarantee no protection, the sexes succumb equally and no age is exempt. Weight gain during ascent means water retention, which bodes ill.

Preventing AMS

- Allow ample time at various levels to acclimatise. AMS is more likely to occur the higher, the faster, the harder, and the longer the climb. Cold and wind, fear and fatigue, dehydration during rapid ascent and strenuous exercise soon after, and upper respiratory infection, all predispose to AMS.
- Climb without haste: above 3000m gain height slowly and steadily, ideally at around 300m a day; take a rest day about every 1000m.
- Avoid strenuous exertion soon after arriving at altitude.
- To help the process of acclimatisation hike up high but sleep low.

- Drink sufficient fluid: four to five litres daily should balance the heavy losses caused by strenuous breathing in cold, dry, thin air, and allow clear, colourless, copious urine. Dark yellow urine usual indicates dehydration.
- Avoid alcohol and coffee, they dehydrate.
- Eat a high-calorie diet, with plenty of carbohydrate before and during ascent. A good appetite suggests good acclimatisation.
- Don't eat too much salt or take too many sedatives.

If, despite these precautions, a trekker gets sick and does not improve on rest, descend quickly until they start to feel better. Even 300m will help; 1000m may save their life. If the person feels ill and does not improve quickly on descent, insist that they do not re-ascend on that expedition.

To quote the wise words of Rex Munro, the Australian record holder for guiding the most treks in the Karakoram: 'There are two ways to get up a hill: slowly or not at all'.

Mild AMS

Many people who climb high (over around 2500m) are fit on arrival but feel ghastly over the next couple of days, with headache, breathlessness, insomnia (sleeplessness), fatigue, poor appetite, nausea and dizziness. As they adapt to the altitude, these symptoms usually wear off.

Mild AMS has vague symptoms but can drift subtly into severe AMS, which can be fatal. Some people never get used to the altitude, their symptoms worsen, and death is possible from HACE (High Altitude Cerebral Edema) or HAPE (or High Altitude Pulmonary Edema).

Symptoms of mild AMS

These develop 12–48 hours after arriving at altitude.

- Headache, usually at the back of the head and often developing during the night so that it is present on waking (the head feels tight, the sufferer may feel giddy and light-headed)
- Fatigue, sleep disturbance
- Appetite loss, nausea and indigestion
- Shortness of breath on exertion (dyspnoea): the chest feels uncomfortable and tight, but quiet, easy breathing resumes after rest
- Shortage of fluid (dehydration): urine output is low for 24 hours
- Swelling: face puffy; rings on fingers feel tight

Action

Rest, wait and see. Additional oxygen may fool you into thinking the victim is better. If they have not improved within 24 hours assume they have severe AMS, so descend.

Mild AMS may blend unnoticed into severe AMS. HACE or HAPE manifest depending on whether body

Crossing Jutmal Glacier (Trek 1, Stage 9; photo: Jasmine Star)

water settles in the brain or lungs, or both. The entire drama can unfold within hours, and usually does so at night.

Severe AMS

Anyone venturing into the high, cold, thin air is wise to study AMS, which can kill the unwary, the bold and the previously healthy. It affects those who ascend too high too fast, and is usually cured by immediate descent. Severe AMS can kill quickly, so act decisively.

The main dangers of severe AMS are High Altitude Cerebral Edema (HACE) and High Altitude Pulmonary Edema (HAPE).

Symptoms of HACE

HACE is like an exaggerated form of mild AMS and usually occurs above 3600m.

- Headache: severe and constant. No relief from paracetamol, codeine or a night's sleep.
- Lack of coordination (ataxia): the victim staggers as if drunk, and fumbles fine movements such as handling a camera.
- Languor: extreme fatigue is not reversed by rest. The victim won't talk, eat or drink; they lie curled up in a sleeping bag and are irritable and confused. If still active, they may show poor judgement and thus make bad mountaineering decisions. Sleep is fitful and punctuated by bad dreams. They may hallucinate. They may be incontinent.
- Vomiting: severe vomiting leads to dehydration, which cannot be reversed by drinking. Urine is scant and dark yellow.

- Coma: drifts into coma and may die. Convulsions are rare.

Symptoms of HAPE

In HAPE the lungs become waterlogged. HAPE is rare below 3000m; it begins 36–72 hours after arriving at altitude and is cured by descent. Rest and oxygen may help temporarily. It affects children more than adults, men and women equally. It may be related to severe exertion and rate of climb. It worsens at night.

- Shortness of breath (dyspnoea): occurs on slight exertion and is even present at rest. Breathing is irregular and fast at more than 25 breaths per minute. The victim does not improve with rest, and is hungry for air. The chest feels full and tight.
- Cough and sputum: early cough is tickling, hacking and dry – without sputum. Later the sputum is frothy and pink. (By contrast sputum in pneumonia or bronchitis is yellow-green.)
- Chest sounds: crackling, moist sounds (crepitations) can be heard by placing an ear against the back of the victim.
- Cyanosis: at rest the lips, face and fingernails look blue.
- Accelerated pulse: the pulse will be rapid, more than 110 beats per minute.

Action in the case of severe AMS

Descent usually cures severe AMS miraculously. Do not delay. The victim should descend at least 300m, preferably 1000m. The greater and faster the descent, the swifter the recovery. Once down the victim should stay down and will have to wait some days before flying home. (Note that you are not allowed to take an oxygen canister onto a flight in many countries.)

The forms of treatment listed below buy you some time but should never take preference over evacuating the victim immediately to a lower altitude.

- Rest: prop the victim up and keep him or her warm and relaxed.
- Oxygen: give 100 per cent oxygen. A change in the victim's colour from blue to pink shows the effectiveness of oxygen, which may relieve headache and help pulmonary edema.
- Fluids: drink (four to five litres daily) enough to maintain a copious flow of urine (one litre daily minimum).

REMEMBER

With good sense AMS, HACE and HAPE should not occur. But if they do, prevent their deadly consequences by rapid descent to a lower altitude.

Part of the Trango group seen from near Liligo: (L to R) Trango Monk, Trango Tower or Nameless Tower, Great Trango, Trango Castle (Trek 2, Stage 3)

- Acetazolamide (Diamox): 125–250mg once or twice daily, a mild diuretic that appears to help acclimatisation without masking the symptoms of AMS (unlike steroids), and diminishes the incidence and severity of AMS symptoms of headache or nausea. Do not give Diamox to someone with a known allergy to sulpha drugs. Diamox can also be taken in preparation for high altitude.
- Dexamethasone (Decadron): 4mg twice daily starting on the day of ascent and for three to five days.
- Gamow bag: a portable, inflatable pressure chamber can lower the virtual atmospheric pressure while the patient is in the bag.

USING THIS GUIDE

The main section of this guide describes the itineraries of three treks in the Karakoram and two, with variations, in the Pakistan Himalaya. The overview map at the front of the guide will give you a feel for where you base yourself for each trek. At the start of the trek is an information box giving general information about the whole trek, including start and finish points, trek length in days and other information where available. The treks are illustrated with maps which show key landmarks, altitudes, and route lines to help you envisage your itinerary more clearly. Note that these maps are not detailed enough to navigate by, and you should not attempt to trek independently without an experienced trekking guide.

TREK GRADES

Descent of Gondogoro La (Trek 3, Stage 8; photo: Tom Richardson)

Treks have been given a rough grade to give you an indication of the effort required. Since all treks, except one, are strenuous and more there is only a strenuous grade explained here. Expect one or more of the following descriptions to apply for the trek of your choice: high altitude, high passes, high camping, camping on ice, difficult trails, millions of possibly loose stones (large and small) along the trail, glacier travel, possible river crossings, long days, long treks, hot and no shade, long distance between water refilling, technical in some cases demanding climbing gear, only for well-prepared trekkers.

Each trek is broken down into day stages, but these divisions are suggestions only – you can split the days up as you choose and stay at different places for the night halt, if the local infrastructure permits. In most cases, the description of each day stage starts with another information box giving (if available) walking time, walking distance, ascent, descent and altitude gain/loss. (Altitude gain/loss given is the difference in sleeping altitude.) The day's route description follows, with details on what to expect along the way and on points of interest to be seen during the day. Some days also offer suggestions for side trips or alternative routes. Ideas for combining treks are also given where appropriate.

The information given here is as accurate as possible. However, it is bound to be out of date in some places due to the ever-changing nature of the environment, human influence, and costs of services.

Throughout the book, names for places, campsites, mountains and given heights are based on most used and most commonly found in literature and maps. Often several names and heights are indicated throughout this book. To complicate matters, even more different names and heights can be found or are used by locals. Use some common sense and be a bit creative with names and heights to finally find the closest correct information – it is called adventure travel. Eric Shipton's *Blank on the Map* is a title which sometimes can be used literally when moving around in the Karakoram and Himalaya. Enjoy!

GPX tracks

GPX tracks for the routes in this guidebook are available to download free at www.cicerone.co.uk/1056/GPX. If you have not bought the book through the Cicerone website, or have bought the book without opening an account, please register your purchase in your Cicerone library to access GPX and update information.

A GPS device is an excellent aid to navigation, but you should also carry a map and compass and know how to use them. Do not rely on GPX files when crossing glaciers. GPX files are provided in good faith, but in view of the profusion of formats and devices, neither the author nor the publisher accepts responsibility for their use. We provide files in a single standard GPX format that works on most devices and systems, but you may need to convert files to your preferred format using a GPX converter such as gpsvisualizer.com or one of the many other apps and online converters available.

Lukpe Lawo Brakk on the right (Trek 1, Day 6; photo:Colin Prior)

ALL ABOUT THE KARAKORAM

Near Paiju camp (Trek 2, Stage 1)

PEOPLE AND POPULATION

Pakistan is one of the most populated countries of the world (number 5). The population is young and growing fast, but not evenly spread around the country. The mountainous areas towards the west and north are less densely populated, but the fertile Punjab province counts more than 390 people per km^2.

Growing urbanisation is, like in so many countries, an ongoing process. Pakistan has 10 cities with populations exceeding one million, but the two largest are Karachi (approximately 15,000,000) and Lahore (approximately 11,000,000).

Life expectancy is about equal for women and men, namely 66½ years old. In 1984 it was 57 years old.

Most Pakistani people come from the Indo-Iranians group. The biggest population group is Punjabi followed by Pashtuns and Sindhis. There are three major languages spoken in Pakistan: Punjabi (87 per cent), Saraiki (10 per cent) and Pashto. But English is the official language of the government and therefore widely spoken throughout the country.

Foreigners living in Pakistan are mostly from Iraq, Uzbekistan, Bangladesh, Somalia, Tajikistan, and Burma. In the 1980s Pakistan received about three million Afghan refugees, followed by another wave in the 1990s. Several millions have moved back but presumably just as many have stayed in Pakistan. A new wave of Afghan refugees began in 2021.

About one million Pakistani live and work around the Persian Gulf and Middle East, as well as a large number in the UK.

People and population of the Gilgit-Baltistan areas

Note: this book is dealing with the eastern part of the northern areas, therefore concentrating on the people from Gilgit and Baltistan.

The Tibetan origins (animist and shamanist traditions), Buddhist past, and the Muslim present have all shaped the Balti and their culture through the centuries into today's form, a unique cultural mix. The Balti dialect is related to Tibetan.

GILGIT

Gilgit, the capital of the Gilgit–Baltistan region, counts more than 330,000 inhabitants. It is located in a broad, irrigated valley at the confluence of the Hunza and Gilgit rivers, along the Karakoram Highway (KKH). The city has developed vastly since the opening of the KKH in 1978.

The mountain Haramosh (7409m) guards the entrance to the Gilgit Valley, with Diran (7266m) and Rakaposhi (7788m) looming over Gilgit town. Gilgit Valley is a desert with little rainfall. A genius irrigation system of long water channels provides the fields with snowmelt, making it possible to grow some produce.

Bridge near Joila camp (Trek 2 approach)

Fruits, such as apricots, are popular in the region.

Gilgit has historically been of significant strategic importance, as proven by a long list of books and articles. One of the more famous books is *The Gilgit Game* by John Keay (1979).

Gilgit is near the meeting point of the Himalaya, Karakoram, Hindu Raj, Hindu Kush, and nearby Pamir, which also means a meeting point of different inhabitants, tribes, traders, travellers, warriors and others. One of the Silk Road routes went through Gilgit, encompassing diverse cultures, regions, ethnicities, and religions. According to Chinese Tang annals, Gilgit was Buddhist from the 4th to the 11th centuries and together with Yasin was called 'Little Bolor', while Baltistan was 'Great Bolor'. Slowly and finally after the 15th century the whole area gradually converted to Islam. Shina dialect is the most important dialect of Gilgit, introduced in the 10th century.

The Indus River is close and the territory west of the Indus up to Afghanistan was usually grouped together under the title Yaghistan, meaning 'the land of the uncontrollable' – of the savages.

Further north up the valley from Gilgit, John Keay describes the following from 1866:

> In Hunza captured soldiers of the Maharaja of Kashmir were used as human fireworks and in Yasin the natives were said to pluck out their hearts and eat them raw. Other tribes were supposed to be devil worshippers who offered human sacrifices. Any caravan that ventured into their valleys was immediately plundered and the only trade that could be said to flourish was the slave trade. In fact, in the absence of coin, mankind was the common currency; a hunting dog cost one male slave and a sturdy pony two females, preferably fair and fourteen.

After some influence of the British colonial power, and a political Great Game blowing over the area, the Gilgit district became part of Pakistan in 1974, but only after the kings of the seven feudal kingdoms along the Hunza and Gilgit rivers were relieved of their power by the government of Pakistan.

SKARDU AND BALTISTAN

Spreading over an area of about 26,000km^2 and situated in the heart of the Karakoram, Baltistan is a region of the Northern Areas and the home of lofty peaks and long glaciers. It borders with Ladakh in the east, Gilgit–Hunza in the west, the Xinjiang Province of China in the north, and Kashmir in the south.

The indigenous features of the population, cultural traits, and the similarity of the Balti language to archaic Tibetan has earned this area the nickname of 'Little Tibet'.

From earliest times, it was in the cultural sphere of northern India. Alexander of Macedon (356–323BCE) subdued Baltistan and brought Hellenic influence to the area. Thereafter, Baltistan was part of Gandharan culture and was an important centre of Buddhism. It was only in the 8th century that Tibetan tribes made inroads into the region and became a dominant part of the population. Ladakh and Baltistan remained under the Central Tibetan dynasty for a very long time.

The majority of people converted to Islam when it came to Baltistan in the 13th century, during the rule of the Makpon dynasty. It is often said that it was only with the Makpon rulers that Baltistan acquired its identity. Ali Sher Khan Anchan was the greatest ruler in the Makpon dynasty. The period of his rule is considered to be the golden period in the history of Baltistan. His rule spread from Mansroar, a lake in Tibet, to the valley of Kalash, Chitral in the east-west, and from the Karakoram mountain range in the extreme north to the northern boundaries of the present-day Kohistan Hazara. Their rule lasted until 1840, when the Dogras under the rule of Ghulab Singh Maharajah Jammu and Kashmir, seized the area.

The ethnic and cultural bonding between Baltistan and Ladakh deepened during the Dogra period (1842–1948), as the Dogras consolidated both regions into one province called the Ladakh Wazarat. The union of Ladakh and Baltistan within one administrative setup was successful as both regions have a similar culture.

Ladakh Wazarat was the largest province of the unified Jammu and Kashmir, and was six times larger than the total area of Kashmir province. It was divided into Leh, Kargil and Skardu districts. Skardu, the capital of Baltistan, was the winter capital of the province while Leh, the capital of central Ladakh, was the summer capital.

Baltistan remained part of Kashmir until 1947. The partition of Ladakh Wazarat in 1948 led to the separation of Ladakh and Baltistan, when the local Baltis fought for freedom from the Hindu Dogra regime to join Pakistan. Baltistan was later annexed by Pakistan and incorporated into the Northern Areas.

Skardu, at an altitude of 2340m, is the capital of Baltistan. It is located at the confluence of the Indus and Shigar Rivers, and counts a population of 26,000 people (up from 10,000 in 1975). The valley is a high-altitude desert, like most of Baltistan, and measures 10km wide by 40km long. Growing crops is only possible by using some ingenious irrigation systems, as in other places of Northern Pakistan.

Skardu (and Baltistan) never had the strategic importance of other places, such as Gilgit, due to the fact that it is only accessible via nearly impossible routes. When building the Karakoram Highway, a side-road

In Skardu – try to find the author?

was built which originates just before Gilgit and reaches Skardu after 200km (three to four hours' drive).

Polo in Baltistan

Polo is one of the world's oldest known team sports. Played on horseback, teams of 4, 12 or 14 players compete, using long-handled mallets to thwack a small, hard ball into the opponent's goal. There are several variations, but the games usually last no more than an hour on a pitch around nine times the size of a football ground! The team with the most goals, wins. Any player wishing to participate must demonstrate excellent horsemanship and it is worthwhile trying to spectate, even if you only see a practice game. Just about every village has a polo ground in Baltistan. Some call it a 'gentlemen's game' and this 1909 description by Filippo de Filippi gives some context:

> At four o'clock in the afternoon a game of polo was organized in honour of the Duke [of the Abruzzi]. Twelve players took part. In the excitement of the game horses and men totally changed their aspect [...] 'It is, however, improbable that polo was, as K.E. von Ujfalvy would have us believe, invented in Baltistan, a country so rough that, with few exceptions, there is no place for galloping outside the polo grounds themselves, which are levelled and beaten on purpose. The origin of the game is certainly remote. It seems to have been common at the court of the Mogols. Then the tradition was lost in India, and only kept up at Manipur (on the confines of Burma), in Baltistan, Ladakh and Gilgit. The English of Calcutta learned the game in Manipur and were so attracted by its fine and manly qualities that they made it their own and have diffused it throughout the world.

Skardu fort

Anyone who sees the old fort of Skardu, carved entirely into the rock and dominating the Indus Valley like an eagle's nest, believes absolutely in its impregnability. The fort is known as Karpochu, Askandria or Mindoq Khar. In Buddhist times, a monastery stood here, followed by a fort from the 15th century, after which the present fort was built during the 18th and 19th centuries. Today, unfortunately, much of the fort has deteriorated.

However, it is possible to visit the fort. Allow one to two hours for this trip. Bring some cash for the entrance fee (find out if the caretaker is at the entrance before hiking up). Walking to the top of the Skardu rock is possible but not easy.

The views over Skardu, the valley and its surrounding mountains, and the Indus River are impressive.

Skardu Fort has been described by several authors, including Filippo de Filippi in 1909:

> Upon the detached rock between Skardu and the Indus stands an ancient fort built about 1610 by Ali Sher, the first of the dynasty of independent Mohammedan chiefs which came to an end when Ahmed Shall was conquered and dethroned by the Sikhs in 1840. The fort is now abandoned, and another was built by the Sikhs at the foot of the rock, on the verge of the plain. The legend of Alexander the Great, which is so living throughout central Asia, has penetrated even to this remote spot, and tells us that Skardu is a mere corruption of Iskandaria, or city of Alexander. The tradition is, however, quite baseless. It is true that early travellers called the town Iskardo, but according to Thomson the real Tibetan name is Skardo or Kardo. The place seems to have been far more prosperous and civilized in the past than at the present day. Thomson, who made a long stay there, spending the whole winter in 1874, found ruins of buildings constructed of quarried stone, marble fountains, hanging gardens, aqueducts...

RELIGION IN THE GILGIT-BALTISTAN AREAS

In Baltistan, in the arid valleys of the Karakoram, lies the historic junction of the Buddhist and Islamic worlds. Some historians claim that the original inhabitants of Gilgit and Baltistan were the so-called Aryan Dards, and that there was once a centre of Bon shamanism, the indigenous religion of the Himalaya.

Animist traditions are still around. The water spirit Lu, dwelling in the trees, should not be disturbed and therefore trees close to springs are left untouched. Ibex statues, symbols of fertility, can be found in pastures, where livestock are breeding. The connection between household and field is important, symbolised by a ripe stalk of wheat extracted from the field and tied around a pillar of the house. Threshed wheat is often placed in amulet charms to invoke nature's support for a bountiful harvest.

In the 3rd century BCE Buddhism arrived in the Indus Valley. It spread around in Baltistan when the route, through the Karakoram between Yarkand and Kashmir, was much used for trade, starting from the 2nd century. From the 2nd century BCE to the 5th century CE northern Pakistan was the centre of Buddhism, and from here the religion/philosophy spread to China and Tibet.

Near Skardu, the Manthal Buddha or Satpara Buddha (from between 700 and 1000AD): Sakyamuni Buddha is surrounded by twenty similar Buddhist and Tibetan inscriptions at the foot

Today ornamental motifs, auspicious symbols (such as the lotus flower, swastika, endless note and sun), can be found on pillars, cupboards, and wooden walls. They suggest Tibetan origins and are supposed to protect and bring fortune.

Islam was introduced to Baltistan around the 16th century but can be traced back as far as the 14th century. Islam is now the state religion of Pakistan and around 96 per cent of the population are Muslim, with Sunni making up 70 to 80 per cent of the Muslims, beside Shias and Ismailis. Nowadays 60 per cent or more of Baltistan's population is Shia (or Shi'ites).

Religion is taken seriously in Baltistan. Days of celebrations can be expected throughout the year when everything is put on hold.

CULTURE AND ARCHITECTURE

Pakistan has been ruled by cultural and nature-loving Mughal Emperors and British colonialists. Such a rich history has left behind many religious and military landmarks all over Pakistan like mosques, national monuments, forts and museums.

In and around Lahore most monuments can be found like the Shalimar Gardens, the Pearl Mosque, and the Badshahi Mosque. There are a couple of fine museums throughout the country. The Lahore Museum, the

Taxila Museum near Islamabad, and the Lok Virsa or Heritage Museum in Islamabad.

Mughal heritage can also be found in art and literature (notably poetry). Dancing and singing are an important part of Pakistani culture and as a trekker in the mountains there should be some opportunities to enjoy this.

Onc of the more impressive art forms is the decades-old, costly decoration of trucks and buses crossing the country, making Pakistan's traffic some of the most colourful in the world. A guess could be that a truck without decoration would take up 20 per cent less space!

In the Northern Areas

Further back in history another important period took place in Pakistan where Buddhism flourished. This can be seen for example at the ruins and in the museum of Taxila, a day's outing from Islamabad. Buddhism travelled through the Northern Areas leaving traces behind, like rock paintings and carvings.

In the Northern Areas several small kingdoms existed like Hunza, Gilgit, Yasin, Gupis, Rondu, Skardu, Shigar, and Khapalu all of which had their own culture. Numerous impressive ruined and renovated palaces and forts can be found in these districts, some have even been turned into

Near Concordia, on the way to Broad Peak Base Camp and K2 Base Camp (Trek 2, Stage 7)

museums and/or hotels. In Askole a well-illustrated local museum is open for visitors.

Spectacular ancient mosques and religious buildings can be found throughout the Karakoram. Many of these buildings are often decorated with fine wood carvings.

An interesting group of people are the Kalasha people, who live close to the border with Afghanistan in the Chitral district. Their mythology and folklore are likely influenced by the presence of Alexander the Great and his army from Greece.

TIMELINE OF EXPLORING AND CLIMBING HISTORY IN THE GILGIT-BALTISTAN AREAS

This selective timeline covers some of the most significant expeditions of the past, and is far from comprehensive. The focus here is on trips for which there was a written record, first ascents and trips for which the main purpose was recreation or exploration. For more detail on local and Pakistani climbing, see 'Pakistan high-altitude climbers and porters'.

Year	Expedition
1254–1324	Marco Polo travelled along the northern border of the Karakoram and is probably the first western person to give a written account of the range since ancient times.
1820	William Moorcraft was the first European explorer to visit the Karakoram and gave it its name, which means 'black gravel' in Turkish.
1835	British botanist-geologist Godfrey Thomas Vigne visited Skardu, spotted Nanga Parbat and penetrated the Karakoram.
1856	Three German brothers named Schlagintweit crossed the Karakoram Pass and New Muztagh Pass. Adolf repeated his trip alone and when reaching Kashgar he was beheaded without a trial as a suspected spy.
1856	Survey officers Thomas Montgomerie and William Johnson are likely the first Europeans to see K2 from 150 miles or 240km distance. Montgomerie labelled the peaks with the letter 'K' for Karakoram, for example K1 or Masherbrum, K2, K3 or Gasherbrum IV, K4 or Gasherbrum II, K5 or Gasherbrum I. A few 'K' peaks are left these days (like K2, K6, K7, K12).
1860–1861	Henry Haversham Godwin-Austen explored the Hushe Valley and several remote valleys of northern Baltistan and climbed some peaks near Skardu. He was the first westerner to sight the Hispar Glacier, fixed the height of Ogre at 7285m, visited the Baltoro Glacier and high on a spur of Masherbrum where he had an excellent view of K2.

Year	Expedition
1887–1889	Captain Francis Edward Younghusband is the first confirmed westerner to see K2 from the north when travelling up the Sarpo Laggo Valley leading to the Old- and New Muztagh Pass. Younghusband was the first European to cross the Old Muztagh Pass.
1888–1889	Bronislav Grombchevsky seen as the Russian counterpart of Younghusband, led several expeditions along the Chinese border near Kasghar and Tien Shian mountains, Pamirs, Muztagh Ata Peak (7548m), and reached the foot of K2 in 1889.
1892	William Martin Conway conducted several expeditions. Baltoro Karakoram was his first. From Gilgit they travelled north to Hunza and up the Hispar Glacier, crossing the pass and following the Biafo Glacier all the way to Askole; the first westerner to do so. They spent 84 days on snow or glacier.
1895	Nanga Parbat 8126m: Albert Mummery, Geoffrey Hastings and J. Norman Collie, after assuring themselves that the Rupal Face was not even worth considering, crossed over the Mazeno Pass to the Diamir Face where a height of 6100m was reached.
1898–1912	American couple Fanny Bullock Workman and Dr William Hunter Workman contributed considerably to opening-up unknown far corners of the Karakoram and Himalaya with all their travels and books. They were accompanied by the Swiss guide, Mattias Zurbriggen.
1902	Brit Oscar JL Eckenstein was the leader of the first serious attempt to climb K2 on the Northeast Ridge. Other team members were experienced climbers Aleister Crowley, Guy Knowles, Heinrich Pfannl, Viktor Wessely and Jules Jacot Guillarmod. At the beginning of the expedition Eckenstein was arrested and accused of being a spy. The team left Askole with more than 150 porters moving three tons of luggage. The team reached a height of about 6550m after lots of bad weather and internal conflicts.
1909	Luigi Francesco di Savoia-Aosta, il Duca d'Abruzzi. One of the main objectives for the Duke choosing K2 was to return to Italy with a first ascent and surpassing the altitude record of that day which was 7338m. Two months after sailing from Marseilles they camped at the foot of K2 using 260 porters to move 4752kg of luggage. They were defeated on several different routes.
1934	Nanga Parbat (8126m): under the leadership of Willy Merkl, the expedition climbed high but were struck by death, due to sickness and storm at high camp (approximately 7500m) on the Silver Saddle. Sixteen men were at high camp when an enormous storm hit. Four climbers and six Sherpas perished.

Year	Expedition
1936	Henri de Ségogne led a French expedition to attempt Gasherbrum I (8080m) (Hidden Peak or K5), giving up due to a long period of bad weather.
1937	Eric Shipton and Bill Tilman made a major reconnaissance and surveying expedition in the Karakoram: Skardu, Askole, Paiju, Muztagh Pass, and recounted their exploits in the classic book, *Blank on the Map* by Eric Shipton.
1953	Nanga Parbat (8126m): first ascent by Austrian, Hermann Buhl. An Austrian-German team led by Dr Karl Herrligkoffer including a fine team of climbers, accompanied by Hunza porters put Buhl on the summit after an epic climb. The return trip to the camp at around 6900m took Buhl over 40 hours, including a standing bivouac.
1954	K2 (8611m) – first ascent – Italian expedition led by Professor Ardito Desio placed Achille Compagnoni and Lino Lacedelli on the summit on 31 July, only possible with the enormous support of Amir Mahdi and top alpinist Walter Bonatti, under some controversial conditions. More than 500 porters were employed, an available budget around £1.2 million, and loads of free equipment made this a rather large-scale outing.
1956	Gasherbrum II (8035m) – first ascent – Austrian expedition by Josef Larch, Fritz Moravec and Johann Willenpart
1957	Broad Peak (8051m) – first ascent – Austrian expedition by Hermann Buhl, Kurt Diemberger, Marcus Schmuck, Fritz Wintersteller.
1958	Gasherbrum I (8080m) (Hidden Peak) – first ascent – US expedition led by Nick Clinch put Andy Kaufmann and Pete Schoening on the summit.
1958	Gasherbrum IV (7925m) – first ascent by Italians Walter Bonatti and Carlo Mauri.
1960–1974	Access to the Karakoram was prohibited because of international tensions in the area.
1977	K2 (8611m) – Ashraf Aman became the first Pakistani to climb K2, as part of a Japanese expedition,
1977	Ogre (7285m) (Baintha Brakk) – first ascent by Doug Scott and Chris Bonington with a more than dramatic finish (see Trek 1, Day 3 description).
1978	K2 (8611m) – American expedition led by Jim Whittaker succeeding after 40 years of American K2 expeditions placing four climbers on the summit: on September 6 Louis Reichardt and James Wickwire, and on September 7 John Roskelley and Rick Ridgeway (Reichardt is the first to summit without supplementary oxygen).

Year	Expedition
1982	K2 North side climbed by a Japanese expedition.
1985	Gasherbrum II (8035m) – Mohammed Karim or better known as 'Little Karim' (from Hushe) climbs his first 8000m peak without oxygen. He has an impressive list of climbs and supporting expeditions.
1986	K2 (8611m) – Polish Wanda Rutkiewicz, the first woman to climb K2.
1999	Broad Peak (8051m) – Qudrat Ali from Pakistan-Shimshal climbs his first 8000m peak after having climbed some lesser peaks and followed by many more impressive climbs, including the 8000m peaks of Pakistan and an attempt on Manaslu (8165m) in Nepal.
2021	K2 (8611m) – Nirmal Purja climbs K2 with nine fellow Nepali climbers In winter. A first winter ascent of K2 and the last 8000m peak to be climbed in the winter, Purja didn't use supplementary oxygen.
2022	An amazingly successful season. More than 400 climbing permits were issued for K2. On the 22nd of July more than 90 people summited K2 in one day; it took 40 years to complete 100 summits of K2 with nearly the same milestone achieved in a single day! Around 200 summited K2 in 2022. Over 1000 people climbed across several peaks with the majority on the five 8000m peaks. And only very few fatal accidents.
2023	Norwegian Kristin Harila, together with Tenjen Lama Sherpa, completed all 14 8000m peaks in just 92 days, with K2 as her final summit on 27 July. All peaks were climbed with Sherpa support.
2023	Many successes despite suboptimal weather. Estimated successful summits include: K2 112+, GI 63+, GII 65+, Broad Peak 61+, Nanga Parbat 60+.

PAKISTANI HIGH-ALTITUDE CLIMBERS AND PORTERS

The well-known high-altitude (support) climbers from Nepal (best known by the name Sherpas), also exist in Pakistan. Foreign expeditions in Pakistan employ Sherpas, but also Pakistani high-altitude climbers. We don't hear so much about these Pakistani climbers but there are many, coming from areas like Shimshal, Gilgit and Baltistan. Living at altitude in remote areas, you are exposed from an early age to walking long distances at altitude and carrying loads or herding animals on steep slopes in a variety of weather conditions. A combination that easily forms some hardy mountaineers.

Pakistani climbers are not generally recognised in their own country, unlike the west, where mountaineers and climbers are often celebrated as heroes. A small number of Pakistani climbers have received international attention and recognition, usually

Looking west along Hispar Glacier (Trek 1, Stage 9; photo: Jasmine Star)

for a first ascent of one Pakistan's many mountains, or those who have accompanied foreign climbers and supported (or sometimes rescued) climbers.

There is such an enormous world of difference between climbers from the west and those from Pakistan: long preparation time versus none; lots of training versus none; hobby versus job (except for professional climbers); amount of money used for a climb; self-promotion before and after a climb. Some of these differences also exist between Sherpas and Pakistani altitude climbers.

In Shimshal a mountaineering school was set up in 2009 to help male and female climbers develop better technical skills. The oldest mountaineering school is the Balti Yul Mountaineering School (BYMS) in Khaplu, with experienced mountaineer Muhammed Khan as climbing teacher.

PAKISTANI CLIMBERS

This list, by no means exhaustive, highlights some key achievements by Pakistani climbers. It does not include mention of their incredible amount of hard work carrying gear to high camps to facilitate climbing expeditions, or their rescue efforts.

- **Ashraf Aman** – first Pakistani to climb K2
- **Nazir Sabir** (Hunza) – joining several expeditions, Japanese expeditions, first Pakistani to climb Everest (described climbing on K2 as 'we perform under the shade of death'[sic])
- **Meharban Karim** (Shimshal) – impressive list of climbs

- **Amir Mehdi** (Hunza) – joining the first successful Nanga Parbat 1953 and K2 1954 expeditions
- **Samina Baig** (Shimshal) – first Pakistani woman to climb Everest in 2013
- **Rajab Shah** (The Crown of Karakorum) – first Pakistani to summit all five Pakistan 8000m peaks
- **Fazal Ali** (Shimshal) (The K2 King) – summiting K2 four times (out of eight attempts)
- **Sirbaz Khan** (Hunza) – climbing 10 of the 14 8000m peaks
- **Naila Kiana** – female climber who climbed all five of Pakistan's 8000m peaks and as of 2023 has climbed nine peaks over 8000m

For more information on Pakistani climbers and porters, see Lara Lee's 2015 documentary *K2 and the Invisible Footmen* or the book *And death walks with them* by Christiane Fladt.

It's worth noting that this list would be longer if foreign expeditions would allow the Pakistani climbers to join the final summit push more often.

In Pakistan the porters are organised in a union. Porters should be equipped by the local tour operator. Make sure they have been supplied with some warm clothes and sunglasses for a simple trek, and more equipment for technical trips.

Some of the amazingly hard-working and ever-so-friendly porters and staff at Broad Peak Base Camp, with K2 in the background (Trek 2, Stage 7)

Porters claim that, due to the toughness of their jobs, their life expectancy is 10 to 20 years shorter than the average Balti. Especially if they are made to carry 40kg instead of 25kg.

Porters are tough. On one of my Biafo–Hispar crossings, when camping on top of the Hispar Pass (5151m), a snowstorm struck during the night. The porters had built themselves a reasonably comfortable shelter; a square hole about one metre deep in the snow, covered with a huge, well-fixed tarpaulin. However, the wind picked up and the tarpaulin blew off. Hearing it blowing over my tent, I rushed out, got hold of the tarpaulin and went to the porters, expecting to see them bewildered in the open air with a snowstorm blowing around them. On the contrary, they were still fast asleep. With some help the tarpaulin was fixed back again and everybody had a good night's sleep. The porters best of all!

Besides high-altitude climbers there are so many other Pakistani staff doing an excellent job, providing different services on trek. The kitchen crew, for example, are up long before trekkers and climbers, preparing breakfast, lunch to-go, and taking down camp. They then walk the same distance as trekkers do, arrive at camp in advance of the main group and prepare everything all over again.

OTHER ADVENTURE ACTIVITIES

Besides trekking and mountaineering, mountain biking is popular in the Karakoram. The 1300km-long Karakoram Highway (KKH), connecting Pakistan with Xinjiang, China, and crossing the Khunjerab Pass (4714m), is one of the highlights of a mountain bikers' life. The KKH has recently been repaired and made wider. This could make it more dangerous to bike since it might mean trucks, buses and other drivers want to speed up. There are many other possible routes to bike in Pakistan besides the KKH.

Rafting and kayaking are getting more popular. If you go trekking to K2 or on the Biafo–Hispar route you will follow the Braldu Gorge where some professional kayakers have managed to kayak the wild 78km-long Braldu River (you can check out some clips on YouTube). In 1978 a UK team failed: too much water. But in 1984 a US team including Andrew Embick succeeded – with only two broken paddles!

Skiing is done, but it is no big business. Some other activities on offer are: motor-biking tours, heli-trekking, jeep safaris, hunting, cultural and archaeological tours, and paragliding.

THE LANDSCAPE OF THE KARAKORAM

Vigne usually calls the country Little Tibet, and both the people and the terrain are distinctly Tibetan in appearance. The valleys are perhaps deeper and steeper than further east, and they are separated not by rolling plateaux but by lofty spurs. Yet there is the same overall impression of rock and sand, harsh white light and biting dry wind. Natural vegetation is a rare and transitory phenomenon; cultivation just an artificial patchwork of fields suspended from a contour-clinging irrigation duct or huddled on the triangular surface of a fan of alluvial soil washed down from the mountains. The water is an icy grey mercury fresh from the glaciers and glittering with mica. Shade, the other essential, is either the dappled pallor afforded by willow and apricot tree or the deep and shivery gloom of a Balti house.

John Keay, When Men and Mountains Meet

The Karakoram range contains the greatest concentration of high mountains, and high-altitude glaciers in the world and, geologically, has a longer and more complex history than the Himalaya. The Karakoram is on the same latitude as Tibet, both being north of the Indian plate Himalaya and the Indus suture zone that divides the two terranes. This fact may suffice to explain the climate differences between the Karakoram and other well-known section of the Himalaya, making the Karakoram in general colder.

GEOLOGY

Karakoram geology includes Paleozoic and Mesozoic mainly sedimentary rocks and their crystalline basement, as well as their metamorphosed equivalents. Metamorphism results from increased pressure and temperature due to plate collision and the processes of crust thickening. Dating of metamorphic rocks shows that major events occurred both before the India–Asia collision (50 million years ago), and after, during the Cenozoic period. The metamorphic events culminated in widespread melting of the lower crust, which resulted in the intrusion of a large-scale granite batholith (Baltoro granites).

The trek along the Baltoro Glacier to K2 crosses the southern Karakoram metamorphic complex (Shigar–Askole–Paiju), the Baltoro granites (Trango Towers, Masherbrum range) and the northern sedimentary units (Gasherbrum range). K2 is an isolated inlier of deep crustal metamorphic rock and granite intrusions. The Gondogoro La trek from Concordia on the Baltoro Glacier over the pass crosses back from the northern sedimentary units (Hidden Peak, Broad Peak and the Gasherbrum range) to the granite intrusions around Laila Peak and the upper Hushe valley. The Baltoro granites comprise most of the backbone of the Karakoram with the spectacular spires of the Trango Towers, Shipton Spire, Uli Biaho Spire north of the Baltoro Glacier and the Biarchedi–Masherbrum massif to the south.

The Biafo–Hispar trek starts from the Dassu–Askole region along the Braldu valley and turns west along the Biafo Glacier. This part of the trek traverses the metamorphic rocks with granite dykes and veins, then crosses into the Baltoro granites at the junction of the Uzun Brakk and the Biafo Glaciers. Peaks to the north of the Biafo, including Ogre (7285m), Conway's Ogre/Uzun Brakk (6422m) and the Latok peaks are all composed of the young Baltoro granites, which intruded around 20–15 million years ago. The granites contain red garnets, black tourmaline crystals as well as milky white feldspars and translucent quartz. Some pegmatites (coarse-granites) also contain rare gem-quality blue aquamarine (beryl) crystals. Trekking along the Hispar Glacier towards Nagar and Hunza, the high peaks to the north, including Pumari Chhish (7491m) and Khunyang Chhish (7852m) are granite batholiths.

Nanga Parbat is not strictly in the Karakoram range but forms the western extension of the main Himalaya. The Nanga Parbat massif is entirely composed of metamorphic rocks and migmatites (partially molten metamorphic rocks) with a series of granite dykes intruding. These rocks have undergone the entire burial and metamorphic history seen along the Greater Himalayan ranges following the collision of India and Asia, but also show an even younger phase of high-temperature metamorphism dated at between 7–0.75 million

Cleaning the campsite at Paiju (Trek 2, Stage 2)

years. These granite melts containing red garnets, green cordierite and pale muscovite mica show that the rocks forming the upper part of Nanga Parbat were buried to depths of about 20–25km, metamorphosed and partially melted around one million years ago, then returned to the surface in the last one to two million years. These rocks on Nanga Parbat are the youngest metamorphic rock on Earth and show the highest and fastest exhumation rates.

The Karakoram is an active young mountain belt that extends west into the Hindu Kush along the Pakistan–Afghanistan border region. Although the Karakoram has relatively few earthquakes, the Hindu Kush–Pamir region has an extremely seismically active zone of earthquakes as deep as 250km. These deep earthquakes are caused by the rapid subduction of the Indian plate crust to 250–300km and are the deepest known earthquakes anywhere on the continents. These deep earthquakes are generally less destructive that the major Himalayan earthquakes, such as the 2015 Gorkha earthquake, which are generated by slip along the Main Himalayan thrust, where the Indian plate is sliding beneath the Himalaya (see *Colliding Continents* by Mike Searle for more details).

GLACIERS

With 7253 known glaciers, including 543 in the Chitral Valley, there is more glacial ice in Pakistan than anywhere on Earth outside the polar regions, according to various studies. Those glaciers feed rivers that account for about 75 percent of the stored-water supply in the country of at least 180 million.

(Tim Craig, in an article in The Washington Post in 2016)

The glaciers of the whole of the Himalaya and Karakoram are a critical water source for millions of people living across eight different countries, or for ten major river systems. These populated countries south of the Himalaya and Karakoram create a lot of air pollution, depositing black carbon and dust on the ice, hastening the

Ice sail and author on Baltaro Glacier

thaw (black absorbs sun heat). A very pessimistic scenario predicts that with a 2°C increase of global temperature, the glaciers will have disappeared by 2100. Water supply is an ever-increasingly hot topic in this area.

However, there are reasons for hope: the 'Karakoram anomaly' is a phenomenon indicating that the glaciers in this region are retreating more slowly than in other parts of the world. Landsat images, taken as part of a 10-year study of the Karakoram Park glaciers from 2001–2010, showed that ice cover has remained largely the same.

The high degree of glaciation in the Karakoram is due to the northern location – compared to Nepal – and lower average temperatures. While the mountains in Nepal lie on a latitude around 28 degrees north, the Karakoram ranges between 34 and 37 degrees north. This colder climatic zone also causes the tongues of the large glaciers to descend to much lower altitudes, like the Baltoro Glacier at 3600m, the Biafo Glacier at 3100m and the Batura Glacier even at 2600m.

Some of these glaciers are huge: up to 70km long and several kilometres wide and often have extremely rugged surfaces with mountain-like moraines, which are so unusual that newcomers generally completely underestimate the challenges that these glaciers demand. The melting of the huge glacier masses in summer means that the mountain streams or glacial streams on the surface become dangerous obstacles. Treks such as K2 and crossing the Hispar Pass involve walking for many days and many kilometres on these ice highways.

On a list of the seven longest glaciers on Earth in non-polar regions, Pakistan ranks number three, five and seven. Some of the larger glaciers in the area include Biafo ($333km^2$), Hispar ($280km^2$), Baltoro ($236km^2$), Chogo Lungma ($131km^2$), Virjerab ($62km^2$), and Braldu ($48km^2$).

Glacial Lake Outburst Floods (GLOF) have occurred 35 times in the last 200 years.

Ice sails

Ice sails are an impressive ice phenomenon, that can be encountered while trekking on the Baltoro Glacier. They start with ice being covered with 'dirt', absorbing the solar radiation. The glacier warms and melts downwards, except where there are patches of clean ice reflecting the sun's rays. These sections melt more slowly and rise, as everything around them falls, thus creating ice sails. They are also known as 'penitentes', supposedly because they look like a praying monk.

RIVERS

The Indus River crossing Pakistan provides water for roughly 270 million people along its path. From the 10 major river basins originating in the Himalaya–Karakoram–Hindukush range (like the Indus, Jhelum, Ganges, Mekong, Bhramaputra, Yellow River and others) the Indus River is number three on the list of the number of people depending on its water. (The Yangtze is number one, with roughly 605 million people, and the Ganges River close with 600 million people; the 10 rivers together provide water for 1.9 billion people).

When the Indus River reaches the town of Skardu, it is more than 700km from its source in Tibet. Skardu's big valley was once a lake.

The enormous size of rivers, the sheer amount of water, the glaciers, earthquakes and landslides cause an ongoing challenge for people living in this region. Filippo de Filippi chronicled one such event:

> In 1841 a landslide in the deep gorge of the Indus to the west of Nanga Parbat almost entirely dammed up the course of the river, forming a lake about 40 miles long. Months later the dam gave away, and the huge reservoir was emptied in a single day, obliterating every trace of life for 800 miles of valley. With ant-like industry the inhabitants have succeeded in wresting their nurture from the terrific nature round them. They have caught every trickle of water, every rivulet fed by high névé or glacier, and have led it for miles through carefully constructed conduits to a point where little sloping ledge, or more often the surface of an alluvial delta, permitted of irrigation and culture.

Fresh landslide area (Trek 1, Stage 8; photo: Jasmine Star)

MINING

Controlled mining takes place throughout the CKNP and the Northern Area of Pakistan, with local councils issuing permits. It is a paradise for gemmologists: around 25 different types of minerals and precious gemstones can be found, such as beryl-aquamarine, albite, topaz, aquamarine, tourmaline, quartz, emerald, ruby, sapphire, amethyst, epidote, olivine peridot, mica, zircon, garnet and moonstone.

This hunt for hidden treasure is a centuries old practice, although it has always been done on a small scale. Even today it is not as developed as it could be, mainly due to lack of funding, modern equipment and skilled labour. More recently investors from various countries have shown interest in providing money and basic equipment. The growing mining activity has some negative impact on the fragile mountain ecosystems.

Mining is a dangerous occupation; blasts and falling rocks can be fatal. The miners have set up an association to protect their interests and to help newcomers get established.

NATIONAL PARKS IN THE GILGIT-BALTISTAN AREAS

Pakistan boasts the impressive number of 219 protected areas: 29 National Parks, 100 Wildlife Sanctuaries and 90 Game Reserves. The treks in this guidebook cross some of the protected areas. There are a handful of wildlife conservation organisations operating in Pakistan.

The oldest National Park, Lal Suhanra, dates back to 1972 and is

From Concordia: K2 and Broad Peak, with Gasherbrum IV in the clouds (Trek 2, Stage 5)

in the populated province of Punjab. Since then, 28 more National Parks have been created throughout Pakistan, with the majority to be found in the northern area of the country.

Ecological or life zones

Mountain areas often have a large variation in plants and animals. At the foot of the mountains, deep in the valleys, the climate is dry and warm with forests and abundant undergrowth. At the highest altitudes, a polar climate makes it nearly impossible for anything to grow.

There are several known factors making it nearly impossible for most living organisms to survive at altitude. Some of these include: reduced oxygen levels and temperature levels (average temperature drop of 0.6°C per 100 metres of ascent); enormous temperature differential between day and night; less air dust pollution resulting in more intense sunshine and increased UV intensity; varying levels of humidity, with or without cloud cover; amount of precipitation as rain or snow.

Plants and wildlife for the northern area are described separately in their respective chapters.

Central Karakoram National Park

In 1993 the Central Karakoram National Park (CKNP) was established: the largest park in the country and one of the highest parks in the world.

The CKNP is in the Gilgit–Baltistan region, covering an area of more than 10,550km^2 (half the size of Wales). The altitudes range from 2000m to 8000m+ with four

of the world's fourteen 8000m peaks included: K2 (8611m), Gasherbrum I (8080m), Gasherbrum II (8035m) and Broad Peak (8051m). The area is covered with trekking routes enjoying the rich biodiversity, natural beauty and scenery and is surrounded in a unique cultural heritage.

Roughly 40 per cent of the Central Karakoram National Park is covered by ice forming more than 700 glaciers. The park can proudly boast some of the longest glaciers in the world: the Biafo (63km), Baltoro (63km) and Hispar (49km) Glaciers. (To compare with some other glaciers around the world: the Antarctic Lambert Glacier is 96km; the Siachen Glacier in the Karakoram – but not in the CKNP – is 76km; the Aletsch Glacier in Switzerland is 23km long).

In general, the area has low precipitation and experiences relatively humid westerly winds. The Central Karakoram National Park can be divided into two ecological zones: Gilgit and Skardu. The first zone (Gilgit) is warmer and gets more rain resulting in more forest and natural vegetation, and the second zone (Skardu) is essentially the opposite. However, agricultural lands and pastures can be found throughout the park. Crops include potato, maize, wheat, and fruits like apricot and pomegranate.

The Karakoram mountain range is rather young with steep valleys and a nearly absent soil layer resulting in a sparse vegetation that has to deal with extreme temperatures. The Park has several distinct vegetation zones, each

Gasherbrum IV and snowy GII peeping out behind IV from Baltoro Glacier (Trek 2, Stage 6)

with its own plant life, which thrives or survives according to the climate, aspect, altitude and topography.

- Crops such as potatoes, wheat and maize are grown in the **valley bottoms** where the villages are located. Pomegranate and apricot trees are also plentiful.
- The **alpine steppe** zone is on the lower slopes of the mountains. Here the surface consists of gravel and moraine soil, which support sparse grass and scrub.
- Beside rivers and streams and in the shelter of gullies and ravines, bushes and small deciduous trees grows on the **sub-alpine scrub-land**. These plants provide grazing for livestock and wild ungulates.
- The **alpine meadows and alpine scrub zone** are higher up the slopes: here there is high pasture (for summer grazing) and open coniferous forest.
- Above this, from around 4200m to 5100m, are **permanent snow-fields** and **cold dry desert**. Here only isolated patches of stunted grass and hardy, low vegetation can grow.

Management of the park

The park has been divided into two other types of zone to facilitate land management. Firstly, the core zone, spanning around 7600km^2, which comprises the mountain peaks, glaciers and high-level mountain areas, and their fragile ecosystem; secondly, the buffer zone which comprises around 3000km^2 of mainly lower-lying areas. This buffer zone is concentrated around human settlements and acts, as the name suggests, to protect the more fragile ecosystems above from unsustainable human-related impact, as well as providing access via established corridors to the core zone beyond.

In February 2015, after a year-long consultation period with local communities and other stakeholders, a management plan for the park was put into place, centred on the sectors of vegetation, wildlife, medicinal/aromatic plants and non-wood forest products, pastures and livestock, agriculture, water, mining, tourism, local community involvement and research.

At the entrance point to the Park beyond Askole, leading to Hispar and K2, there is a rather large centre. Here permits are checked and there are some educational materials displayed on the walls. The environmental protection in the Park along the route to Concordia has unfortunately been deteriorating over the years. A very long list of new plans and a strategy to get back on track is in the pipeline. Let's see if they will be implemented.

Some other facts about the park:

- In 1992 the Concordia Rescue Team was established due to the lack of a first aid service within the park.
- Hunting of Himalayan Blue Sheep and the Himalayan Ibex and Tahr is allowed with permission.

- Mining in the CKNP is happening: see the previous section on Mining.

Fairy Meadows National Park

Fairy Meadows National Park, established in 1995, is located at the foot of the north face of Nanga Parbat (8126m), the ninth highest mountain in the world. The name Fairy Meadows (*Märchenwiese*) has its origin in the German expeditions visiting Nanga Parbat. The local name is *Joot*. At an altitude of 3295m, the beautiful Fairy Meadows are surrounded by thick alpine forest and the towering 4800m-high face of Nanga Parbat with impressive hanging glaciers. Brown bears have been seen around in the area, but not for some time. Musk deer can be spotted.

Khunjerab National Park

Khunjerab National Park was established in 1975 and is located in the extreme north. It is the third largest national park covering 2270km^2 and reaching altitudes of 7700m. The park is connected to the north with the Chinese Taxkorgan Reserve (14,000km^2), established in 1984.

The famous wildlife biologist George B Schaller proposed the idea of this park in 1973. The main reason behind its conception was to protect the Marco Polo sheep, whose numbers had dropped by more than half when the Karakoram Highway was finished (1978). Other animals protected here are the Himalayan ibex and snow leopard. More than 150 species of flower can be found in the Park.

Deosai National Park

The Deosai National Park (or Deosai Plains) was established in 1993 (*deosai* means 'the land of giants' or 'giant shadow'). It covers an area of 3584km^2 and is in the Skardu district. The park is at an altitude of 4000m+. From one of the lakes, Sheosar Lake, Nanga Parbat can be seen.

Balti people like to call it 'summer land' because the summer is the only time of year where you can visit the park due to the cold weather conditions during the rest of the year. But even in summer it can start snowing here. Normally there is an eight-month period of snow cover.

The Himalayan Brown Bear (thirty individuals and increasing numbers) has protected status within the Park. The Deosai Plains are also home to other species such as the Gray Wolf, the Himalayan Ibex, Red Fox, Golden Marmot, and Snow Leopard. There are more than 120 species of bird in the Park, (including spectacular birds of prey such as Sparrowhawk, Kestrel, Golden Eagle, Griffon Vulture, Laggar Falcon, Peregrine Falcon), and over 300 species of flower.

Ghizer Gilgit Baltistan Broghil Valley National Park

Ghizer Gilgit Baltistan Broghil Valley National Park or Broghil Valley National Park is located close to the

Afghan–Pakistan border in the Chitral and Khyber district. Elevations range from 3280m to 4300m where the beautiful mountain lake Qurumber (or Karamber) Lake can be found. The landscape is very mountainous with steep mountain valleys and the occasional grassy plain.

It is one of the smaller parks and is not included in any treks in this edition of the guidebook. A popular trek here is crossing the Darkot Pass.

PLANTLIFE

Oleg Polunin and Adam Stainton wrote the definitive book on flowers of the Himalaya, originally published in 1984, and a bit heavy to carry in your daypack. Nearly 100 years older, the 1892 book by Martin Conway *Climbing in the Himalayas* has detailed descriptions of the flowers he found at each campsite.

Like many other aspects of the Karakoram, the plant-growing environment has undergone many changes in the last few decades as road access, erosion, global warming, and human occupation have all dramatically increased.

First impressions for road travellers from the cities of Pakistan to the Karakoram range is a continuous transition of vegetation zones throughout the journey. For the traveller arriving by plane from Islamabad to Skardu, the first things that stand out are the general aridity and lack of vegetation of the valleys and the high snow-covered peaks, the only patches of green being small farms created by humans using irrigation. All this is despite the presence of the mighty Indus River flowing down the centre of the valley in which Skardu is situated.

The tree line (around 3900m) indicates the possible or impossible climate for trees to grow, which at altitude is only for a short period. An average of two and a half months each summer is not long enough to produce trunk, branch or leaf of any particularly impressive size.

Above 3900m smaller trees appear sporadically, typically covered by a layer of snow during many months which actually stops them from drying up. Branches above the snow will desiccate and die off, making trees looked curved.

Most villages and towns run smaller private, or government supported forestry projects to secure the need for building wood. Pine tree needles need a certain layer of wax to stop evaporation. If the cultivating season is too short, the wax layer will be too thin, which results in the trees drying out in the springtime and therefore no usable wood for construction.

Himalayan Cedar, or Deodar, is the national tree of Pakistan. Other trees to be found are West Himalayan spruce, Himalayan white pine, Pashtun juniper, and Pashtun smithiana or evergreen tree. Scattered in between the trees, shrubs and plants can be found, such as wormwood,

Mountain flowers (photo: Dave Morgan) – clockwise from top left: Kashmir Larkspur, Icelandic Poppy, Himalayan Thyme, Himalayan Crane's-bill, Moorcroft Campion, Alpine Ground Daisy, Dane's Dwarf Gentian, Bonnet Bellflower, Tibetan Stonecrop (centre)

milkvetch, wild strawberry, Nepal geranium, wild rose, poor man's orchid, Himalayan thyme, white clover, wild red raspberry, and dandelion.

On east- and south-facing slopes there is sea buckthorn and the medicinal plant barberry. At higher altitudes we find the wild rose and oriental gooseberry.

Some other herbal plants encountered on sparse grassland and often hidden in narrow ravines are elegant willow, bluebell, bunge, Persian juniper, buckwheat, and steeplebushes.

Other herbaceous plants growing on the sparse grassland, especially in gullies and ravines, are *Salix denticulata, Mertensia tibetica, Potentilla desertorum, Juniperus polycarpus,* alpine bistort, *Berberis pachyacantha, Spiraea lycioides* and artemisia.

Jasmine is the national flower of Pakistan, symbolising attachment and representing amiability and modesty.

WILDLIFE

More than thirty different mammals are present in the CKNP, including brown bear, snow leopard, wolf, fox, musk deer, large wild coat markhor, ibex, bharal, urial, woolly hare and marmot.

Snow leopard

Found during the summer at altitudes of over 4000m (and even 6000m), they stay above 1800m in winter and are most active at dawn and dusk. About 100 to 150 snow leopards are estimated to roam the mountains of Pakistan (and 4500 to 6000 in Asia). The two genders look alike, standing 40–50cm tall at the shoulder, with tails almost one metre in length and a body length of 75–130cm.They can weigh up to 70kg. Their feet are large, helping them to walk on snow, and their tail is long and flexible, enabling them to maintain their balance while chasing prey on steep ground. Snow leopards are well adapted to the cold with thick fur, sturdy bodies and small rounded ears to reduce heat loss.

The leopard has a very large hunting territory (around 1000km^2), mainly due to the scarcity of prey – largely blue sheep and (baby) yaks – at high altitude. They can survive two weeks on one kill before they need to hunt again. Vegetation, like grass and twigs, is also on the menu.

The snow leopard's coat is extremely beautiful and, as such, the animal is a target for hunters. Hunting or poaching does occur in Pakistan, even though it is forbidden according to the Wildlife Act of 1975. (There is a £215/€251/$275 minimum fine; between 2005 and 2017, there were 101 recorded arrests for snow

Snow leopard (photo: SLF Pakistan Snow Leopard Trust)

leopard poaching, each incurring a £392/€457/$500 fine).

The snow leopard population is in perpetual conflict with farmers living in the mountains. The cats frequently kill domestic goats and sheep. The snow leopard has little choice of food since its natural prey, like wild goats and sheep in the mountains, has been hunted (by farmers and others).

Baltistan Wildlife Conservation and Development Organisation (BWCDO) has a unique approach to the farmer/snow leopard conflict and towards protecting the cat. In 1999, the BWCDO started Project Snow Leopard in Rondu Valley, establishing an insurance scheme that provided compensation to farmers who lost their farm animals and funding for them to build predator-proof cages for livestock. Villagers pay a premium amount per head of livestock. More than 18,000 animals are now insured in 26 villages (over 50 valleys) and this amount keeps growing, not only in Pakistan but also in other countries with snow leopards. Since 2006 roughly £13,500 (€15,500/$17,000) has been paid out in compensation to farmers in Pakistan.

Only the yeti would be more difficult to photograph than the snow leopard. The local name for the snow leopard is *Barfani chita* (Urdu) or *Ikar* (Balti).

Lynx

The lynx inhabits the barren highlands in the Karakoram, avoiding forests and deep valleys. It is a medium-sized wild cat, with a body length the same as a snow leopard but weighing half as much, or even less than that. Lynx have a short tail, with powerful legs and large furry paws hitting the ground with a spreading toe movement functioning like natural snowshoes. The lynx is a skilled hunter with incredible eyesight, able to spot small prey 75 metres away, and ears that have a specific black hair tuft giving them excellent hearing ability. On the menu for lynx are rabbit, hare, mouse, marmots, grouse, and occasionally sheep and foxes. They are capable of killing prey that is three or four times their own weight.

The local name is *Tsogde* (Balti). Lynx numbers are growing throughout Asia.

Bear

The Himalayan Brown Bear or Himalayan Red Bear (called *Dremos*, by the locals) has a sandy or reddish-brown colour, and males can weigh anything from 135kg to 390kg (double that in autumn). Bears live by themselves, except females when they have cubs. They feed on grass, roots, bulbs, fruit, ants, fish, small mammals like marmot, and sometimes even ibex or Marco Polo sheep can be on the menu.

There are not many bears in the wild anymore, not only due to hunting but also because they are caught to perform in circuses and shows. Apparently, there are more bears on the streets of the big cities of Pakistan than in the wild. However, the Deosai National Park counts more than 30 bears. **Warning:** give all bears a wide berth should you see one: every year locals are mauled in encounters with bears when they get disturbed.

Alexander Kinloch writes in his 1885 book *Large Game Shooting in Thibet, The Himalayas, and Northern India*:

> The Snow Bear, Brown Bear, Red Bear, or White Bear, as it is variously called, inhabits most of the highest forest-clad ranges, but it is by far most numerous in Kashmir. In that country, in 1864, a friend of mine saw twenty eight in one day, and shot seven. I have myself seen thirteen. Forty years ago, the country must have been literally swarming with them, and I have heard that the people were afraid to go from one village to another after dark. Now-a-days everyone who visits Kashmir shoots a few Bears, and the only wonder is that the race is not quite exterminated.

Marmot

Marmots are widespread in the mountains. The marmot is a member of the squirrel family, growing to a length of about 60cm with a tail around 10cm long.

They live in areas of summer grazing, near cattle and humans. They live in large colonies, digging into sunny slopes at altitudes from 1400m to 5200m. They hibernate in winter in deep holes, so in spring they have to work hard to procure food, eating

Blue sheep or Bharal

grass, leaves and roots. Their holes not only damage pastures but can also cause yaks to break their legs. A disturbed marmot will sit up and tweet, then give a loud whistling scream to send its companions scurrying back to their holes.

Ibex

The ibex is part of the goat family and lives at an altitude of 3600 to 5200m. With the beard and long, gracefully-curved horns, it is easy to identify. Some horns have been measured up to 140cm long! Ibex weigh anything between 35kg and 130kg and can reach a shoulder height of up to one metre. The female ibex is about a third smaller, with no beard and with shorter and smaller horns.

The ibex is an excellent climber, traversing precipitous and dangerous ground, making it a wonderful sight. They are hunted by snow leopard, wolf, lynx and humans.

Urial sheep

The Urial (Oorial) sheep, or *Shapu*, is a medium-sized sheep, that can measure up to one metre to the shoulders. They weigh between 40 and 60kg. The male Urial is a noble animal and a highly-prized trophy for hunters because of his beautiful horns. The horns are a little like those of the domestic ram, but have only one curve, which can grow all the way round to form a circle. They attain a length of 65–80cm. Urial live in open areas at lower altitudes, making it easier for them to be hunted.

Marco Polo sheep

The largest living wild sheep named after the Venetian merchant and adventurer Marco Polo, who crossed the Pamirs in 1273. They are also called *Pamir argali*. They can measure up to 125cm to their shoulder, weigh up to 160kg and their horns can reach a length of 180cm. Marco Polo sheep have long legs which are needed to out-run predators. This sheep is remarkably well-equipped to deal with all kinds of weather at very high altitude (5000m).

Markhor

The markhor is the national animal of Pakistan. It is part of the goat family, has long (up to 160cm) corkscrew-shaped horns, stands about one metre high and can weigh up to 100kg. The colours are seasonal: with a long, grey silky coat in the winter that turns reddish brown in summer.

They live in herds in the low-lying dry cliffs and eat shrubs.

Blue sheep or Bharal (Burrell)

The blue sheep looks like a sheep but behaves like a goat. Blue sheep stand about a metre high at the shoulder and weigh well over 70kg. Both sexes carry a pair of dignified horns measuring about 60cm.

> The horns are peculiarly shaped: they are set very close together, and at first diverge horizontally in two round arches; then sweep backwards, upwards, and outwards, in a shape different to those of any animal with which I am acquainted.

Kinloch: Large Game Shooting in Thibet, The Himalayas, and Northern India

Their coats undergo seasonal colour changes – slate blue in summer and slate grey during the winter. Rams have a black stripe along their back, but ewes do not.

Herd size and composition varies from 50 to 200 individuals. Generally, males separate from the females when the rut is over, when they form their own groups until next rut. A few males, however, remain with the females throughout the year. Blue sheep are known to consume a broad range of alpine herbs and shrubs.

Thanks to their impressive horns, the blue sheep has become a worthy trophy animal and is now on the endangered list. According to Kinloch:

> An old Burrell's head is a trophy worth working for; and the meat is excellent, the flavor being a happy combination of Highland mutton and venison. Late in the year, Burrell become extremely fat, and a haunch is then hardly to be surpassed for tenderness, juiciness, and flavor.

Musk deer

The deer is 80–100cm long and stands around 50cm high at the shoulder. Its coat has a somewhat greyish-brown colour – the chest features a wide vertical whitish-yellow band, which extends up the throat to the chin. Its body slopes forward, since the forelegs are one third shorter than the hind legs. Both sexes have strong upper canines, reaching a length of seven centimetres in males, and they stick out from the mouth a bit like fangs.

The musk deer is most active between dusk and dawn, and it lives at an altitude of 2500–4000m. It is superbly adapted to its surroundings: it has a well-insulated coat of hollow hair which, a bit like a sleeping bag, traps air to allow the animal to lie on cold ground – even snow – with minimal heat loss. It is also incredibly sure-footed – the envy of any climber – as it nimbly bounds over the rockiest ground and most precipitous slopes. The deer eat leaves, grasses, moss, lichens, shoots and twigs.

The musk deer's aromatic name comes from its distinct smell. Musk, a brown waxy substance, is produced in a gland of the males. The musk produced is highly prized for its cosmetic and supposed pharmaceutical properties.

BIRDLIFE

More than 360 species of bird are known to exist in the Gilgit–Baltistan area (including the Central Karakoram National Park) and 780+ in the whole of Pakistan.

Around 90 species of migratory, breeding, and resident birds are known to be in the CKNP itself. Some of these include: Goldcrest, Common Raven, finches, buntings, warblers, redstarts, pipits, larks, pheasants, pigeons, doves and woodpeckers. In the waterfowl family there are ducks and geese, waders, gulls, terns, grebes, egrets and herons. As for birds of prey, there are up to 19 different hawks and eagles, five species of vulture, nine species of owl, and six species of falcon.

Some excellent birdwatching books can be found (see Appendix D). In this guidebook only few birds will be described.

- **Chukar partridge** or **Chukar pheasants** (the national bird of Pakistan) can be up to 39cm. A medium-sized bird, with a dull brown-grey body, but some surprising features like a black stripe over the eyes and around a small white area under the red bill, and black-brownish rib-like bars on the flanks.
- **Himalayan Griffon Vulture (1)** is the largest of all species with a rounded tail and a wingspan ranging from two and a half to three metres and inhabits the high mountains between 1500m and 4000m. White on underwing with contrasting dark flight feathers and tail.
- **Bearded Vulture** or **Lammergeier (2)**, is a very large bird of prey

weighing an average of 6kg, up to 125cm tall, and with a maximum wingspan of 280cm. The body is small in comparison with the size of the bird. Small-headed but with a powerful neck, it has slender grey coloured wings and a pointed tail. The adult is mostly dark grey, rusty, and whitish in colour. The acid concentration of the bearded vulture stomach and a kind of churning of its contents, means the bird can digest large bones in about 24 hours.

- **Golden Eagle (3)**, or 'Master of the Sky', can grow up to 90cm tall with a wingspan of 180–230cm and reaching speeds of up to 320km/hr. Spends long periods soaring around mountain crags with wings held in a very shallow 'V', looking for medium-sized prey, and sometimes birds, lizards, and snakes. Common at high altitude.

Birds of Gilgit-Baltistan (images: Professor Zahid Mirza)

Chukar partridge (photo: Imran Shah/Wikipedia Commons)

- **Eurasian Kestrel** can be found up to altitudes of 4000m, feeding on small mammals. The kestrel (or small falcon) can be 35cm tall, has distinctive male plumage, grey head, rusty back, grey tail with broad black tip and rather pointed wingtips.
- **Black Kite (7)** with a shallow V-shaped tail, is dark rufous brown with some white spots at the end of its underwings. It can be 55–70cm tall with a wingspan of up to 150cm.
- **Himalayan Snow Cock (4)** is about the size of a duck (70cm) and can be found at altitudes up to 4500m, producing a furious whistling cry. It has a beautiful combination of stripes over its body in black, white, grey, and brownish tones.
- **Red-billed Chough (8)** is a medium-sized (40cm) bird, totally black except for a red bill and red legs, and can be found up to 4000m.
- **Eurasian Hoopoe (6)**, an elegant bird with distinctive black and white stripes, fawn head and fan-shaped crest and a light-coloured orange head. It can be 30cm tall.
- **White-capped Redstart (5)** is a common resident near mountain streams up to 4000m and can be 18cm tall. It has a white cap, with the rest of the head black down to the breast. The rest of the body is a beautiful orange-chestnut colour, except for the black end of the tail, bill, and legs.

THE TREKS

On the Khunyang Glacier on the penultimate day of Trek 1 (photo: Jasmine Star)

GETTING TO ASKOLE – THE STARTING POINT FOR THE KARAKORAM TREKS

The ancient kingdom of Baltistan was founded where sands and snows meet in the heights of Central Asia.
Galen Rowell

The starting point for the Biafo–Snowlake–Hispar, Gondogoro La, and K2 treks is Askole (3045m) (or Askoley), the last and only village on the K2 route. The Nanga Parbat treks normally start with a drive from Gilgit after catching a domestic flight to Gilgit; see Getting to Gilgit in the Introduction. If a trek finishes in Joila or Askole it should be possible to find transport to Skardu.

Weather permitting, a short, impressive flight covers the distance from Islamabad (around 500m) to the Baltistan capital, Skardu (2230m), in less than an hour; otherwise, it's a long journey overland to Skardu before the final six hour jeep ride to the village of Askole. From Islamabad to Skardu it is 300km by air, and a whopping 635km by road. Four-wheel drives (jeeps) are needed for the drive to Askole and can be booked in Skardu. Be aware, departure from Skardu can be delayed due to some time-consuming permit signing issues or religious festivals.

After a short drive east from Skardu towards Hushe the road will split and turn north crossing the Indus River, then across the Sarfaranga cold desert, over a small pass and down into the fertile Shigar Valley, known for its abundance of apricots, mulberries, walnuts, and grain. Once across the small pass, the vista over the fertile Shigar Valley opens out, with Marshakala Peak (5153m) visible and located either to the right of Shigar town (2230m) or straight north from Skardu. The peak was first climbed in 1861 by Godwin-Austen; from it, he had grand views towards K2, Masherbrum, and Nanga Parbat. Shigar has a 450-year-old fort. It is known as *Fong-Khar* and has been renovated together with the 17th-century Raja Palace located in the same compound, into a luxury Serena Hotel.

Not far after Shigar there is a route crossing the Skoro La (5073m) that leads to Askole. It's an alternative high route, only accessible on foot, hardly used these days, and bypassing the difficult Braldu Gorge.

Dassu offers a lunch-stop possibility. Opposite Dassu, and beyond, dynamite blasts might be heard from the crystal and mineral mines (see Geology section).

The road beyond Dassu is still prone to landslides but even in its poorest condition, no more than a few hundred metres of brisk walking across landslides is usually required and there are now several good bridges crossing the river.

The road to Askole is an adventure. Driving through the Braldu Gorge you are left wondering if this road leads to any civilization. If you suffer from vertigo, then be prepared. The drive is normally conducted by experienced drivers who are immensely proud of the most beautiful, polished jeeps. Whenever there is a stop, a driver will always look after – or will remain in – his jeep. It takes a good car and a good driver to handle the rough road through the narrow Braldu Gorge, a road which can be blocked by landslides. Accidents do happen. As American climber Galen Rowell describes his driver: 'He negotiated the rough road at full throttle, and we had the combined sensations of being in a sports-car race and riding down rapids inside a barrel'. Reaching Askole and beyond by jeep is by no means guaranteed: the road was blocked for several months in 2022.

Before the village of Askole are a couple of hot springs – in the old days this was a welcome place for a good wash, as can be seen in photos in some old expedition books.

GETTING TO ASKOLE IN THE PAST

Prior to 1947, Baltistan, also known as 'Little Tibet', was part of the royal state of Jammu and Kashmir. Located between China and Indian-held Kashmir, Baltistan has always been difficult to get to. To the north the Karakoram mountains block the way, with impossible passes and over 100 mountains above 7000m. The Indus River crosses the area; with some difficult gorges along the river and, to the south, the uninhabited Deosai Plateau, so there were no routes entering Baltistan from this side either.

For many expeditions, getting to Askole was the start – and finish – point of their adventure. A famous expedition leader once said, 'an expedition to the mountains around Concordia starts and finishes at Askole'.

Karl Eugen von Ujfalvy (Austrian–Hungarian explorer), writes in 1884: 'On the third day, after crossing the Braldu on a primitive wooden bridge and a strenuous day we reached the small, wildly romantic fortress of Askole, which lies almost at the foot of the Biafo-Ganse Glacier from which you can see the Karakorum sea of ice as never seen before'.

In 1909 the Duke of the Abruzzi was received in all the towns en route to Askole with enormous fanfare, gifts, food and – of course – a polo game. Hunting ibex and markhor was popular in this region, both for locals and any English officers on leave to escape the heat of the plains.

Until the early 1990s the road terminated at a point beyond Dassu and any trek included several extra days of walking (180km to K2 base camp) including bypassing the notorious Braldu Gorge climbing high, crossing the river on a cable in a box or on an 80-metre-long vine and twig bridge (three ropes in the form of a 'V', the lowest rope for the feet and the upper ones for hands and arms).

Askole village

ASKOLE – GATEWAY TO THE KARAKORAM

Askole has been called 'the world's end'. Eight villages with roughly 450 houses are scattered around Askole in a fertile broad valley. Askole itself is a flourishing village of 60 houses and about 600 inhabitants, and is surrounded by well-looked-after fields growing wheat, buckwheat, peas and turnips irrigated by ancient, canal-based systems (Pakistan has the largest canal-based irrigation system in the world). Essential livestock for the village are sheep, goats, cattle, yak and dzo (a yak/cow hybrid). Askole is famous because so many (high-altitude) porters come from this valley.

The village has several shops, two mosques, a medical centre, and two restaurants. There is a large school for boys and girls in the village, which is getting some support from a UK-based organisation (The Juniper Trust) to ensure female teachers are employed and receiving wages.

Askole has two enclosed campsites with a toilet building and a very basic shower facility. Around camp it will be busy with people organising porters, porters arranging loads, last-minute shopping, locals exchanging the latest news and gossip.

Take time to stroll through the village (modestly dressed), get 'lost' and enjoy the scenery and friendly people (sometimes too friendly if your

HISTORY OF ASKOLE

Some sources say Askole is about 900 years old, based on a local legend when a prince from Nagar (Hunza), fearing for his life, fled across the Hispar Pass and discovered the flat valley of Askole. He married a girl from Shigar and settled down with her in the isolated valley. Besides expeditions, trekkers, and military personnel, Askole used to be frequented by traders from China using the two Muztagh passes until, around 1750, conditions in the glaciers made the passes impassable for pack animals. Several explorers have tried crossing the Muztagh passes since (see Trek 2 K2 Base Camp section for more detail).

When the Duke of the Abruzzi visited the village in 1909, Askole had some stray dogs that were as large as wolves – a rare sight in a Balti village. Conway saw dogs in 1861, which were kept for hunting and trained to flush out the ibex.

personal items are in high demand!). Some corners of the village seemed to be totally unaffected by modernisation. Women can be seen wearing jewellery fashioned out of seemingly random objects such as spoons, forks, zips, coins, small sea shells, brass pins, or indeed anything shiny! An old belief is that these items protects the wearer against disease. Visit the interesting and well-illustrated Askole House Museum.

At the time of publication, work is underway to extend the road beyond Askole, with the aim of making Paiju accessible by road one day. This could mean that a K2 trek would be several days shorter than it has been for the last couple of decades: up to five days shorter if a K2 return trek is the chosen route. However, travel by jeep beyond Askole is currently forbidden by authorities and locals. Locals would lose the Askole camping fee and porter wages would be cut due to losing out on some stages' trekking.

In 2023 around 1400 trekkers visited Pakistan. 1084 did the Gondogoro La Trek; 115 the K2 Trek, and the rest went to different destinations, including 3 or 4 groups who completed the Biafo–Hispar Trek.

Lukpilla Brakk (The Ogre's Thumb), Baintha Brakk (The Ogre) and Latok II from the Biafo Glacier (Trek 1, Day 4; photo: Colin Prior)

TREK 1

Snow Lake and the Biafo and Hispar Glaciers

Start	Askole (3045m)
Finish	Hispar (3250m)
Distance	115.8km
Ascent	2526m
Descent	2271m
Grade	Strenuous and technical when crossing pass
Days	12 + 2 rest/acclimatisation days
Highest point	5151m
Permits	An open trek needing no permit
Warning	Conditions of the glaciers around the pass might make it impossible to cross. Check with local agencies if the trek is possible (in 2023 several groups crossed).

This trek has been described as crossing the greatest area of glaciation anywhere outside the Polar Regions, a spectacular white highway across the heart of the Karakoram and the quintessential Karakoram traverse. It is usually undertaken

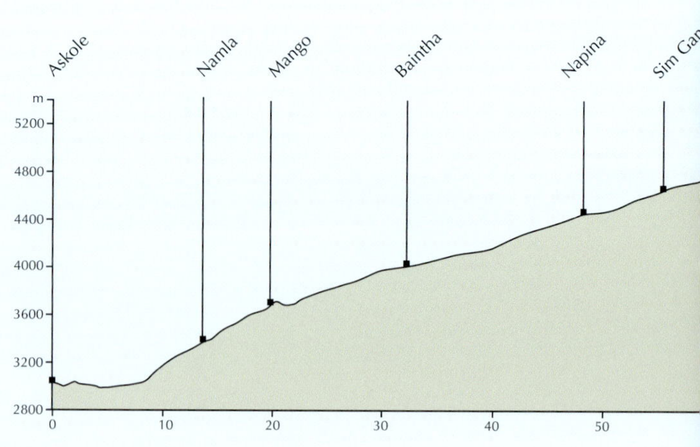

from Askole to Hispar, not least because of the greater availability and ease of hiring porters on the Askole side.

At a bridge a few kilometres from Askole, the trekking route branches off from the K2 Base Camp trail, and it is altogether a much less frequented and more remote undertaking.

The trek will take 13 or more days, depending on the length of trekking days, rest days, side trips and weather, although expect to pay porters for more than this as it includes up to twenty-two official day stages for porters. It is wise to have some days in hand to use as rest days, acclimatisation days or unplanned rest days due to bad weather.

Your journey begins with a full day of driving from Skardu to Askole and finishes with a similar length drive from Horo via Nagar or Karımabad to Gilgit. A bus service is available from Karimabad to Gilgit, otherwise pre-booked private jeep hire is necessary.

Travelling up the glacier, the environment turns from lush-green to sandy, and from rocky campsites to finally camping on ice. The Biafo Glacier is as smooth as the Hispar is twisted and churned – fed by several smaller and bigger side glaciers coming in from the north. This makes the going rather hard. The southern side of the Hispar Glacier is prone to avalanches from 6000m peaks and therefore used less. At the end of the Hispar Glacier, roughly 115km away, the village Nagar is located.

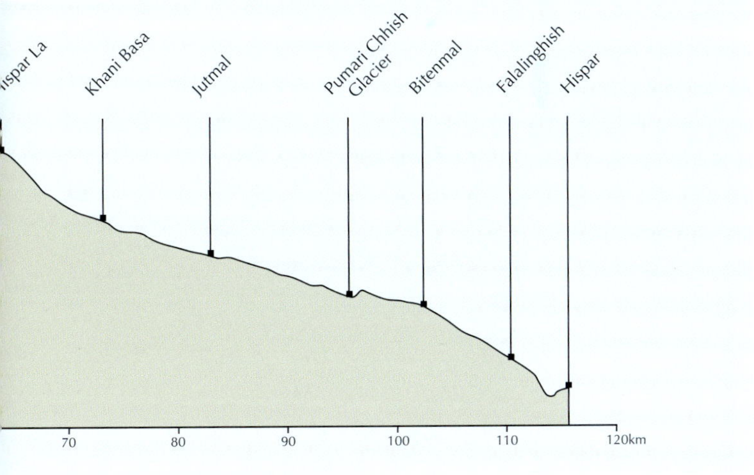

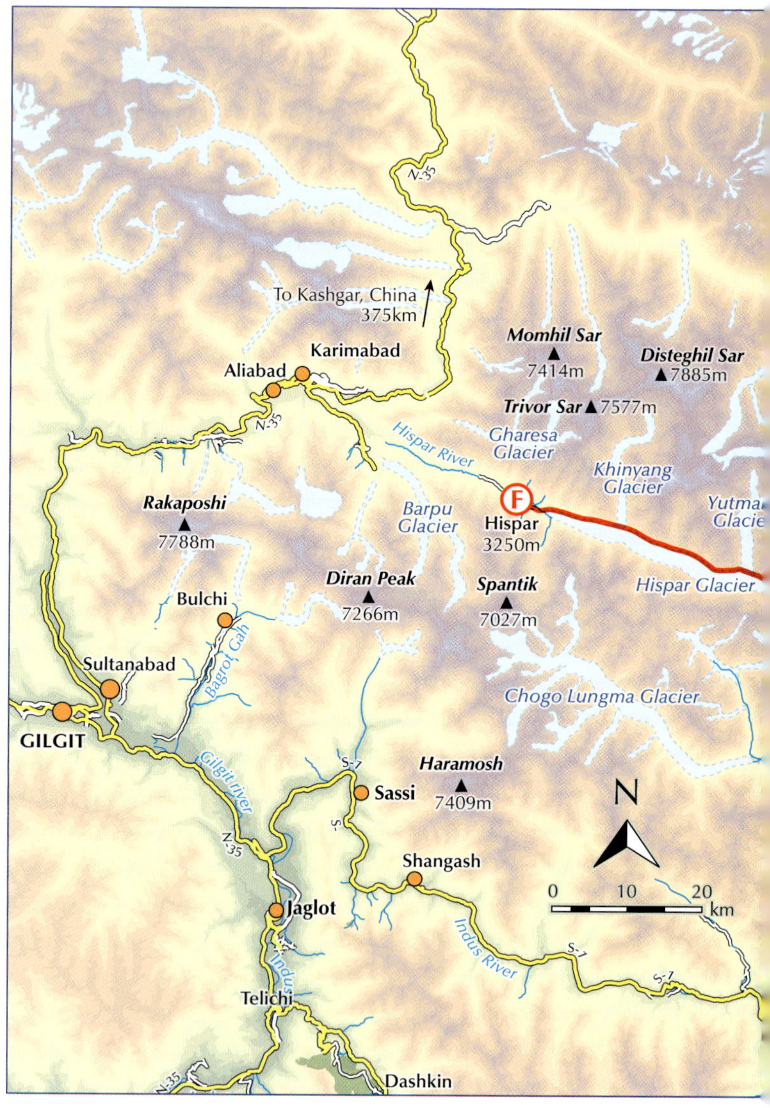
To Kashgar, China
375km
N-35
Karimabad
Aliabad
Momhil Sar
7414m
Disteghil Sar
7885m
Trivor Sar 7577m
Hispar River
Gharesa
Glacier
Khinyang
Glacier
Yutma
Glacie
Hispar
3250m
Barpu
Glacier
Rakaposhi
7788m
Hispar Glacier
Diran Peak
7266m
Spantik
7027m
Bulchi
Bagrot Gah
Sultanabad
Chogo Lungma Glacier
GILGIT
Gilgit river
Haramosh
7409m
S-7
Sassi
N
Shangash
0
10
20
km
Jaglot
Indus River
Indus
Telichi
Dashkin

Kanjut Sar
7760m
ani Bass
Glacier
Braldu
Glacier
Snow Lake
Hispar La 5151m
chori Sar
5949
Sim Gang
Glacier
Ogre
7285m
olu
acier
Choktoi Glacier
Panmah
Glacier
CHINA
K2
8611m
Biafo Glacier
Feriole
Glacier
Hoh Lungma
Glacier
isko
Dassu
Braldu River
Askole
3045m
Joila
Surungo
Braldu River
Sino
Kurpe
Korophon
Tisar
To
Skardu
Shigar
River
PAKISTAN

WARNING

Travelling on moving glaciers means existing 'trails' are prone to changes. Route indicators might be old ones, showing a 'wrong' way. Don't travel alone on the glaciers. Changing trails might also influence the timing and distances indicated each day. Carry some flexibility along in your pack!

A high point of the trek is the legendary Snow Lake (so named by the first known foreign explorer Sir Martin Conway in 1892, and recounted in his book *Climbing in the Himalayas*), the local original local name being Lukpe Lawo. It is an ice mass at an altitude of around 5000m covering an area of about 50km^2 and is 1000 metres deep. Both the Hispar and Biafo Glaciers (among others) flow out of the lake, stretching for a total distance of nearly 130km. It is surrounded by high jagged granite peaks, once described as 'being like standing in a shark's mouth'.

The geographical highpoint of the trek is the Hispar La (5151m), a pass that links Snow Lake with the Hispar Glacier. The condition of the glacier on the pass varies each season. Climate change might have an influence on the condition as well, resulting in large crevasses opening up and making the crossing impossible. Trekkers and their porters should always be suitably equipped to travel and sleep on these glaciers with ropes, ice axes, suitable footwear, crampons, sunglasses, gloves, head lights, and warm sleeping gear. They should also be proficient in crevasse rescue techniques.

Until the early 1990s, the few trekkers and mountaineers who passed this way regularly had visits to their camps from Himalayan brown bears and snow leopard prints were often spotted, but with the increased interest in climbing, trekking and exploration, such sightings are now rare.

TRAVEL LITERATURE

Sir Martin Conway recounted his experiences in the Karakoram in *Climbing in the Himalayas: Climbing and Exploration in the Karakoram-Himalayas*, published in 1894. He was followed in 1899 by the adventurous American couple Fanny Bullock Workman and her husband William Hunter Workman. Later in 1937 and 1939, Bill Tilman and Eric Shipton trekked, explored, and mapped the area and vividly wrote about it in the classic book *Blank on the Map*.

In Catherine Moorhead's book, *The K2 Man (and his Molluscs)*, there are excerpts from never-before-published private papers of Haversham

Godwin-Austen. He wrote in 1864 that 'hundreds of people from Nagar crossed the Hispar pass to loot the villages in the Braldo area, up till 1840, carrying off about 100 men and women, cows, goats and sheep'. The Hispar Pass was also called the 'robber road' according to a local from Chongo. Conway picked up the following story in Askole: 'the leader of the 1840 band was called Wazir Hollo, who, with his band came in the autumn to Askole because their own harvest was bad. The Baltis gave them provisions but on their return crossing the Hispar pass they all perished in the snow, except their leader'.

According to Conway, the Askole men told him (in 1892) that long before the last raid in 1840 from the Nagar people they came over the Hispar and brought with them a Shoti (leather worker), who built the stone hut called Lancum I Brangsa, and decorated its roof with ibex horns, or made the roof of them. The hut still exits somewhere by the Biafo Glacier.

DAY 1

Askole to Namla via Kesar's Polo Ground

Start	Askole (3045m)
Finish	Namla (3380m)
Distance	13.9km
Ascent	540m
Descent	205m
Time	5–7hr
Altitude gain	335m
Note	This day could be made 1hr or 1hr 30min shorter if you are allowed to drive beyond Askole to the split in the road near a bridge – see description below.

After leaving Askole a drivable dirt road leads out from the irrigated fields surrounding the village to the newly built **CKNP office** where documentation must be completed. Toilets are provided in the building, the last such facility – in fact the last building – until Hispar village at the end of the trek.

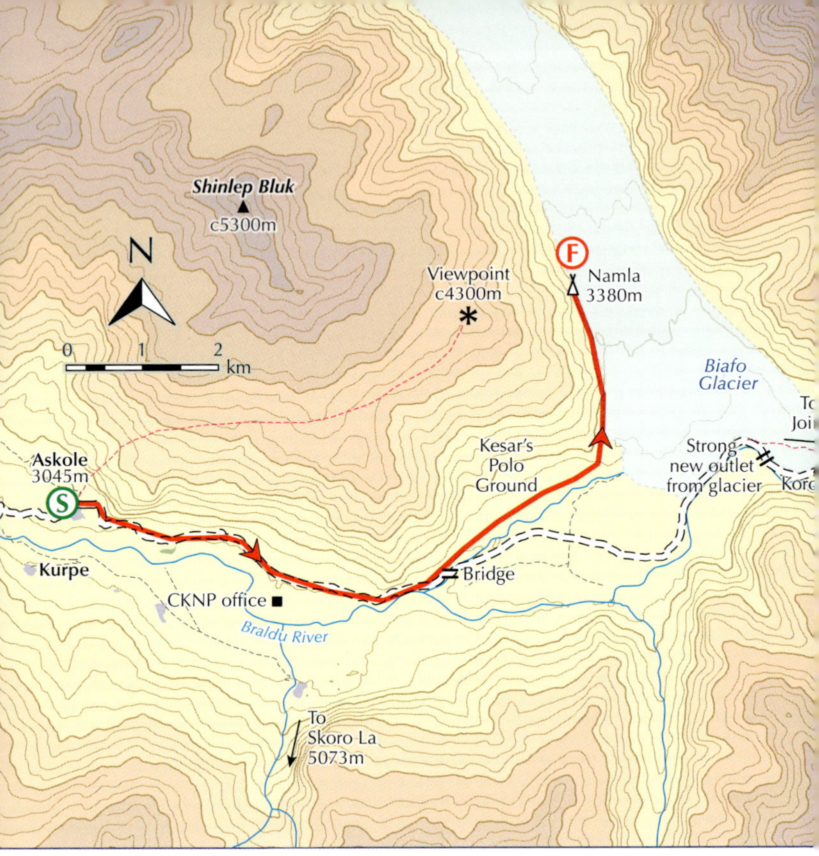

After completing the formalities, join a trail outside the office and cross some fields. Follow the river around the corner on the dirt road. A once rickety, but now driveable, road bridge crosses the Braldu River here en route to K2 Base Camp and Concordia. Do not cross but continue on the same side on a smaller path above the river. The path is vague in places until you reach a huge flat camping area called Kesar Shaguran (**Kesar's Polo Ground**) which is a possible camp for the night (less than 2hr from Askole).

According to local **legends** and as told in Isobel Shaw's trekking book, King Kesar, a mythical ruler with magical powers, rescued his abducted wife from an evil giant. She had given birth to two children by this giant – Kesar beheaded them both and played polo with their heads on this ground!

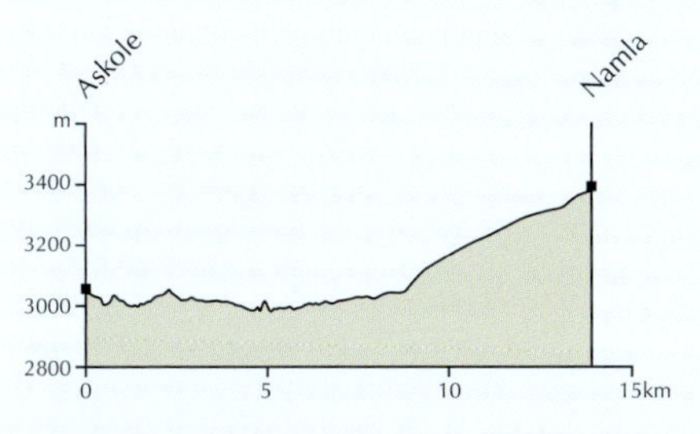

Cross the flat area and aim for a small gorge whereafter the several-days-long hike on the Biafo Glacier starts.

At the gorge, the remains of some **stone huts** can be found, built by the British glaciologist Kenneth Hewitt for his winter scientific expedition in 1961–62 (Hewitt researched the Karakoram glaciers for more than 45 years).

BIAFO

The name Biafo means 'rooster' in the local Balti language as it describes the cockscomb shape of the snout of the glacier. At this point the snout is covered in rocks and little ice is visible, it does however nearly bulldoze its way onto the Braldu River below.

As Karl Eugen von Ujfalvy described in his 1884 book, *Aus dem Westlichen Himalaja*: '...and once you see a glacier, it appears as big as a European kingdom. Our Alps are just a delicate pocket edition of the Himalayas and the Karakorum'.

Namla is a couple of hours further along. With many boulders to negotiate and a low-altitude heat, the last couple of hours for today are tough, although the trail is shaded in the afternoon. The trail turns north following rocky goat-herders' tracks clinging to the edge beside the Biafo Glacier. When the path ends, cross onto the ice and trek with more difficulty over boulders and around crevasses. Return to the lateral moraines and on to **Namla**, which is not obvious from the glacier but is a pleasant grassy spot for a campsite. The local porters will be able to assist if the trail is not clear.

DAY 2

Namla to Mango

Start	Namla (3380m)
Finish	Mango (3725m)
Distance	6.6km
Ascent	345m
Descent	Negligible
Time	4–6hr
Altitude gain	345m
Note	Reaching Mango camp is getting more and more challenging due to changes in the glacier. Count on having to walk onwards to Shafung camp (3950m; see Day 3), crossing the glacier, making the day 6–7hr long.

The day begins on the highest ridge on the rubble-covered glacier.

The **view** ahead is of the Latok group, with Latok I (7145m) the highest at the centre, Latok II (7108m) to its left, and Latok III (6949m) on the right. Latok IV (6456m) and Latok V (6131m) are not quite visible.

A view from the viewing point at 5100m above Baintha Camp (see Day 3), with Latok II, Latok I and Latok III

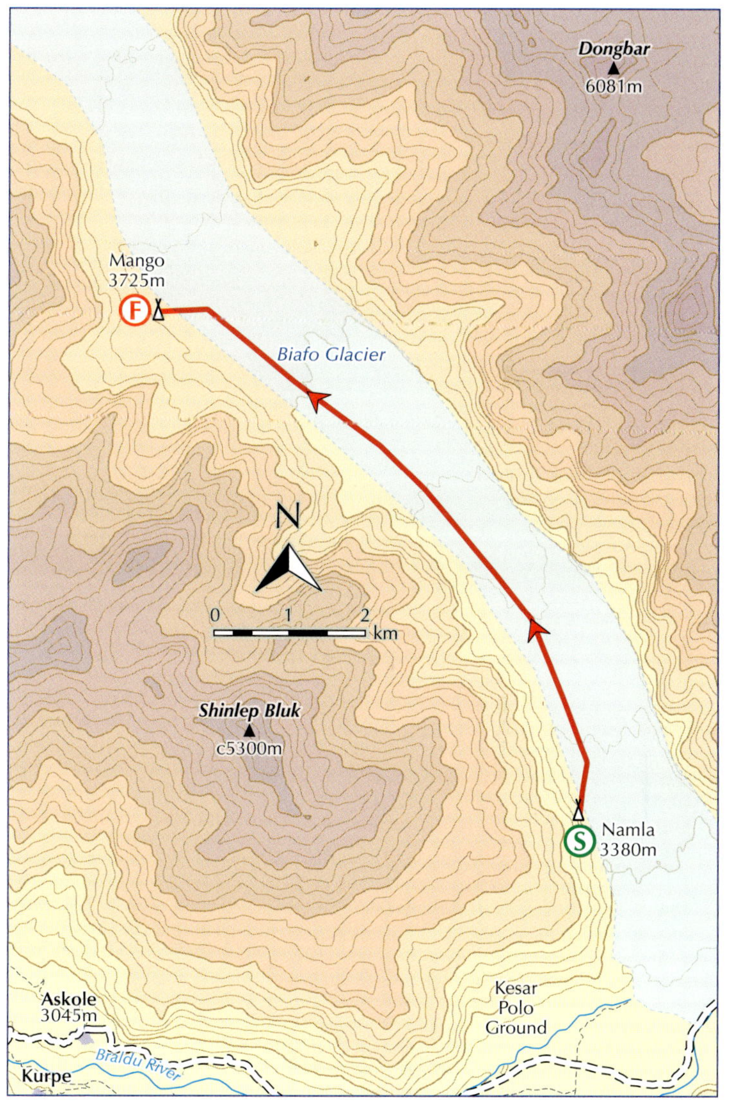
Dongbar
6081m
Mango
3725m
F
Biafo Glacier
N
0
1
2
km
Shinlep Bluk
c5300m
S
Namla
3380m
Kesar
Polo
Ground
Askole
3045m
Braldu River
Kurpe

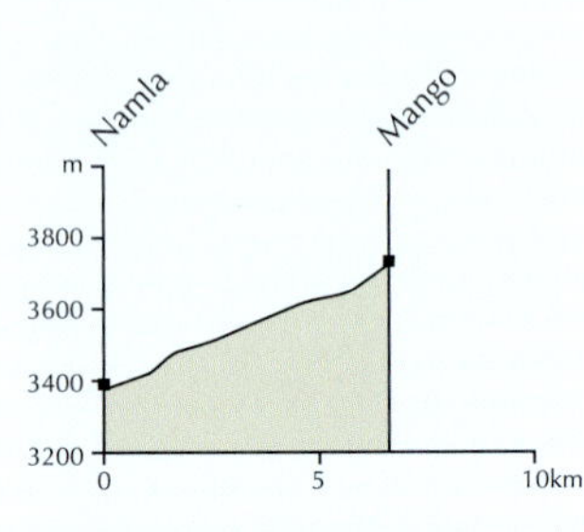

Climb steadily for a couple of hours on unstable rock ridges then turn left across the crevasses to an ablation zone called Mango which is also a good camping place (there are three possible camp sites close to each other; the last one has the better water normally). It is a shortish day to **Mango** (3725m) to aid acclimatisation, but also a challenging day with all the loose rock along the 'trail'. Some groups who have limited time make a long tough stage by continuing to Baintha.

EVER-CHANGING GLACIERS

Glaciers are changing non-stop, as Swiss guide Mattias Zurbriggen noted in 1899 and as described by Fanny Workman Bullock: 'Zurbriggen, who was with the Conway expedition in 1892, said the changes in the glacier at this part were such, as one would not believe could take place in seven years. It had receded greatly and become much more crevassed and broken, and passage was now barred, where it had then been easy'.

DAY 3

Mango to Baintha

Start	Mango (3725m)
Finish	Baintha (4020m)
Distance	12.2km
Ascent	340m
Descent	45m
Time	4–6hr
Altitude gain	295m

Beyond Mango the route starts in the ablation zone until a small lake is reached. It then takes the bare ice on the so-called Miracle Highway up the centre of the glacier and eventually crosses to the true left bank (the right side as you ascend and the northern edge) and continues to Baintha where the Baintha Lukpar

Baintha Peak
5100m
F
Baintha
4020m
N
0
1
2
km
Chaunpisha
5129m
Sokha Lumbu Glacier
Miracle Highway
Shafung
3950m
Sokha Lumbu
5501m
Soblung Lukpar Glacier
Mango Brakk
c5400m
Mango
3725m
S
Gama Sokha Lumbu
6282m

Between Mango and Baintha camp on Biafo Glacier (photo: Jasmine Star)

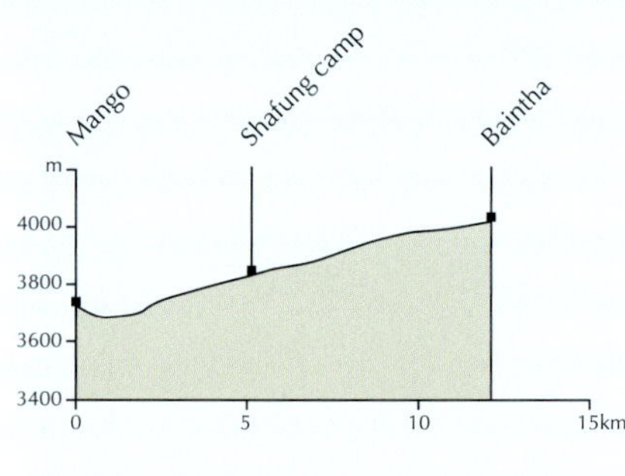

Glacier joins the Biafo Glacier (after crossing Biafo there is a campsite called **Shafung** (3950m); check if water is available). Baintha is a splendid place with some flat camping places, stone walls used by porters, grass and flowers. From the centre of the glacier, you get the first view of Hispar La. Baintha is also known as Conway's Camp.

One year we had to descend for about a metre on steps hacked out of the ice into a crevasse to reach an enormous boulder jammed in the deep-looking crevasse, cross the boulder and climb out of the crevasse again. Today's route finishes above the glacier on a trail that runs through an expanse of beautiful wildflowers in spring and early summer.

At **Baintha** expect flies, as Fanny Workman describes in *In The Ice World of Himalaya*:

We were here greatly troubled by flies, some of them small, and some larger than horse flies, which, entirely reckless of danger devoted their attention to us with a persistency, that indicated, they desired to make the most of this one opportunity of their lives to form the acquaintance of humanity. Their well-meant attentions met with rather an inhuman reception and the list of the slain was large. No prisoners were taken.

RECOMMENDED REST AND ACCLIMATISATION AT BAINTHA

Baintha is a popular location for rest, acclimatisation, exploration, spotting bears and the 'Dremo' (Baltistan Yeti), or reading the epic 1977 Ogre expedition report. Nearly all groups will spend at least one rest day here. The porters will also be very keen to stop as they will bake their chapati bread supplies, slaughter and prepare a goat and other food, and eat some good meals prior to the harsher conditions ahead. The mountain scenery is already spectacular from camp, with snow-capped peaks along the horizon. It also marks the last green vegetation until well down the Hispar Glacier on the other side. Doug Scott counted more than thirty five different kinds of flower during his stay at Ogre Base Camp. Keep an eye open for ibex around the camp.

One idea for an acclimatisation day is to make the stiff hike up Baintha Peak (5100m) to attain impressive views of the upper Biafo and Uzun Brakk Glaciers, the Latok group and Ogre (7285m). Latok I (7145m) was first climbed in 1979 by a Japanese expedition, Latok II (7108m) in 1977 by an Italian expedition, Latok III (6949m) in 2001 by a German–Swiss team, and IV (6456m) by a Japanese team. The group is separated from its neighbours by the Baintha Lukpar Glacier and the Choktoi Glacier. Conway in 1892 called the Latok peaks 'The Five Virgins'. He also gave the name 'Ogre's Fingers' to a group of jagged peaks around Ogre.

At one corner of Snow Lake is the infamous peak, Baintha Brakk (7285m), (aka Ogre, again a name given by Sir Martin Conway, meaning 'the man-eating monster'). It was first climbed by Doug Scott and Chris Bonington in 1977, and was also the location of a major epic when Doug broke his legs retreating from the summit and had to crawl down the mountain; Chris broke some ribs, and after their long ordeal descending the mountain, a rescue helicopter transporting only one patient from Askole crashed near Skardu! A measure of the difficulty of the climb is that it was a further 24 years until the second ascent was made by a German–Swiss team, with Thomas Huber and others. In between, twenty other attempts had failed. As Huber writes: Ogre is possibly more a 'spirit-eating' mountain since so many aspiring climbers have failed.

BAINTHA TO HISPAR LA

To reach the top of Hispar La (5151m) from Baintha, you can count on three to four days. There are four or five campsites to choose from: Nakpogoro (4240m), Napina (4470m) or Makpogoro; Karpogoro, Sim Gang (4685m) and a Hispar La Base Camp (4700m) below the pass.

DAY 4

Baintha to Napina

Start	Baintha (4020m)
Finish	Napina (4470m)
Distance	16km
Ascent	450m
Descent	Negligible
Time	4–6hr
Altitude gain	450m
Note	Some parties carry on beyond Napina camp after just having had a rest day.

Within 1hr of leaving camp, Ogre and the Latok group peaks appear making a vista for some fantastic photos. It is hard to comprehend the scale.

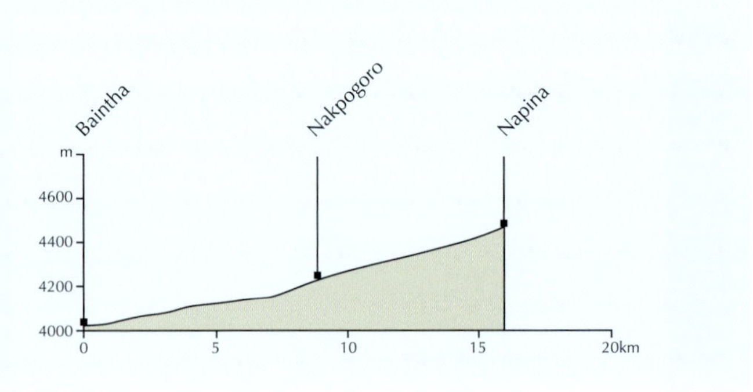

Biafo Glacier ice highway (photo: Jasmine Star)

Two glaciers from the east, Baintha Lukpar and Uzun Brakk join the **Biafo Glacier** here. The Biafo Glacier itself is five kilometres wide here as it emerges from Snow Lake, and is moving at a pace of about 100 metres per year.

Much of the route is along the central moraine on the glacier which, after meeting the Sim Gang Glacier junction on the next day, crosses over to the right bank. After about 2hr 30min, little-used **Nakpogoro** camp (4240m) is bypassed.

The newly visible **peaks** towards the west are part of the West Biafo Wall, including Ghur (5794m), Pamshe Peak (6023m), and lastly 'Fairy Tale' Sosbun Brakk (6413m).

There are several large crevasses to be circumnavigated before camp is reached. They are at their biggest and most exposed from late August onwards. In bad weather or snow cover it is essential to rope up all members of the party. Crossing in the dark should not be attempted.

There is a good campsite known locally as **Napina** (4470m) (or Morfogoro or Makpogoro, meaning 'red stones') with the possibility of water below a prominent rock tower called Uzun Brakk (6422m).

Uzun Brakk means 'steep mountain' or 'sheer mountain'. It was formerly known as Conway's Ogre, and has had several ascent attempts: in 1980 a

Sim Gang Glacier
Ogre
Base Camp
Uzun Brakk
(Conway's Ogre)
6422m
F
Napina 4470m
(or Makpogoro)
Uzun Brakk
Glacier
Biafo
Glacier
5470m
Pamshe
Peak
6023m
Miracle Highway
Nakpogoro
4240m
Ogre Camp
used in 1899 by
Bullock Workman couple
Ghur
5794m
Ho Blük

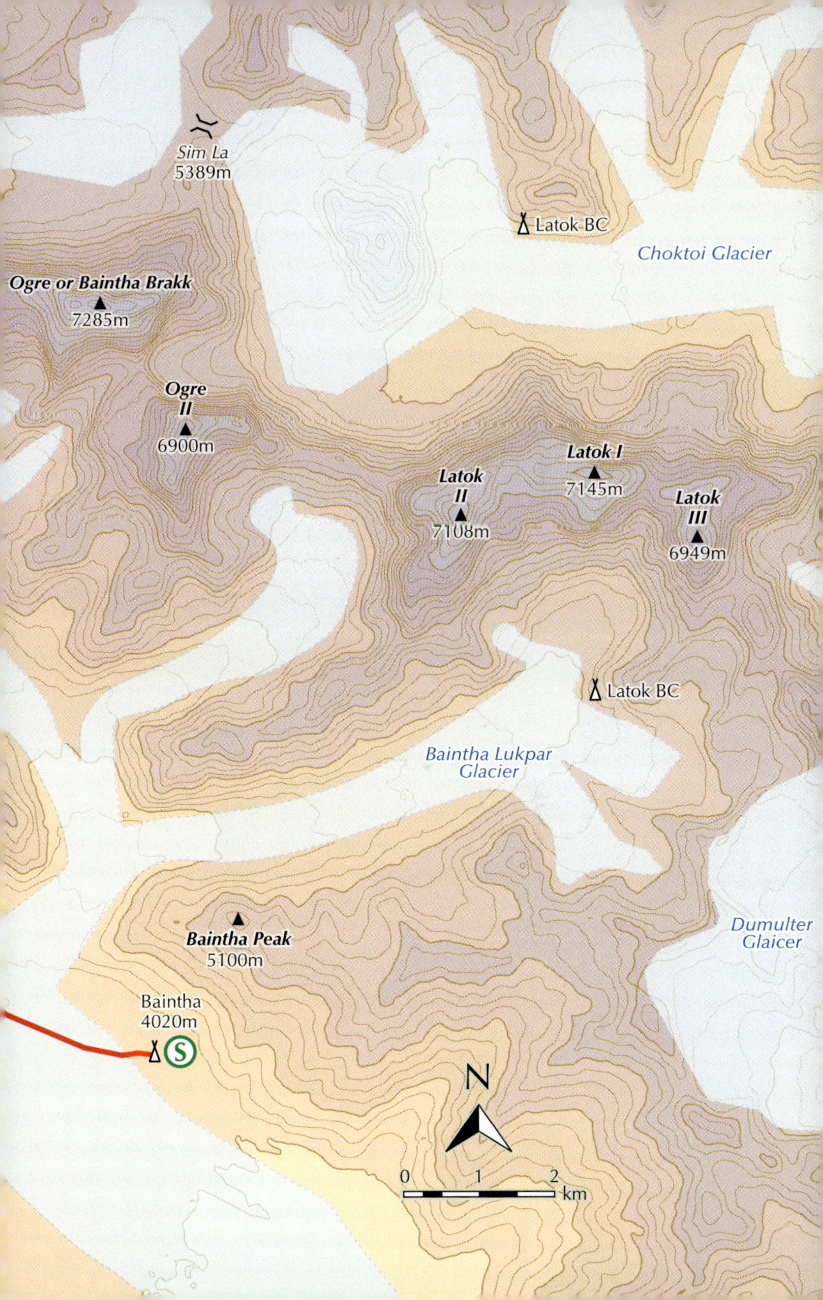

Sim La
5389m
Latok BC
Choktoi Glacier
Ogre or Baintha Brakk
7285m
Ogre
II
6900m
Latok I
7145m
Latok
II
7108m
Latok
III
6949m
Latok BC
Baintha Lukpar
Glacier
Dumulter
Glaicer
Baintha Peak
5100m
Baintha
4020m
S
N
0
1
2
km

British party tried the east face, in 1993 an American party attempted the southwest face, and finally Czech climbers reached the summit in 2013.

DAY 5

Napina to Sim Gang

Start	Napina 4470m
Finish	Sim Gang 4685m
Distance	7.9km
Ascent	215m
Descent	Negligible
Time	4–5hr
Altitude gain	215m
Note	This day could finish at four possible camp sites. 1. Karpogoro at 4580m: 3hr. 2. Sim Gang camp 4685m: 4–5hr. 3. Hispar Pass Base Camp at 4750m. 4. Top of the Hispar Pass 5151m: making a long day of 6–8hr. A camp in between Napina and Hispar La is advised in order to acclimatise.

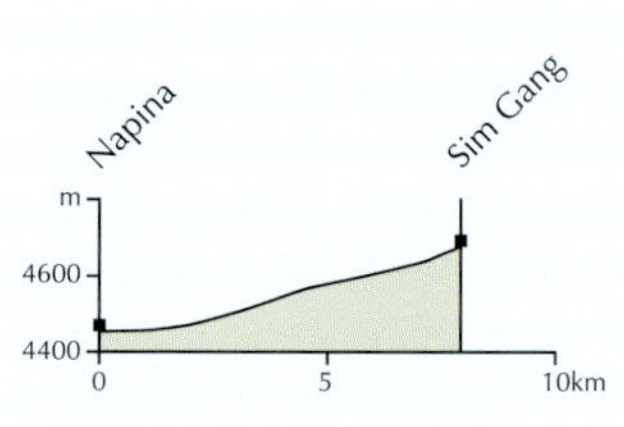

Back onto the glacier, the Biafo loses its debris of stones and turns now into a river of white ice. **Karpogoro** (4580m) camp on the rocks can be reached 3–4hr from Napina. It is a small campsite and water is not always easily available. If this camp is not being used, the route crosses over an area of the Biafo Glacier with lots of crevasses. Groups should walk together, roped up, and remain alert. The trekking is relatively easy.

Enjoy the **views** towards Sosbun Brakk (6413m), attempted in 1976 by a German party and climbed by a Japanese party in 1981. To the right of this peak a steep snow 'technical trail' leads to a pass called Sokna (or Sokha) La (c5500m) which leads to the Basha Valley in three days, and which was traversed for the first time in 1937 by HW (Bill) Tilman.

The **Sim Gang** camp itself is on the west corner of the Sim Gang/Snow Lake basin, affording stunning views. The camp is on platforms amongst a ridge of rocks and extreme care should be taken when moving around camp on Snow Lake to avoid unseen crevasses.

Looking towards Snow Lake and Ogre from near the top of Hispar La (photo: Jasmine Star)

Following his 1937 expedition into this area – a region in which at least no foreigners had ventured for nearly 40 years – **Bill Tilman** reported seeing yeti footprints in this region. Apparently, they were of the man-eating rather than yak-eating variety (the author has seen some yeti prints in the Rum Doodle bar in Kathmandu!).

Tilman solved the mystery as to whether Snow Lake was an ice cap. He discovered that it was just an extra-wide glacier of only thirty square miles.

POSSIBLE REST AND ACCLIMATISATION DAY FROM SIM GANG CAMP

There are almost limitless exploration possibilities from camp. Some people even bring cross-country telemark skis for use early in the season. However, in addition to requiring the skills to both ski and move together roped up it does add considerably to the loads to be carried by porters up to and over the pass.

To the east is the Sim Gang basin which leads via the Sim La to the Choktoi Glacier, Ogre and Latok group, the Skam La to the Nobande Sobande Glacier and the Lukpe La and eventually to the Shimshal Valley. Weather and time permitting, at least one day should be allocated to exploration of the area and the route ahead. Many weeks could be spent here mountaineering and exploring without ever crossing the Hispar Pass to the Hispar Glacier.

DAY 6

Sim Gang to Hispar La via Snow Lake

Start	Sim Gang (4685m)
Finish	Hispar La (5151m)
Distance	7.4km
Ascent	466m
Descent	Negligible
Time	3–5hr
Altitude gain	466m

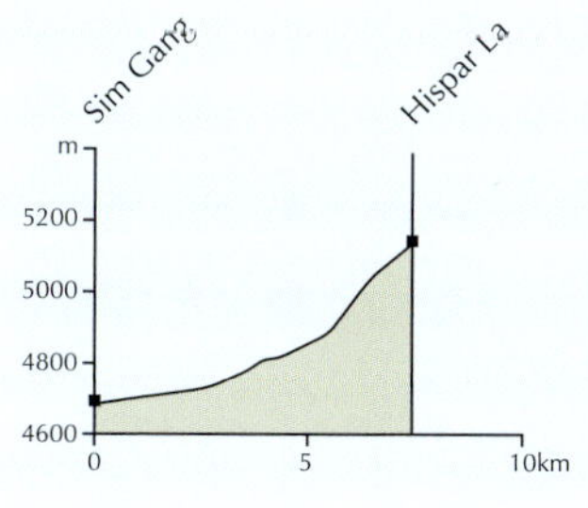

Cross the Sim Gang Glacier and Snow Lake (4870m) and ascend to the high point of the whole trip, the Hispar La (5151m). It requires a very early start to get the safest snow/ice/crevasse conditions. The way through the crevasses is not obvious and a zig zag route around each is necessary. This section should be undertaken roped up. A reconnaissance trip the day before can often save time. The route moves from generally flat to a steeper climb with some big crevasses, finishing with a 30min flat piece reaching the pass.

Possible camp below the Hispar Pass, on the Hispar side (photo: Jasmine Star)

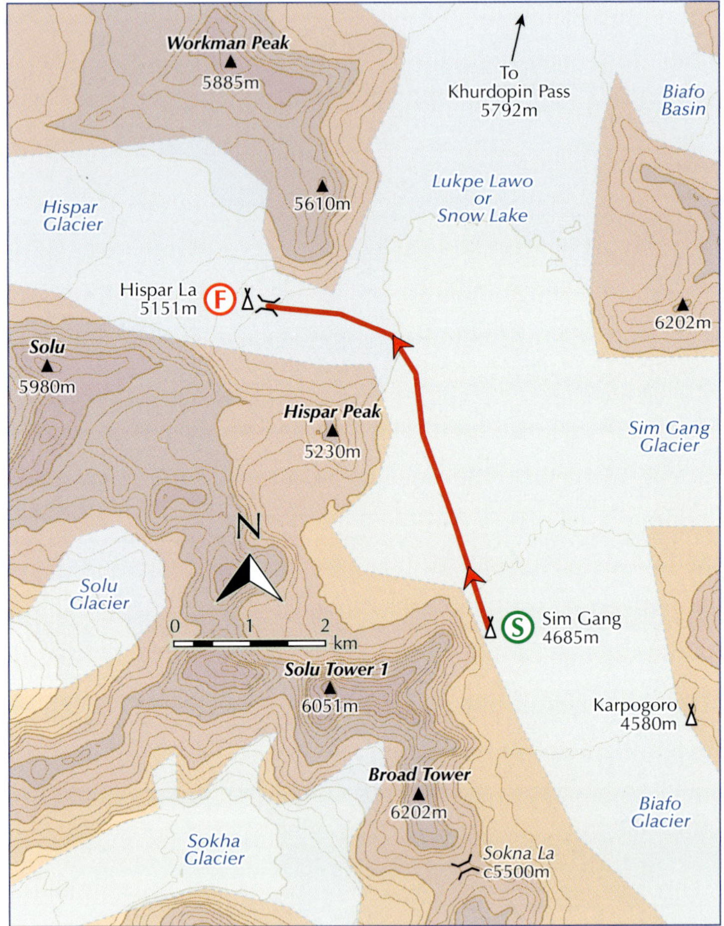

In the 1980–90s there were few difficult crevasses in this area, and they did not present a serious obstacle. In recent years however, the crevasses have been such that parties have not been able to cross the pass and have had to return down the Biafo Glacier. In the summer of 2018, a group did make a route through the crevasses and reopened the pass crossing.

If the conditions are suitable a magnificent high camp can be experienced on top of the pass with either a view down the Hispar Glacier or back towards Snow Lake, depending on the choice of campsite location. Camp is normally made on top of the **Hispar La** pass. Porters will dig themselves a kind of one-metre-deep pit covered by a tarpaulin, and cook and sleep quite comfortably close to each other in this pit. Tents should be fixed extra securely, to stop them blowing away.

FIRST IMPRESSIONS

On reaching the pass from the west in 1892, Conway was transfixed by the expanse of snow and pointy mountains all round. He wrote: 'Before us lay a basin or lake of snow. From the midst … rose a series of mountain islands, white like the snow that buried their bases, and there were endless bays and straits as of white water nestling amongst them'.

Or as the Workman couple described it: 'The pass is a river of pure white, driven snow, less vast only than Snow Lake below, bounded on either side by chains of lofty nameless snow kings'.

Optional excursions from Hispar La

If time and conditions permit, ascend in one day the nearby Workman Peak (5885m), named after the first people to summit, the American Bullock Workman couple in 1899. It is a good 700m of ascent on a snowy slope. It's minimally technical but requires you to rope up and use ice-axe and crampons. From this peak, views extend towards K2, Muztagh Tower, Gasherbrum and Golden Throne.

Another viewing point is on the southern side, just before the pass. A small snowy peak called Hispar Peak (5230m), which should give you a glimpse of Broad Peak (8051m) and Muztagh Tower (7273m) in the far distance, just left of Ogre.

DAY 7

Hispar La to Khani Basa (Baktur Baig)

Start	Hispar La 5151m
Finish	Khani Basa 4525m
Distance	9.9km
Ascent	Negligible
Descent	626m
Time	5–7hr
Altitude loss	626m

The Hispar Glacier, 49km long, is more difficult to travel on than the Biafo. It has four major glaciers that join it from the north on the watershed between the Hispar and Shimshal Valleys. On this watershed lie a series of mountains just under 8000m, Kanjut Sar (7760m), Pumari Chhish (7491m), Khunyang Chhish (7852m) and Distaghil Sar (7885m), the glaciers from which bring down vast quantities of rubble which turn the Hispar into a labyrinthine mass of rock-covered icy mounds and valleys. In contrast the ablation zones that run alongside are green and beautiful and make wonderful campsites.

Travelling along the glacier on the southern side is possible, but trekking parties normally take a trail on the northern side of the Hispar Glacier. The Workman couple travelled the second half down on the southern side using campsites and passing spots with names (according to their map) such as Shenishshish camp (4000m), Markorum (3900m), Gandeshish, and Chokuteris camp (3586m).

An early start from the camp at the Hispar La is again essential for both safety and to see the early sunlight on the mountains that surround both the Hispar Glacier and Snow Lake. Care should be taken moving around camp and packing, and parties should again be roped up for travel. Prepare for travel time to be longer when snow is soft.

The route initially follows the centre of the glacier. The downward slopes vary from straightforward to very steep, sometimes including the need to cross a bergschrund. An additional rope used as a fixed rope will help to safeguard both the

group and porters. There are annual variations, but this is usually the most technical part of the traverse over the pass. Towards the bottom of the slope, where the glacier levels out, the terrain changes from snow to rocky, bumpy moraine. It's another 2–3hr to reach the campsite **Khani Basa** (also called Baktur Baig), which lies on the north side of the Hispar Glacier and on the east side of the tributary

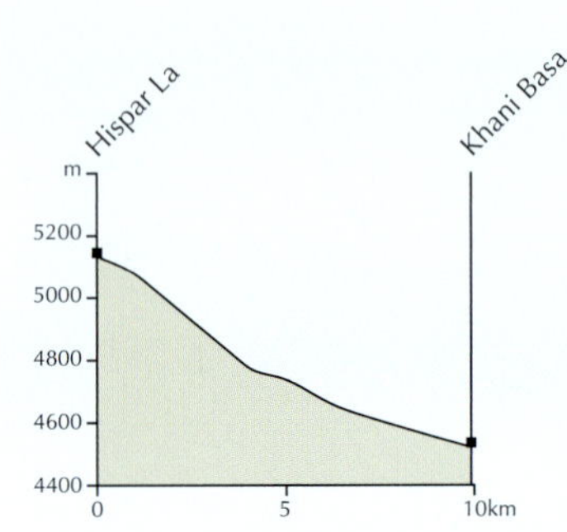

Khani Basa Glacier, nestled in a small ablation valley near a green spot full of flowers. Water may have to be brought up from the glacial pools below.

The 1908 **Bullock Workman expedition** stayed here for 16 days to explore and climb some peaks. Their trip was 51 days long from Hispar to Askole village!

Opposite the camp, views extend towards the impressive snow and ice Balchhish Range with peaks up to and around 6000m height. A rest day here is strongly advised, but 'time is money'!

Optional extension crossing Khani Basa Glacier

If time and energy allow, the Khani Basa Glacier could be crossed in 1hr 30min, to reach the campsite beyond (two additional hours from Khani Basa).

Looking towards Hispar La (photo: Jasmine Star)

DAY 8

Khani Basa (Baktur Baig) to Jutmal

Start	Khani Basa 4525m
Finish	Jutmal 4250m
Distance	9km
Ascent	Negligible
Descent	275m
Time	5–6hr
Altitude loss	275m
Note	Early starts are required every day on descent of the Hispar Glacier to cross rivers and streams when they are not in spate with meltwater in the afternoon. There are several camp sites on the trail between Khani Basa and Yutmaru, so there are options for a strong party or a crowded campsite.

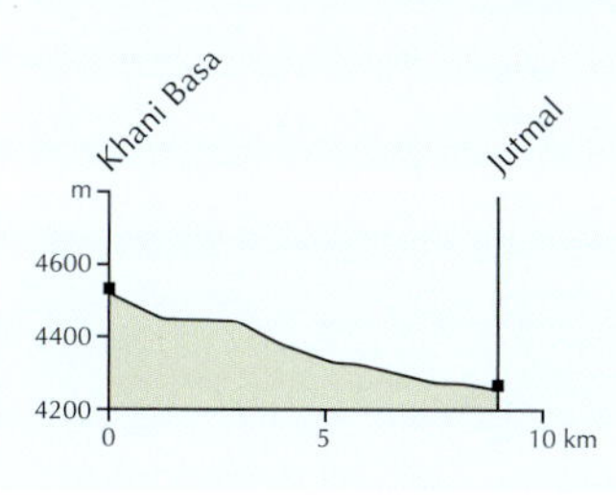

A faint trail leads to the edge of the **Khani Basa Glacier** (around 12km long) where it descends to the jumble of moraine – a result of the collision between this and the Hispar Glacier. Carefully find your way across (around 1hr 30min), but when safe to do so, do not miss seeing the view northwards along the Khani Basa Glacier towards Kanjut Sar (7760m) (climbed for the first time by Italians in 1959 and the 29th highest peak in the world). Once on the other side there is a pleasant lunch spot and fresh water.

The next section of the route crosses several outwash streams. These vary in size and strength depending on the time of day as they are all made up of meltwater: on hot days, or later in the afternoon, they can be in full spate and difficult to cross. It is worth having alternative footwear, such as sandals, for these crossings.

In mid July of 1892, when **Conway** crossed Nushik La pass and camped at Jutmal, they had a clear day: he remarked 'St. Swithin was propitious'.

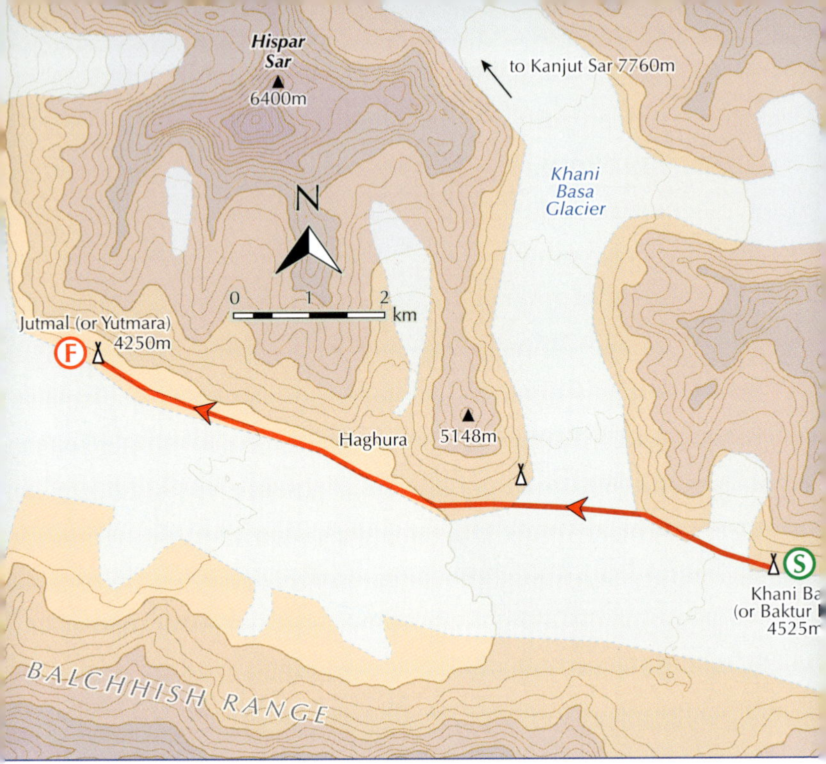

Hispar Sar
6400m

to Kanjut Sar 7760m

Khani Basa Glacier

N

0 1 2 km

Jutmal (or Yutmara) 4250m

F

Haghura

5148m

S

Khani Ba
(or Baktur
4525m

BALCHHISH RANGE

Khani Basa camp (photo: Jasmine Star)

And on crossing the Hispar Glacier in the middle from south bank to north, Conway further commented: 'Thus it is in this county northwards the high mountains seem to have no end. Ridge behind ridge, crest behind crest, glacier behind glacier, they stretch away in monotonous parallelism, through regions uninhabited and even unvisited by man'.

The route then follows the ablation valley that is formed between the sides of the true valley and the lateral moraine of the glacier, passing a place called **Haghura**, or according to the Workmans, Woodline Camp (4428m). The ablation valley on the north bank of the Hispar Glacier can be superb walking, with fresh springs and meadows – a stark contrast to the chaos of rocks, moraine, and ice on the glacier. Choose one of the many campsites. **Jutmal** (or Yutmara) (4250m), is located before crossing the Yutmaru (or Yutmo) Glacier.

DAY 9

Jutmal to Shikam Baris or to camp before Pumari Chhish Glacier

Start	Jutmal 4250m
Finish	Pumari Chhish Glacier Camp 3920m
Distance	12.2km
Ascent	Negligible
Descent	330m
Time	4–5hr
Altitude loss	330m

After 45mins from camp the next, and second, side glacier must be crossed. It is the **Yutmaru Glacier** (or Yutmo; 14km long). The crossing takes 2hr finishing with a steep climb up a moraine.

This impressive glacier is fed by ice from mountains Ali Chhish (6164m), Pumari Chhish (7491m), Yutmaru Sar (7330m), Khani Basa Sar (6441m) and Hispar Sar (6395m). The **Yutmaru Glacier** is about two kilometres wide where it meets the Hispar Glacier.

After crossing the Yutmaru Glacier look to the south, for a pass called **Nushik La** (5275m) (or Kushuk La), an important historic route over which even cattle were probably taken, leading to Arandu in Baltistan. In the old

Ice Cake
6411m
Ali
Chhish
6164m
Pumari Chhish Glacier
Khatumburumbum Glacier
Ghaltza
Dachigan
Pumari Chhish
3920m
Shikam
Baris
Markorum
3900m
Shenishish
4000m
Hispar
Glacier
East Markorum Glacier
Shenishish Glacier
Haigutum
4730m
Haigatum Glaicer
Shirin Chhish
5925m
Nushik La
(or Kushuk La)
5275m

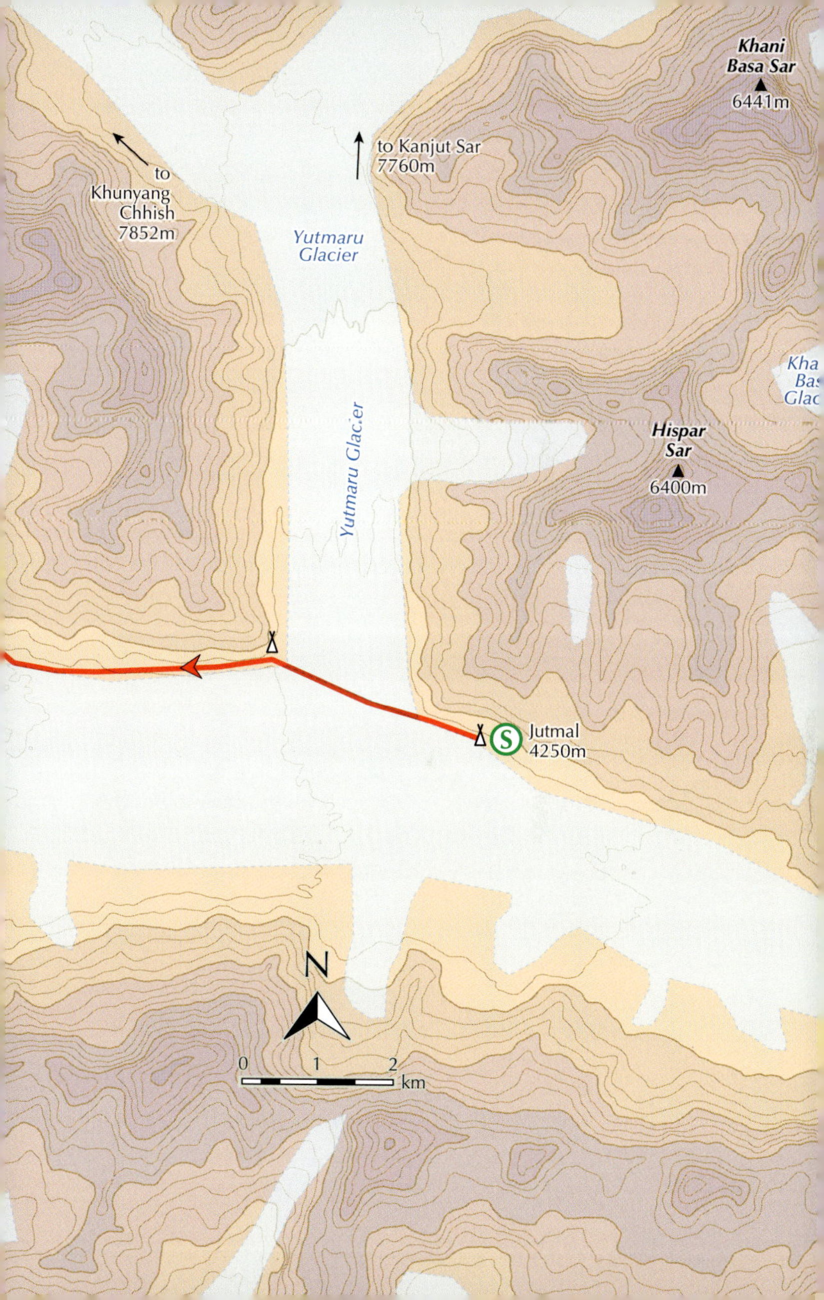

Khani Basa Sar
6441m
to Kanjut Sar
7760m
to Khunyang Chhish
7852m
Yutmaru Glacier
Yutmaru Glacier
Kha Bas Glac
Hispar Sar
6400m
Jutmal
4250m
S
N
0
1
2
km

days locals travelling these areas generally used the Nushik La: although it posed dangers of ice fall and avalanche, it was preferred over the possibilities of fog and bad weather that often prevailed over the Hispar La.

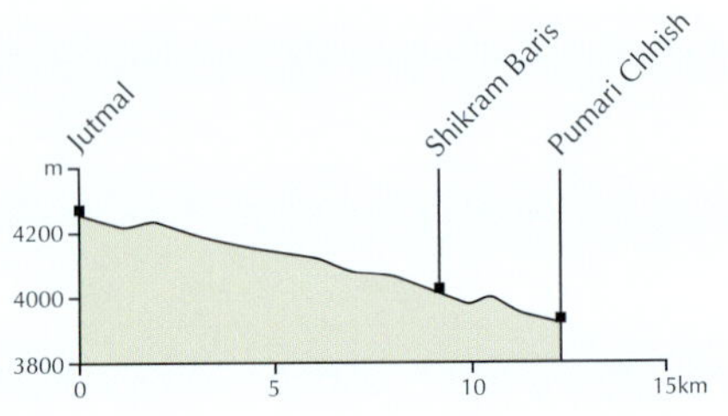

Climb steeply up the moraine to a good campsite and continue trekking a beautiful trail with many possible campsites. **Shikam Baris** (around 4150m) is one of them, a large field with stone shelters and water (4hr 30min from Jutmal). (A stop here would make the route 3.5km shorter.) Depending on availability of water and fitness in group, carry on to a campsite at **Pumari Chhish** close to Pumari Chhish Glacier. The campsites are a delight, and a rest day would be the best.

Looking across the Hispar Glacier (photo: Jasmine Star)

DAY 10

Pumari Chhish Glacier camp to Bitenmal

Start	Pumari Chhish Glacier camp 3920m
Finish	Bitenmal 3810m
Distance	7.5km
Ascent	75m
Descent	185m
Time	4–5hr
Altitude loss	110m

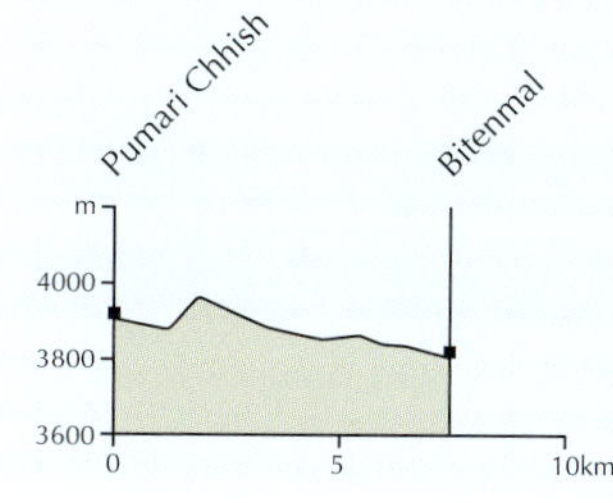

This day starts with a fairly easy walk following the route through the ablation valley to arrive at the tributary Pumari Chhish Glacier. This glacier comes in from the north side, effectively blocking the way so the route has to descend onto the glacier – cross it to reach the other side. The crossing is usually easier than the previous one (across the Yutmaru Glacier), but of course this is still a slowly flowing river of ice and rocks, so every month – let alone year – it is different. On one expedition, a major time-consuming detour had to be made onto the Hispar Glacier to bypass the mess of the Pumari Chhish Glacier, finishing with a steep ascent of the moraine to get back on dry ground.

In 1988 the **Pumari Chhish Glacier** surged three quarters of the way across the Hispar but has slowed now.

A few years later, in 1990, glacial hydrologists measured the depth of the ice on the main **Hispar Glacier** at this point to be 500 metres, it would be interesting to repeat the work now to assess the changes.

A glance of Trivor (7577m), Pumari Chhish (7491m) and Khunyang Chhish (7852m) can be expected. As on the previous day, stop for lunch wherever water is first available in the ablation valley beyond the glacier. A popular spot is the meadow at **Ghaltza Dachigan** (3950m).

To
Distaghil
Sar
7885m
Kunyang
Chhish
7852m
Bularung
Camp
Ice Cake
6411m
N
0
1
2
km
Khunyang Glacier
Daltanas
Bitenmal
3810m
F
Pumari Chhish Glacier
Pumari Chhish
3920m
S
Ghaltza
Dachigan
West Markorum Glacier
Markorum
3900m
Hispar Glacier
Shenishish
4000m
Makrong
Chhish
6511m
East Markorum Glacier
Shenishish Glacier
Shirin
Chhish
5925m
Nushik
(or Kushuk)
5275m

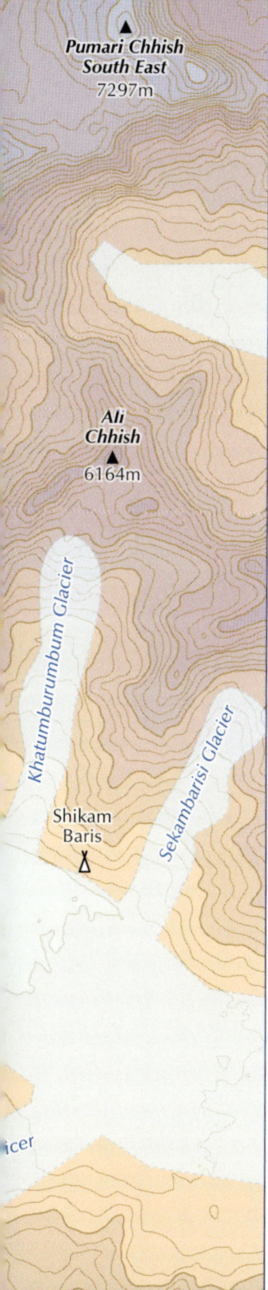

The remainder of the day is pleasant walking through the ablation valley with the ever-present Hispar Glacier flanked by jagged peaks on the left. There is a lower path at glacier level which is best avoided and has a less good view. The camp is situated around 20min before the next major tributary glacier, at an expansive grassy area with a few stone huts used by shepherds (the first buildings since registering at the Central Karakoram National Park office near Askole). This is **Bitenmal** (3810m) (or Bittarmal or Bitanmal) which, as a rough approximation, means 'the home of the witch doctors'!

There is a final climb up to a viewpoint behind Bitenmal that gives an awesome view of the journey just completed and just the tip of the summit of Ogre (7285m). This camp is now beyond the Central Karakoram National Park boundary.

DAY 11

Bitenmal to Falalinghish

Start	Bitenmal 3810m
Finish	Falalinghish 3435m
Distance	6.9km
Ascent	Negligible
Descent	375m
Time	5–6hr
Altitude loss	375m

This is the last day of trekking down the Hispar Glacier, but another big side glacier must be negotiated, and several streams crossed. A final early start is again advisable. The **Khunyang Glacier** has cut deeply into the Hispar Glacier, resulting in a complex ice labyrinth which must be crossed and which is rather time consuming. Tread carefully while enjoying the awesome views of the mountains to your right.

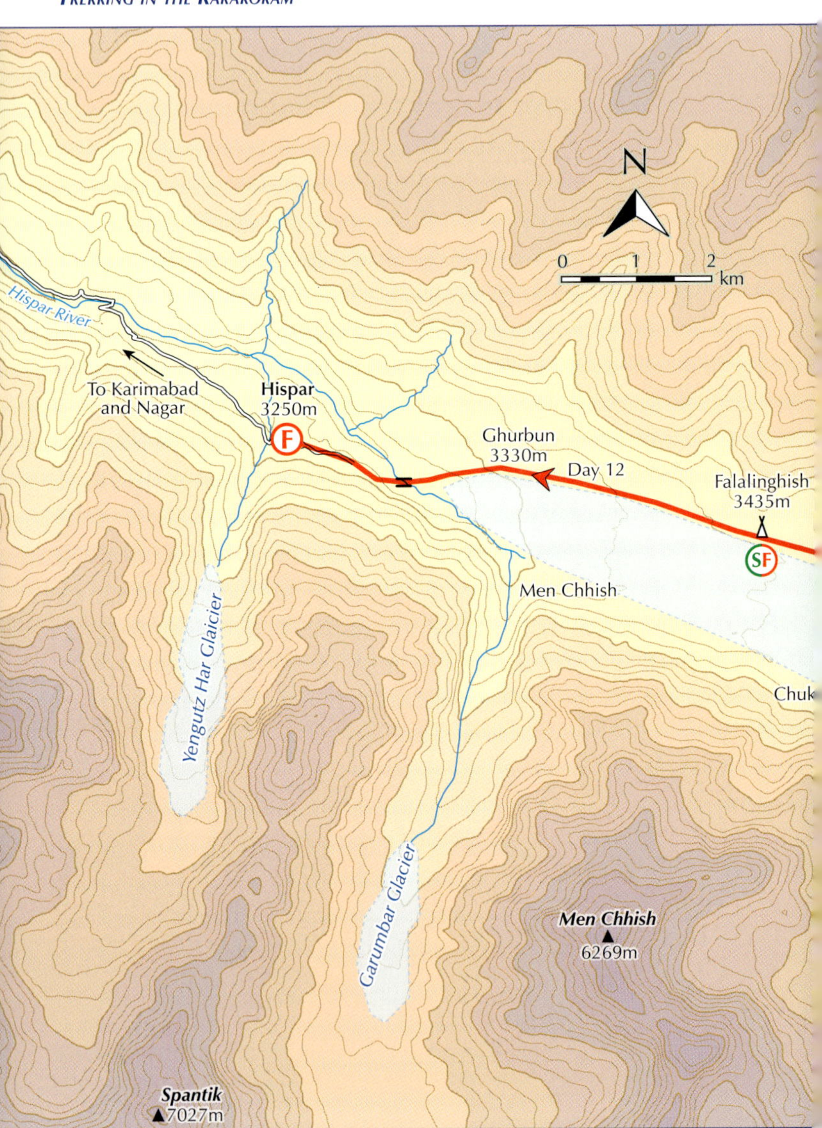
N
0
1
2
km
Hispar River
To Karimabad
and Nagar
Hispar
3250m
F
Ghurbun
3330m
Day 12
Falalinghish
3435m
SF
Men Chhish
Chuk
Yengutz Har Glaicier
Garumbar Glacier
Men Chhish
6269m
Spantik
7027m

Khunyang Chhish
7852m
Distighal Sar
7885m
Faroling Chhish
6187m
5594m
Bularung Camp
Khunyang Glacier
Day 11
Daltanas
Bitenmal
3810m
Turman
Hispar Glacier
West Markorum Glacier
Markorum
3900m
Makrong Chhish
6511m
6210m

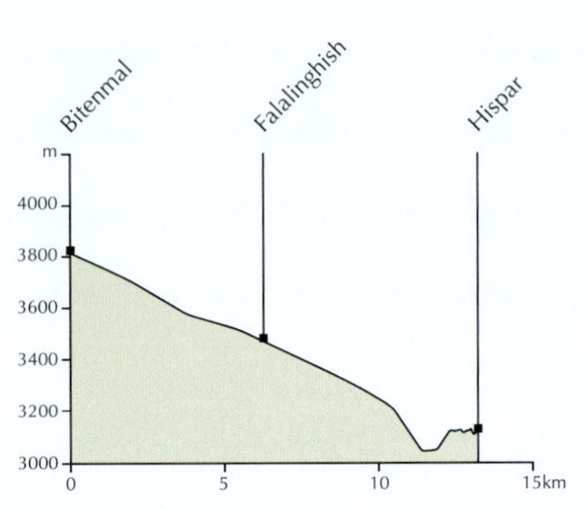

The side glacier is called **Khunyang (or Kanyang) Glacier**, which is fed by mountains like Trivor (7577m), Balarung Sar (7134m), Distaghil Sar (7885m), and Khunyang Chhish (7852m) (first ascent in 1971 by a Polish expedition).

It is difficult to put a time on today's glacier travelling, since the conditions and routes change every year. After a short, gentle walk, there is a steep descent to the Hispar Glacier and the point where the Khunyang Glacier is cutting its way into the Hispar. The unknown time-consuming section starts here. At the end, a steep ascent out of the moraine at **Daltanas**, on the opposite bank of the Khunyang Glacier, leads to a well-deserved easy trail reaching **Falalinghish** campsite (3435m) (or Palolimkish) after about four kilometres.

DAY 12

To Hispar village and beyond

Start	Falalinghish 3435m
Finish	Hispar village 3250m
Distance	6.3km
Ascent	95m
Descent	230m
Time	3–5hr
Altitude loss	185m
Note	For map and profile, see Day 11

Depending on where last camp has been, count on a good few hours of hiking to **Hispar** village (3250m). The village is reached by a footbridge and narrow path at the snout of the glacier.

> **Hispar** is a large village by regional standards and has many acres of cultivated land that stretch out along a huge alluvial fan. It is occupied by Shia Muslims. Negotiating onwards transportation here could result in over-priced services so it is worth arranging to meet your pre-ordered jeep here.

It is a 40km journey to reach the Karakoram Highway (KKH). Make sure there is transport home organised for your porters from Skardu and Askole.

Pastures near Hispar village (photo: Jasmine Star)

Baltoro Glacier, Nameless Tower, Great Trango Tower, Trango Castle and Thunmo Cathedral (Trek 2, Day 3)

TREK 2

K2 Base Camp Trek

Start/finish	Askole 3045m (see note)
Distance	150.7km from Askole (including visit to K2 Base Camp: 175.1km)
Ascent/descent	2295m from Askole (including visit to K2 Base Camp: 2705m)
Grade	Strenuous
Days	12 + 2 rest/acclimatisation days
Highest point	4575m (optional visit to K2 Base Camp: 4965m)
Permits	A restricted trek that requires a permit
Note	In 2023 the route both started and finished in Askole. Anticipate walking between Askole and Joila.

A classic trek, leading to the base camp of K2, the second highest mountain in the world. The landscape is overwhelming, surrounded by so many notorious jagged

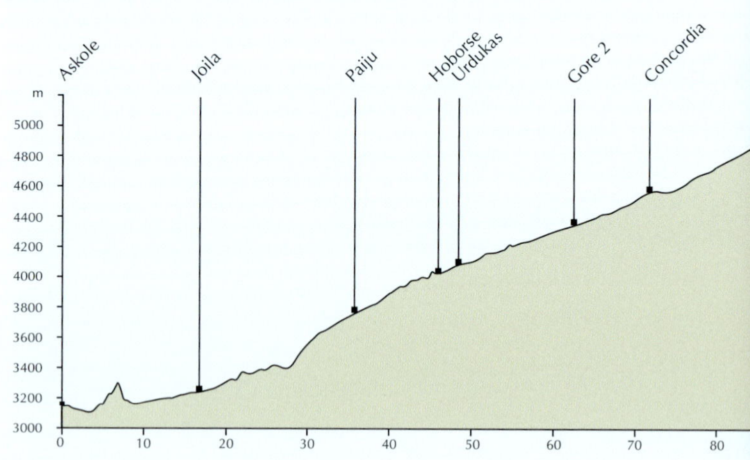

peaks and accompanied by the warmest local staff, that it takes a long time to digest the impressions.

Italian mountaineer Fosco Mariani describes the route as 'The Golden Road to The Seven Giants' (The Seven Giants are: Muztagh Tower, Masherbrum, K2, Broad Peak, Gasherbrum, Chogolisa and Golden Throne).

Getting to the start

See separate information on getting to the start of the trek, Askole. Drive from Skardu (2230m) to Askole (3045m). Be aware of altitude problems that could arise from the altitude gain (815m).

Extra days

Since the K2 trek might get shorter due to road developments, plan extra days besides the trek described here: there's an option to go higher up with an overnight at Broad Peak Base Camp, or a possible two or three days' trek to Gasherbrum Base Camp. Extra days are also needed as contingency in case of landslips, of which there have been plenty in the past.

The trek itinerary

The following trek is described as a 12-day long trek from Askole camp, up and down. Reaching Concordia is normally counted as nine stages for the porters. In

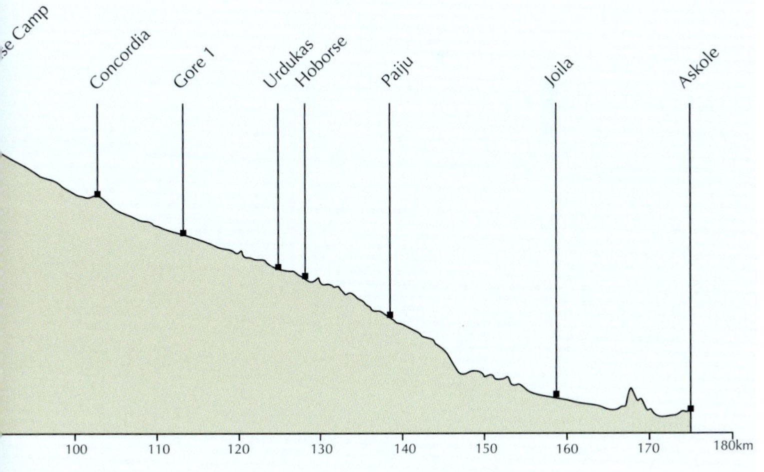

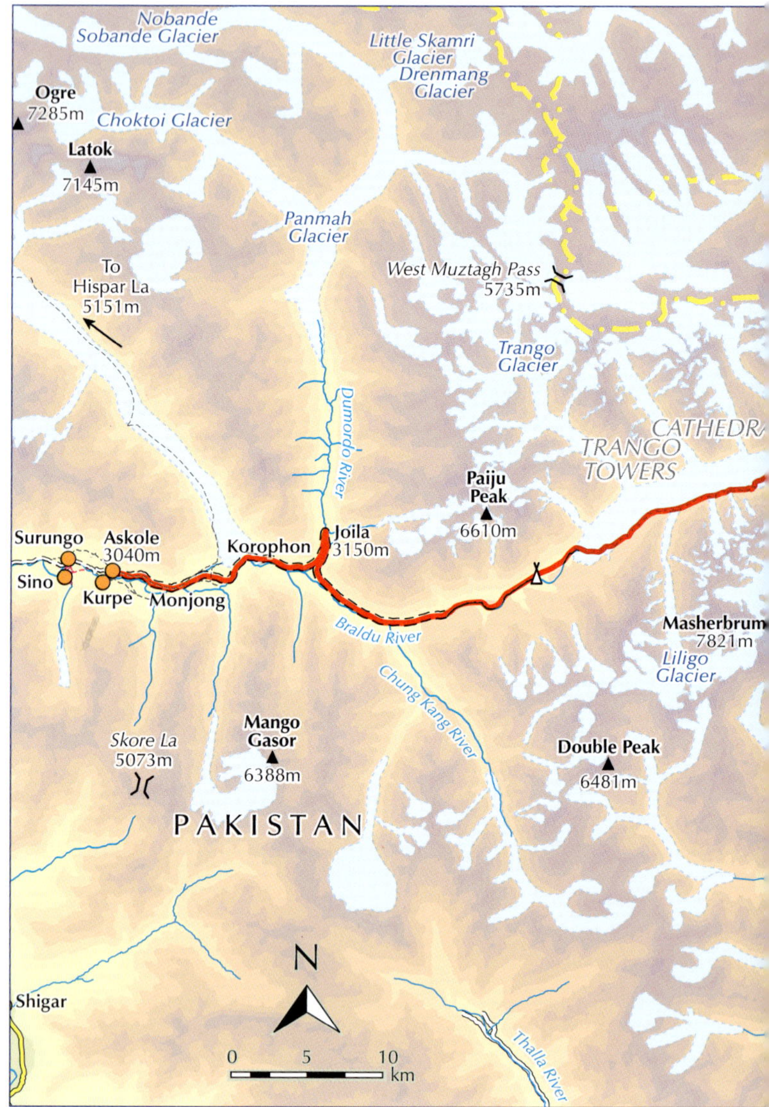
Nobande Sobande Glacier
Little Skamri Glacier
Drenmang Glacier
Ogre
7285m
Choktoi Glacier
Latok
7145m
Panmah Glacier
To Hispar La 5151m
West Muztagh Pass
5735m
Trango Glacier
Dumordo River
CATHEDR
TRANGO TOWERS
Paiju Peak
6610m
Surungo
Askole
3040m
Korophon
Joila
3150m
Sino
Kurpe
Monjong
Braldu River
Masherbrum
7821m
Liligo Glacier
Chung Kang River
Mango Gasor
6388m
Skore La
5073m
Double Peak
6481m
PAKISTAN
N
Shigar
0
5
10
km
Thalla River

CHINA
K2
8611m
Godwin Austen Glacier
Muztagh Tower
7284m
Savoia Glacier
K2 BC
4965m
Broad Peak
8051m
Broad Peak BC
CHINA
Biange Glacier
Gasherbrum II
8035m
Concordia
4575m
Baltoro Glacier
Gasherbrum I
8068m
Upper Baltoro Glacier
Gasherbrum BC
5150m
Sia Kangri or Queen Mary Peak
7381m
Gondogoro La
5595m
Masherbrum La
5364m
Golden Throne or Baltoro Kangri
7300m
Vigne Glacier
Chogolisa
7668m
Siachen Glacier
Ghent
7401m
Kaberi Glacier
Peak 36 Glacier
K6 or Baltistan Peak
7282m
Hushe
Hushe River
Charakusa Glacier
Link Glacier
Sherpi Gang Glacier
Saltoro Kangri
7705m
K6 Glacier

the Karakoram or Himalaya, it is more accurate to measure a trek in days, rather than distance and hours.

POLLUTION ON TREK

Unfortunately, the amount of pollution is increasing on this trek. The area is seeing a growing number of climbers, trekkers and staff which means increasing pressure on nature (there were approximately 1800 trekkers and climbers in 2022, for example, not including local staff). Trekking companies and expeditions should be able to carry away any rubbish their party produces. Still, there is plenty around, especially at campsites. Campsite caretakers do get paid to keep each campsite clean, but this is not always effective. The CKNP organisation, which receives money from each visitor, coordinates clean-up expeditions, with enormous amounts of waste being collected. The toilet facilities at camps are falling apart and are disgusting. Mule and human faeces are all around the campsites, causing extra problems for water supplies at the glacier camps. More and more trekkers have to contend with upset stomachs and end up giving up on their goals. The future of this region and its environmental protection is at stake. CKNP has produced a long list with an environmental strategy and major improvements to hopefully be implemented.

Please travel responsibly, aim to leave no trace, and help to reverse the thoughtless desecration of these wonderful natural surroundings.

DAY 1

Askole to Joila Camp

Start	Askole 3045m
Finish	Joila Camp 3150m
Distance	17km
Ascent	105m
Descent	Negligible
Time	5–6hr
Altitude gain	105m

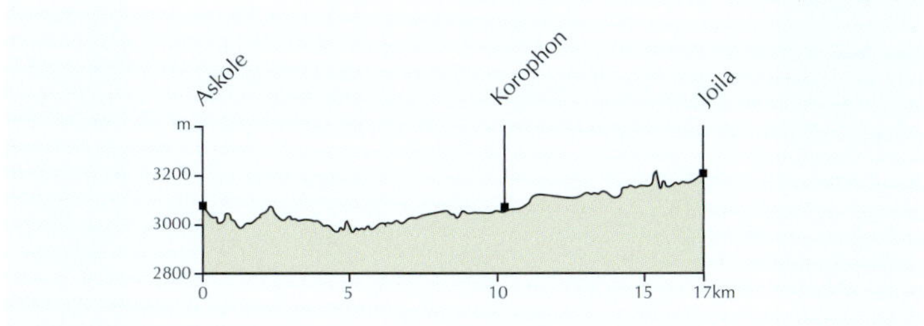

If you start walking from Askole, follow the dirt road enjoying the views towards villages and the last green pastures on the other side of the Braldu River and pay a visit to the **Central Karakoram National Park (CKNP) office** to register, but also to enjoy the posters on display in the main office explaining more about the Park.

On the opposite side of the Braldu River the last village of the valley, **Testa** is located.

Soon a **bridge** is reached crossing the first outlet from the Biafo Glacier. Before the bridge was in, a longish tiring detour had to be made crossing the snout of the Biafo Glacier. Not crossing the bridge will lead to the Biafo–Snow Lake–Hispar route, described in Trek 1 in this book.

When rounding the snout of the glacier keep an eye open for some mountains to be seen to the north along the Biafo Glacier, like Baintha Brakk (7285m) (or Ogre) and Latok (7145m). Cross a recently developed powerful outlet from the Biafo Glacier on a bridge, if it hasn't been washed out!

Suddenly camp **Korophon** appears at 3105m. Some sources call the valley system onwards Biaho Lungma instead of Braldu.

Temporary footbridge near Korophon with Biafo Glacier disappearing on the right

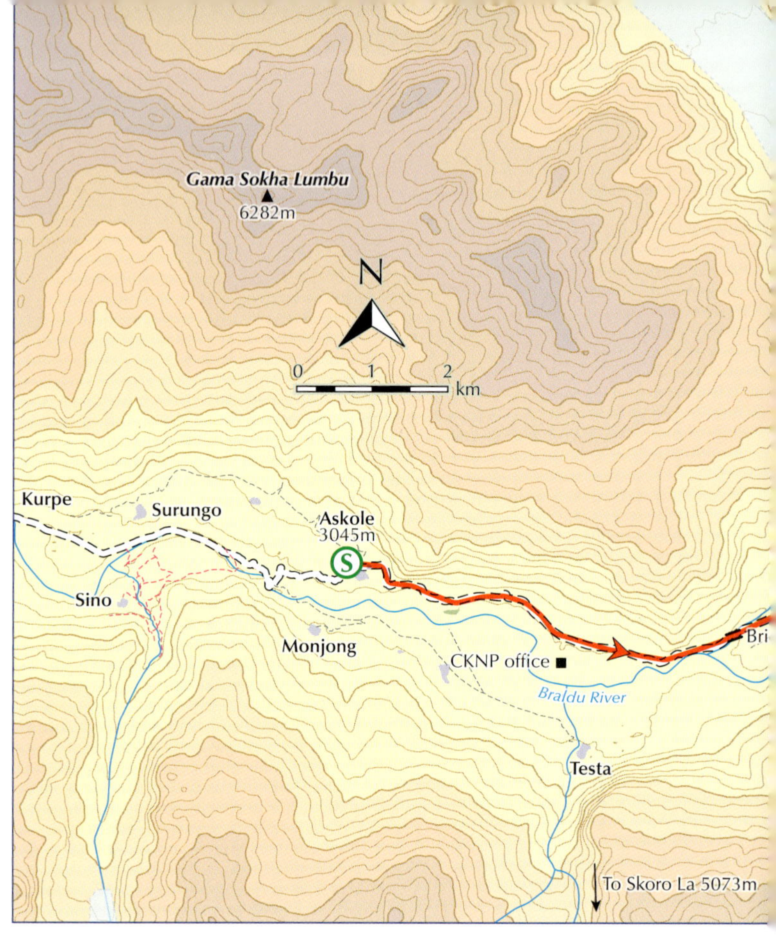

The dirt road follows along the Braldu River turning north after a while, rounding the ridge coming down from Bullah Peak (5950m) leading into the Panmah Valley where camp is located. When moving into the Panmah Valley, a military camp can be seen on the other side of the Dumordo River. To the south the prominent rock peaks Bakhur Das (5809m) and Mango Gusor (6288m) appear.

In previous times this trail was trickier with several options to get to camp or beyond the Panmah Valley. One of them, when the water level was too high, needed a climb and descent over a pass on an exposed cliff crossing the Bullah Peak or Laskam Ridge, leading to the Joila Bridge, a pulley with toll payment per

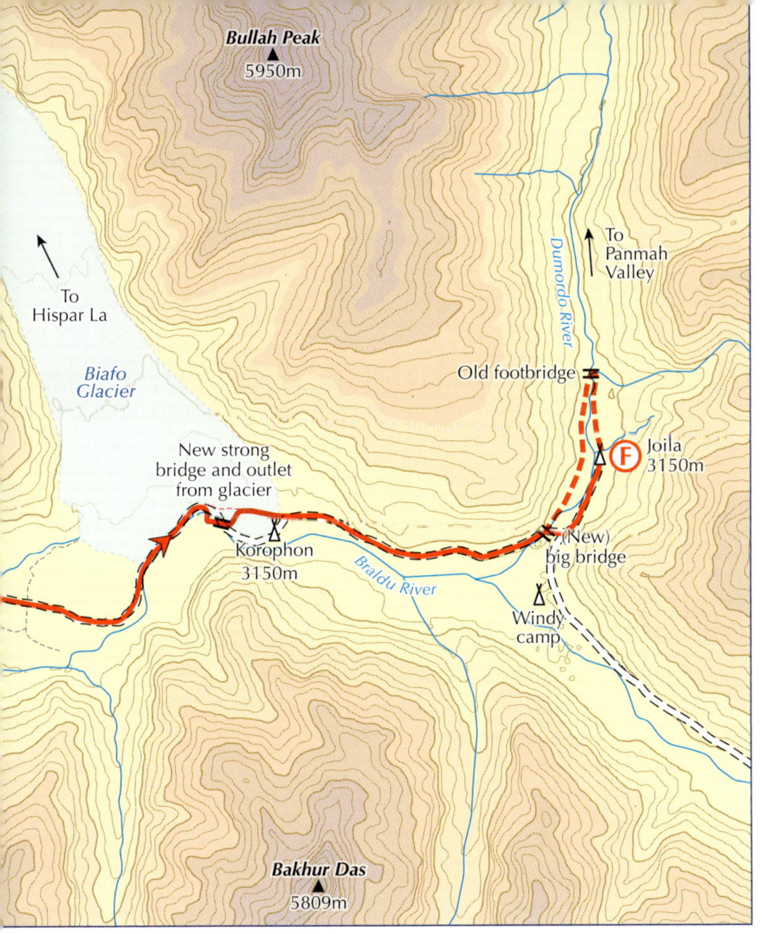

person and per bag. It could take an awfully long time at this pulley bridge if several groups arrived at the same time. Now there is an impressive, fixed bridge for jeeps leading to the military camp. Near the military camp is a camp for trekkers, but there are no toilet facilities, and it often catches the wind (hence the name **Windy camp**).

After crossing the bridge there is a split: to the left leads to Joila camp and the Panmah Valley; to the right the road is under construction towards Paiju. In 2022 the road was open for another 45 minutes' drive towards Paiju, including three Bailey bridges, saving two hours' walk.

Not so long ago reaching Joila camp required four to five days' trek, including tackling the Braldo Gorge and some rope bridges, which according to popular legend were only repaired when broken!

A **rope bridge** was constructed of nine intertwined birch twig ropes to make the footway, and nine lateral ropes to hold on to. Some bridges mix the birch with yak hair: when moistened then dried, it contracts to form a strong, very long-lasting rope.

JOILA CAMP

Joila camp (3150m) (or Jola) has an area with willow trees, many pitches (some protected from donkeys that can make the campsites dirty), water tap, toilet, and shower cabins (the latter not always in a good condition), a caretaker, the caretaker's house and a good cold stream for washing!

Warning: The stream at Joila camp, with clear cold fresh water, often turns murky later in the afternoon.

RECOMMENDED REST AND ACCLIMATISATION DAY AT JOILA CAMP

On a rest day, walk from Joila camp up the Panmah Valley to acclimatise. Walk on a reasonably flat trail towards the snout of the Panmah Glacier. This valley has seen quite a bit of traffic in the past with locals and explorers crossing the West Muztagh Pass (5735m).

The Panmah Valley counts several side valleys, glaciers and passes offering some demanding treks. There should still be some Himalayan brown bears and ibex in the area.

At the end of the Panmah Valley is the Skam La pass (5407m), part of a strenuous 14-day trek from Askole to Snow Lake. In 2018 a team crossed the pass making an excellent movie of it called *Zabardast* (which means 'wonderful' in Urdu) (see https://freeskier.com/stories/skam-la-first-descents-in-remote-pakistan).

Other passes linking with the Panmah Valley include Sim La (5833m), crossing over to Snow Lake, and the West Muztagh Pass, crossing over to China.

DAY 2

Joila Camp to Paiju

Start	Joila Camp 3150m
Finish	Paiju 3395m
Distance	19km
Ascent	525m
Descent	280m
Time	6–7hr
Altitude gain	245m
Note	The length of this day's trek can be influenced by road works and jeep availability. Several bailey bridges are constructed towards Paiju.

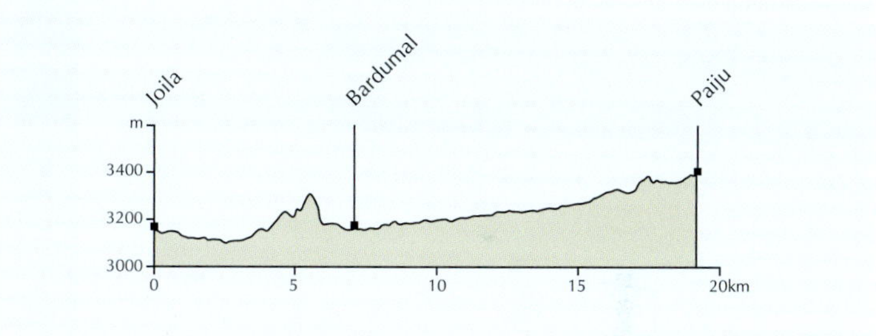

A gentle day for altitude gain but long in distance and tough when the sun is out. Earlier in the season the water level is lower, this means the route can be taken over the riverbed. This avoids the longer riverside path, which has numerous ups and downs. As is often the case with hiking in the Karakoram it is important to leave early in order to beat the heat.

Walk out (south) of the Panmah Valley, next to the military camp spotted yesterday, and turn east passing some possible campsites **Chobruk** (Chobrok), **Bardumal** (3253m) and **Skam Tsok** (3300m). Chobruk camp was used in the old days starting from Askole, in case the Dumordo River could be crossed/waded.

After trekking for 1hr–1hr 30 min, a **valley system**, (not visited on any trek in this book) appears to the south with some impressive peaks called Double

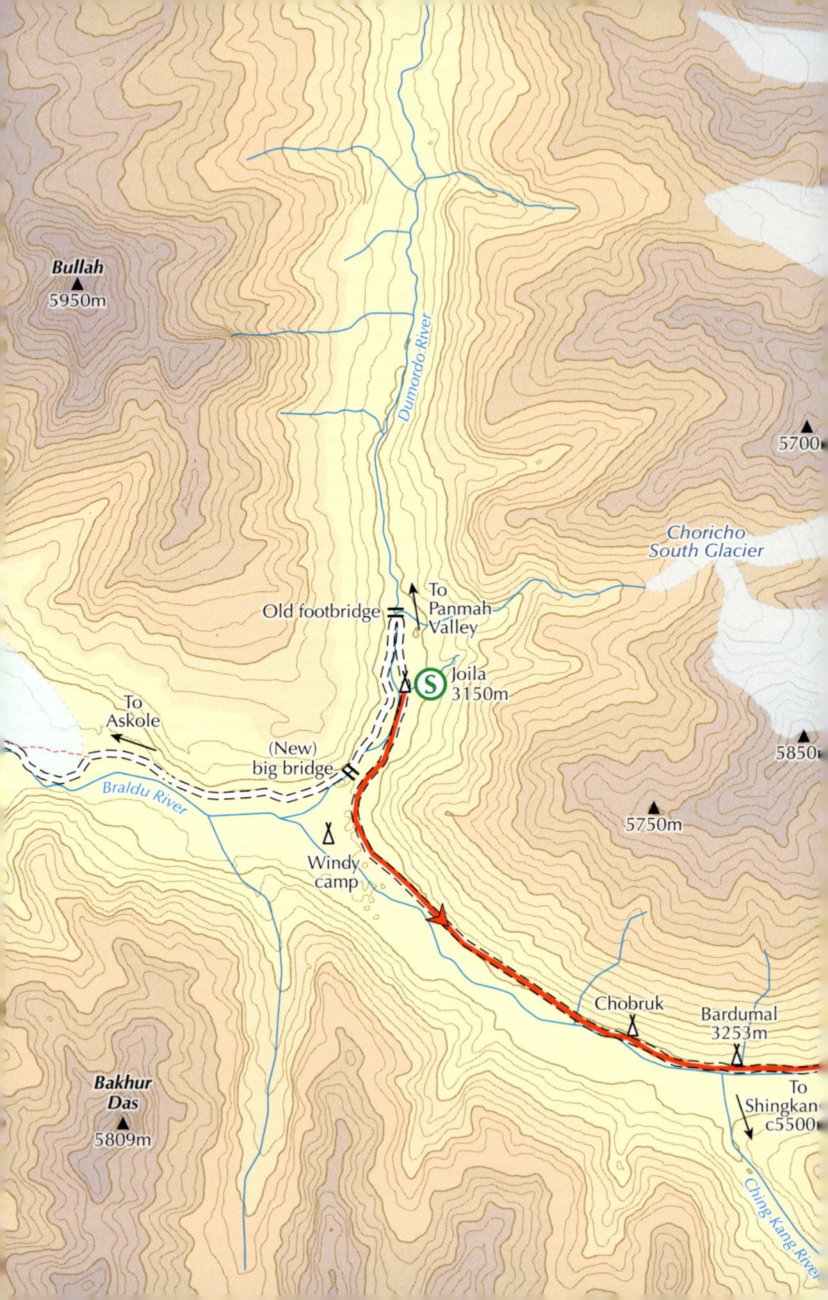

Bullah
5950m
Dumordo River
5700
Choricho
South Glacier
To
Panmah
Valley
Old footbridge
Joila
3150m
To
Askole
(New)
big bridge
Braldu River
5850
5750m
Windy
camp
Chobruk
Bardumal
3253m
To
Shingkan
c5500
Bakhur
Das
5809m
Ching-Kang River

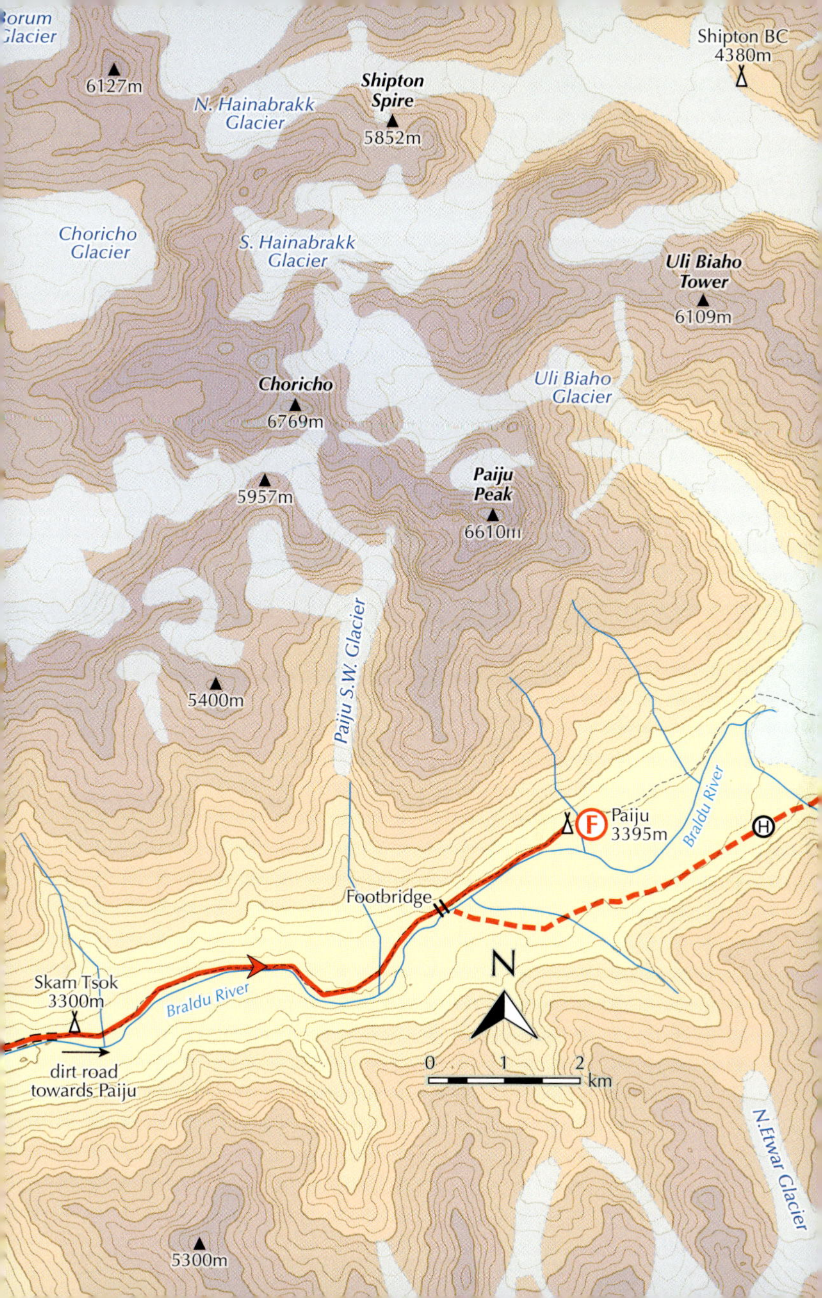

Borum Glacier
6127m
N. Hainabrakk Glacier
Shipton Spire
5852m
Shipton BC 4380m
Choricho Glacier
S. Hainabrakk Glacier
Uli Biaho Tower
6109m
Choricho
6769m
Uli Biaho Glacier
5957m
Paiju Peak
6610m
Paiju S.W. Glacier
5400m
Paiju 3395m
Braldu River
Footbridge
N
Skam Tsok 3300m
Braldu River
dirt road towards Paiju
0 1 2 km
N.Etwar Glacier
5300m

Peak I and II (6700m and 6125m respectively). The valley is called Ching Kang and has a difficult pass at the end called Shingkang La (around 5500m) which leads to the village of Hushe.

Several stretches of this day's route will be very close to the fast and furious flowing Biaho Lungma or Braldu River.

Skam Tsok (Skambosok) is used by some groups these days for camp. There are plenty of flat camping areas, several huts, a toilet building and running water. Many groups stop here for lunch on their way to Paiju.

After Skam Tsok the trail takes some smaller up and downs, crossing dry and wet gullies – with one, sometimes powerful, stream coming down from Choricho Peak (or Paiju I Peak) (6769m); a bridge is sometimes in place.

The glittering reflection on the ground and in some walls is from **mica**, a sheet silicate mineral.

During this section it is possible to see the unmistakable triangle top of K2, the first views of the Baltoro Glacier and some of the impressive rock towers flanking the northern side of the Baltoro Glacier – including Paiju Peak (6610m).

Today's last hour has some small, steep, strenuous up and downs, walking close to, or above the Braldu River, and the shade-promising greenery of **Paiju** camp in the tempting near distance.

Construction work on the new road had reached within 45min of camp in 2023!

PAIJU CAMP

Paiju camp, (*payu* means 'salt' in Balti) 3395m, is a big area with several campsites, some of them with shade from poplars, birches, willows and rose trees. There are several huts with a caretaker, a small mosque, small shop, several toilets and shower cabins which are in a deteriorating state. Porters will form small groups for sleeping and cooking in improvised shelters. Some of the campgrounds have a wire fence around to keep the ground clear from pack animals.

Any infrastructure has been funded by a tourist tax that is paid for entering the CKNP. Normally groups take a rest day here on the way in. People from Askole like to stay in Paiju during the winter since Paiju gets very little snow, and certainly a lot less than Askole does.

At Paiju camp

The pollution at camp can be a problem. There is a large rubbish pit at the camp. An incinerator has been installed to keep the campsite as clean as possible, but it is out of order.

Paiju has been described as 'a place for lovers of myth and saga'. According to legend, Paiju Peak was made of salt and looked totally white. The fairies who lived on the mountain told the people living nearby, that they could take all the salt they wanted as long as they did not sell it. But they did anyway, and the mountain promptly became a rock.

Hunting, now prohibited, was commonplace for locals as well as expeditions. The Duke of the Abruzzi expedition of 1909 killed 30 ibex above camp.

RECOMMENDED PAIJU REST DAY

Aside from a return 3–4hr hike up the hill towards Paiju Peak BC (all the way would make for a very long day), energy could be directed instead towards cleaning the campsite, doing laundry, journal writing, fishing, a cold wash in the river or just enjoying the scenery! To head for a wash, pass the last toilet cabins beyond Paiju and descend to the river where there should be some clear, quiet pools.

The trail to Paiju Peak BC starts on the main trail towards Baltoro Glacier and splits off after 45min, up a steep trail that gets more and more unclear.

A rest day for the kitchen means repacking everything and checking stock. A small depot will be made at Paiju for the return journey. Porters might use the rest day to bake Balti breads and kill the goat supplied by tour operators, and perhaps perform some singing and dancing. In the old days, firewood was collected here by staff for the camps higher up. Firewood has now been replaced by cooking kerosene.

Often at camps, porters will be paid-off since food supplies dwindle and stores for the way down are used. So, expect some farewells during the trek (like here in Paiju) of small groups of porters.

Opposite Paiju camp is a military camp located closer to the snout of the Baltoro Glacier. Helicopters might fly in and out, shifting personnel and supplying provisions (like bringing Coca Cola to sell at campsites).

Besides familiarising yourself with the next day's route getting to the Baltoro Glacier, find some passes on maps that lead to the glacier. Baltoro Glacier can be reached by more than 20 impressive passes. To mention some: Skoro Pass (5073m); Shingkhang La (c5500m, Ching Kang Valley); West and South Vigne Col (c5750m and c5950m); Gondogoro La (5595m); Kaberi La (6400m); Kondus Saddle (6200m); Conway Saddle (6113m); Gasherbrum La (6511m); Sella Pass (6800m); Skyang La (6450m), Savoia Pass (6250m); Steste Saddle (c6400m); Moni Pass (c6450m); East Muztagh Saddle (5389m); Sarpo Laggo (5675m); West Muztagh Pass (5735m); Skam La (5407m); Sim La (5833m); Hispar La (5151m); Hikmul La (5400m). Almost every one of them has some (often old) wild exploring stories attached to it.

DAY 3

Paiju to Hoborse

Start	Paiju 3395m
Finish	Hoborse 3825m
Distance	11.7km
Ascent	485m
Descent	55m
Time	6–8hr
Altitude gain	430m

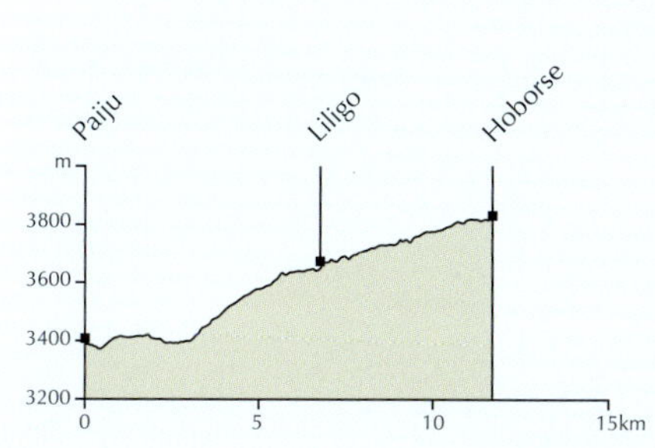

Again a day with reasonable altitude gains, but on the other hand hard ground and a long distance to cover. Expect some moraine walking for the next couple of days, which can be hard, as the Swiss guide Zurbriggen reflected, in 1892: 'In Switzerland if one has to go for an hour over moraine *so flucht Mann* [then you swear], but here one walks over it the whole day and says nothing'.

Start early (5am) and walk for 1hr–1hr 30min on a good trail to the snout of the **Baltoro Glacier** crossing several dry and wet gullies. When tackling the snout, a different colour ice stream joins the Baltoro ice, coming in from the left. This is the Uli Biaho Glacier.

Getting onto the glacier, climbing 100–150m, takes some effort but is not at all technical. There are several trails so make sure to stay close to somebody who knows the way. At the beginning of the glacier is an unclear split with the left branch leading to Trango Towers BC (4050m), Shipton BC (4380m) and the Sarpo Laggo Pass (5675m) and some other passes. Take the right branch. The outlet of the Baltoro Glacier is one of the many dramatic views for the day.

BALTORO GLACIER

The Baltoro Glacier, the fifth longest glacier in the world in non-polar regions, starts 65km upstream at Conway Saddle. The average width is about 2.1km; the maximum is 3.1km at Gore 1. It is one of the world's largest valley glaciers and drains an area of roughly 1500km^2. Part of the glacier is heavily covered by debris (an average thickness of one metre); the depths vary between 23 metres and 85 metres across the lower section and 49 metres and 96 metres across the upper section. The deepest ice covering has been measured at Gore 2 Camp – brown moraine: 171 metres. At K2 Base Camp, the ice is 140–150 metres thick. More than 20 small and big glaciers flow into the Baltoro Glacier, such as Trango, Dunge, Muztagh, Younghusband, Mandu, Yermandu, Biarchedi, Godwin-Austen and Vigne.

The Baltoro Glacier forms the border between Pakistan and China. Check the map and see how close China is. We are now getting deeper and

Hind Hainabrakk Glacier
5810m
Dunge Glacier
Trango Ri
6363m
Trango II
6327m
Trango Tower
6251m
Shipton BC
4380m
Trango Monk
5850m
Shipton Spire
5852m
Cat's Ears Spire
c5360m
Great Trango Tower
6287m
Trango Glacier
S. Hainabrakk Glacier
Uli Biaho NE Glacier
Uli Biaho Tower
6109m
Trango BC
4050m
Trango Castle
5753m
5400m
Choricho
6769m
Paiju Peak
6610m
Uli Biaho Glacier
Baltoro Glacier
N
0
1
2
km
Liligo
Paiju S.W. Glacier
Paiju
3395m
Braldu River
Liligo Peak
6161m

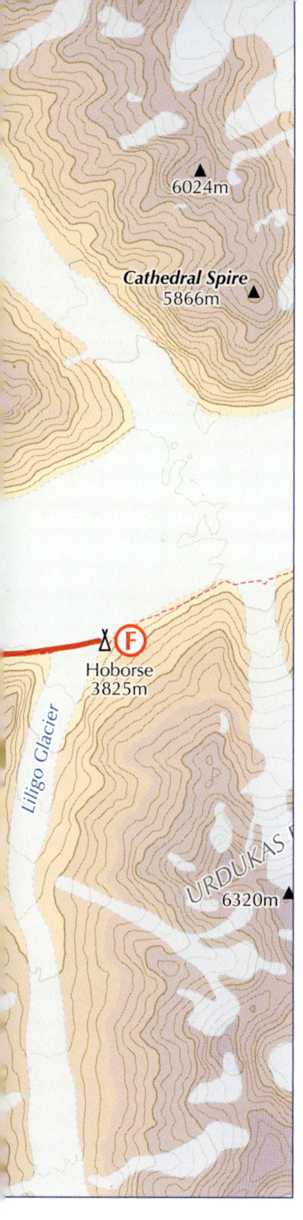

deeper into the heart of the highest mountain range of the planet, the Karakoram, with four 8000m peaks, two more above 7900m, and at least 15 peaks over 7500m.

Explorer Sir Martin Conway describes the snout of the Baltoro Glacier in 1892: 'The foot of the Baltoro glacier is unlike that of any other known to me. Most glaciers seem to lose all their energy at their foot, where, if they have space, they spread out into a sort of jelly-fish termination. This, for instance, is the way with the Biafo; but the Baltoro is busy to its close. It consists of three longitudinal divisions, of which the most northerly is white and crevassed, the central covered with light grey moraine matter, and the southern with dark greyish-brown moraine'.

In the early days, porters would stop before getting onto the glacier, gather and start chanting, a local custom to pray for a safe glacier crossing. Conway's porters asked for a day sewing *pabbus* to protect their feet from the ice (*pabbus*: rough pieces of untanned sheepskin with the woolly side inwards, fastened on their feet with many windings of weak leather thongs. The thongs were always breaking, and they tied the ends together in a 'single sheet bend').

Some of the other highlights today are looking back to Paiju Peak (6610m) and following the Baltoro Glacier to the east to see the Uli Biaho peaks, spires and the tallest in the group, Tower (6109m); Trango Towers (with the highest, Trango Ri, at 6363m); Lobsang Spire; glimpse of Broad Peak's massive bulk (8051m) and Gasherbrum IV (7925m).

After about 2hr, on a NE diagonal crossing of the two-kilometre wide, boulder-covered Baltoro Glacier, including several up and downs, the trail makes a strenuous climb leading onto the side moraine, this is followed by a good section of trail that leads to a great lunch spot at **Liligo**.

Liligo (or Liliwa) was used as campsite but groups now continue to Hoborse because of the danger of rockfall and lack of water. It's not a bad place to have lunch, with views towards innumerable groups of fantastic granite towers on both sides of the Baltoro Glacier, like Paiju Peak 6610m, Uli Biaho Tower 6109m and the group of Trango Towers, with the highest being Great Trango Tower 6287m.

The **Trango Towers** are a complex group of extremely steep rock peaks (more than 15) offering world-class, long, difficult routes at altitude. Since they are different towers, they have different first ascents. Trango Tower (6239m) was first climbed by a British team in 1976, including Joe Brown and others. Great Trango (6287m) was ascended a year later by Galen Rowell and others. Since then, numerous notable new routes have been tried and climbed by top climbers from all over the world.

The trail continues after lunch for a little while along the moraine before meeting the Liligo Glacier from the south. The outlet of this glacier can sometimes be crossed if the stream flow is not too fast and powerful, or if a (toll) bridge is in. If the flow is too fast, a detour must be made on the Baltoro Glacier to reach camp at **Hoborse**. This can be an impressive glacier tour and makes the day easily 30–45min longer.

HOBORSE CAMP

Hoborse (or Khoburtse) camp (3825m) is located on a sandy spot near a good stream, with two military buildings and a very basic toilet building. The stream dries up towards the end of the season but produces more water later on in the day.

There has fairly recently been an issue with the camp being polluted by used petrol jerry cans. In early summer 2019, the camp narrowly missed being destroyed by a snow avalanche! Pack animals wander off high up the ridge behind camp and do sometimes get lost. Keep an eye open for ibex high on the ridge behind camp. And keep your tents firmly zipped up since there are mice in this camp!

The Duke of the Abruzzi learned another name for this camp from his Baltis: 'Machichand'.

Liligo River crossing near Hoborse camp

DAY 4

Hoborse to Urdukas

Start	Hoborse 3825m
Finish	Urdukas 4040m
Distance	5.3km
Ascent	215m
Descent	Negligible
Time	2–3hr
Altitude gain	215m

Today is a short and reasonably easy walk on a good trail along the Baltoro Glacier, mixed with two smaller glacier crossings – all surrounded by a dramatic landscape of rock spires, with a view over the wrinkled, crocodile-hide-like Baltoro Glacier.

Mules and horses often climb up high beyond Hoborse camp to reach the better grazing areas, so this sometimes results in a delay of a few hours while the pack animals are found and herded back to camp.

The two smaller side glaciers to be crossed both descend from the Urdukas Peaks (the first one is bigger and easier, the second one is smaller but more difficult). Urdukas is a green slope of grass and bushes 100m above the Baltoro, directly opposite the Lobsang Spires.

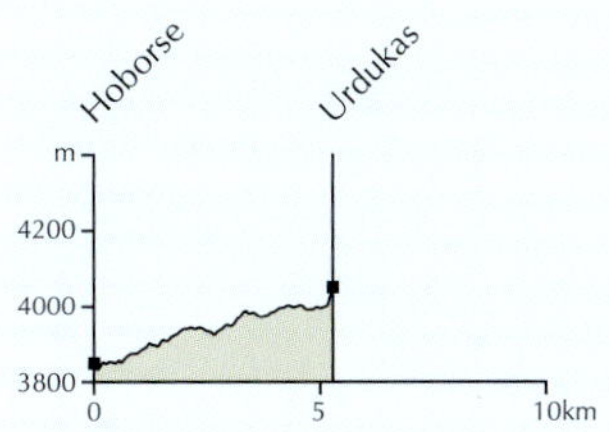

In 1892, Conway described travelling on the **Baltoro Glacier**: 'This glacier is altogether the most inhospitable we have seen. Not only is its surface wholly stone-covered and horribly mounded, but its sides are steep and always difficult to traverse; they are exceptionally barren, with little grass and almost no fuel'.

Urdukas camp is normally reached at lunch time.

URDUKAS/RDOKASS

There are several campsites at Urdukas, not as many as at Paiju though. Beyond camp are some deteriorating toilet cabins. Water is delivered by a pipe coming from a mountain stream. Availability of water can be limited. At camp is a hut, and a caretaker. Porters take shelter near big boulders and some caves. This is the last camp on soil for some days – it will be ice from now on. If it's raining, this camp changes into a mud bath.

Pollution is not as bad as it used to be! However, there are still swarms of irritating flies here. Enjoy spotting the small rodents running around and hiding under stones (locals call them *shippi* or 'whisperers', according to Longstaff). Or enjoy the slopes behind Urdukas as Godwin-Austen did in 1861, giving good views of K2.

Nearby is a military camp with a helicopter landing spot. There is sometimes working mobile coverage near the military camp. From the military camp, Gasherbrum IV and II can be seen. There are rumours that the trekking camp might enlarge.

At Urdukas, the goat that has walked along with you since Askole might be slaughtered, cooked, and served to the trekkers and staff. For every group of five or six porters, one goat is part of the wages. Porters used to join in with eating the meat, but instead get 'meat' money these days.

Urdukas (Rdokass) (meaning 'split rock' in Balti) is an historical place with many expeditions finding a welcome green haven after a long time climbing on ice, snow, and rocks. On one of the rocks an inscription in German reads: 'The end of the world'. Indeed, that is how it feels here. But being high above the glacier with an amazing panorama of towers, buttresses, glaciers, snow, and ice spreading out across the horizon there is nothing more to wish for. These days many expeditions from K2 or Broad Peak opt for the shorter exit to Skardu via the Gondogoro La pass leading to the road end at the village of Hushe.

Rdokass, as Filippo de Filippi calls it, was base camp for the Duke's expedition. Mr Baines (an Englishman living in Kashmir and entrusted with the organisation of the caravan) stayed with 25 porters at Rdokass and was made responsible for supplying the expedition with goods and firewood for the camps higher up. At Urdukas 200 porters who were no longer needed were paid off and sent back. 'Each of them was entitled to 2½ rupees, beside two seers of meal for the return journey; and they were told that the meal would be served out to them as soon as they had been paid. But finding themselves in possession of so vast a sum they were so eager to get home that they all rushed off joyously without stopping for the meal before we were aware of their going, busy as we were in paying out the wages.'

DAY 5

Urdukas to Gore 2

Start	Urdukas 4040m
Finish	Gore 2 4290m
Distance	11.4km
Ascent	290m
Descent	40m
Time	6–7hr
Altitude gain	250m
Note	Sun at camp around 8.30am

Moving on the Baltoro Glacier is like a fine Baltoro ballet, concentrating on keeping your balance and not falling over the endless stones. After an easy day, this one starts with a harder walk crossing to the middle of the Baltoro Glacier for about 1hr–1hr 30min at which point the route turns east. Pass campsite **Gore 1** (or Goro) (4175m) on the way to **Gore 2**. Gore 1, on the glacier, is a typical stopping place for lunch. The glacier is measured to be at its widest here – 3.1km.

On the Baltoro Glacier on the way to Gore 1 and finally Gore 2

MUZTAGH GLACIER

Before reaching the camp at Gore 1, Muztagh Glacier comes in from the north leading to the ancient Muztagh Pass at almost 5800m. A busy pass in the past for travellers from Askole and Yarkand. Sir Francis Younghusband was the first to write about this crossing back in 1887. After traversing the whole of China, leaving Kashgar, he started crossing the Karakoram mountains with only a few porters, no tent, a single sleeping bag, a fur coat, and very little dried food. He ascended to the top of the pass 'by the gentle slope of the Sarpo Laggo glacier, which was deep in soft snow, and descended on the Baltoro side by a steep and broken ice wall, a proceeding both difficult and dangerous for a party lacking the simplest mountaineering equipment. The condition of the glaciers more than justified the abandonment of this pass' (Filippo de Filippi).

The story goes that Younghusband lost his last bottle of fine whisky during the descent when a porter slipped: it was being saved to toast the successful crossing of the difficult pass.

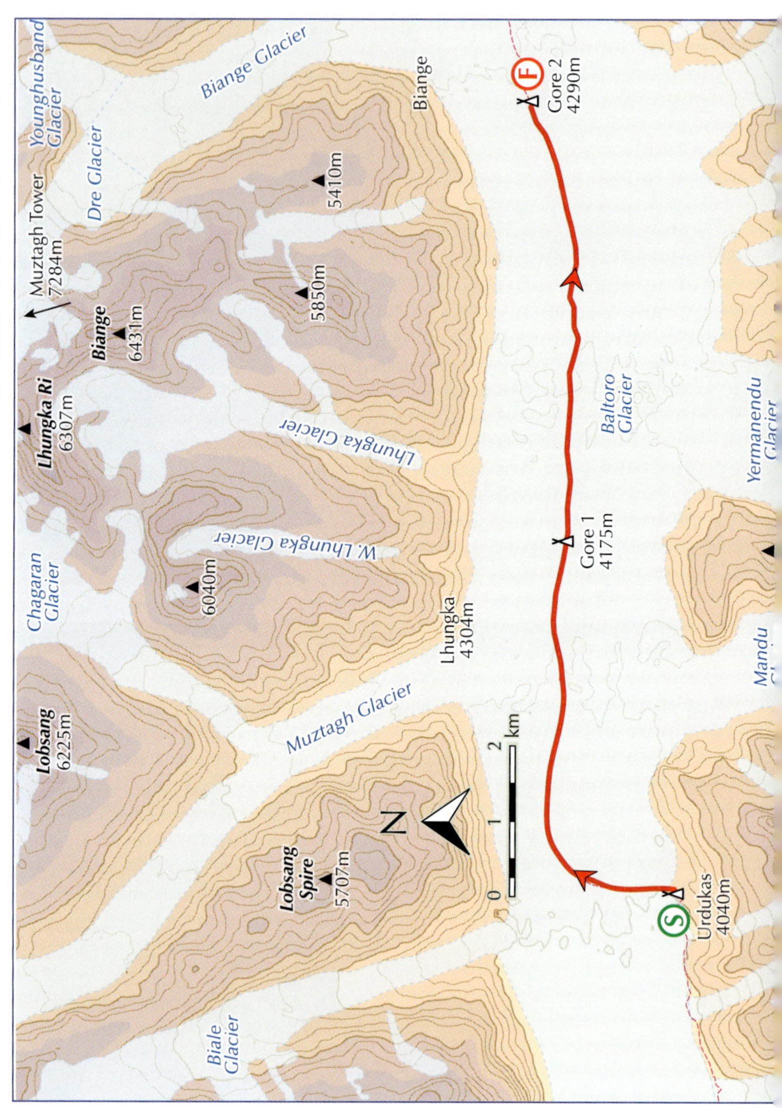

Younghusband Glacier
Biange Glacier
Biange
Gore 2
4290m
Dre Glacier
Muztagh Tower
7284m
5410m
5850m
Biange
6431m
Lhungka Ri
6307m
Lhungka Glacier
Baltoro Glacier
Yermanendu Glacier
W. Lhungka Glacier
Gore 1
4175m
6040m
Chagaran Glacier
Lhungka
4304m
Mandu
Muztagh Glacier
Lobsang
6225m
0
1
2
km
N
Lobsang Spire
5707m
Urdukas
4040m
Biale Glacier

August CF Ferber explored the valley in September 1903, with E Honigmann, and discovered proof of habitation, beyond the valley entrance, at Lhungka (4304m), and Muztagh Spangla (c4650m) with 22 old huts, and Lobsana Blangsa (4855m).

Another discovery was a rectangular field apparently used by Balti and Yarkand people for a friendly polo game. As Ferber jokes 'polo by foot or playing polo while riding ibex'! Not without difficulties Ferber reached the Muztagh Pass (*muztagh* means 'ice-mountain'), but didn't cross due to many technical challenges.

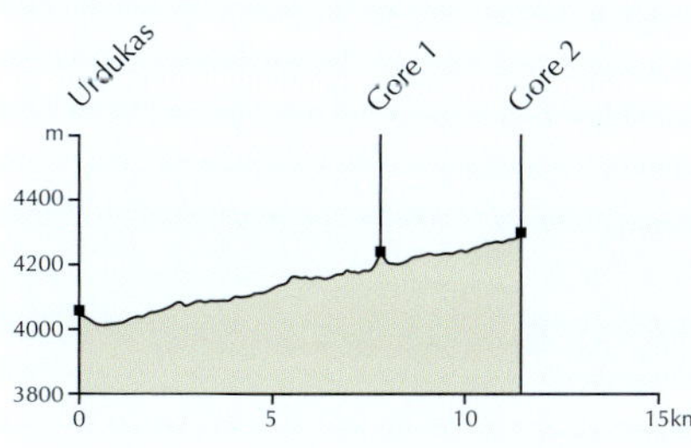

After lunch at Gore 1, enormous **ice sails** make an impressive foreground for pictures of Masherbrum (7821m) and Gasherbrum IV (7925m). Ice sails are ice towers up to more than 10m in height, that are formed by clean ice covered by a thin layer of debris allowing the ice below it to melt faster than the clean ice.

Masherbrum (7821m) is one of the more prominent mountains that will become visible after lunch. Masherbrum, or K1, is the 22nd highest peak in the world. It was climbed in 1960 by Americans Willi Unsoeld and George Bell, and some days later by Nick Clinch and Captain Jawed Akhter (the first Pakistani to climb a major peak). Masherbrum means 'the last sunset mountain'.

If you have a yearning for a tough adventure on the side: crossing Masherbrum La, a 5364m ice-bound pass into the Hushe Valley, will take three to four days with the easy part on the Baltoro side and the technical part on the Hushe side.

Gore 2 camp (4290m) is on the ice with several platforms for tents. The ice here measures 171 metres deep. Camp is located just in front of a pointy brown hill, which can be seen from far. It is an ice-volcano or intrapermafrost ice-cored hill known as a 'pingo'.

It is just about impossible to place a toilet tent on ice and doing so anyway can give rise to many problems by polluting the drinking water. So, at some of the camps on ice, there is an interesting solution: an iron staircase construction leads up to a small platform (a bit like stairs to a pulpit). On the platform is a toilet in a kind of tent, and beneath the platform – a plastic container. Once the container is full a caretaker is supposed to carry the container to the side of the glacier and dump the contents on the moraine, on the sand. In theory it's a good initiative, but one which is lacking sometimes in due care. So be prepared for some exciting toilet visits or decide to take some Imodium for the next couple of days!

Expect some mobile-phone reception from here onwards to Concordia with a local SIM card.

DAY 6

Gore 2 to Concordia

Start	Gore 2 4290m
Finish	Concordia 4575m
Distance	11km
Ascent	295m
Descent	10m
Time	4–6hr
Altitude gain	285m

Today's programme is summed up by the title of Galen Rowell's book *In the Throne Room of the Mountain Gods*. Many of Day 6's surrounding mountains and passes have exciting stories to tell, stories of success and defeat, hardship to the limits, deserving the highest respect.

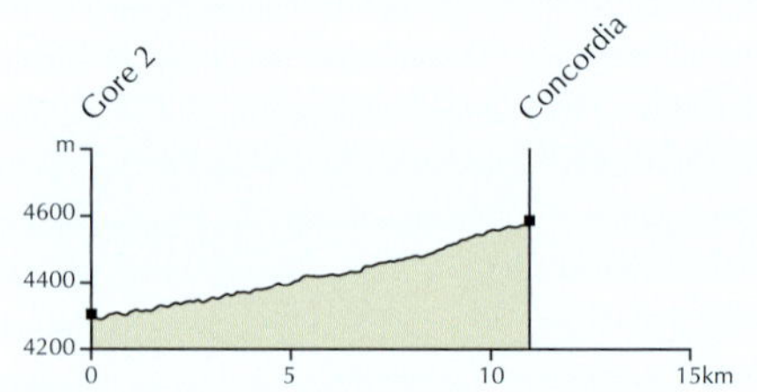

Soon after leaving Gore 2 camp, the route weaves through a labyrinth of ice sails (ice towers). On the left the South Face of

Muztagh Tower (7284m) appears, with the peak on its right side named Black Tooth (6719m).

> **Muztagh Tower** was first climbed in 1956 by the Brits following the Chagaran Glacier route and Northwest Crest, five days before a French expedition that followed the Younghusband Glacier and climbed a more difficult route, the Southeast Crest.

THE SURROUNDING PEAKS

K2 as seen from Concordia and the author

Eyes are needed everywhere today. Looking back, Masherbrum (7821m) is getting more impressive, and ahead the perfect trapezoid of Gasherbrum IV (7925m) and a glimpse of Gasherbrum II (8035m) comes into view. This day will take that last gasp of air desperately needed to get to Concordia. Gasherbrum II is the 14th highest mountain in the world. Only its soaring point can be seen on the right side of Gasherbrum IV.

There are six Gasherbrum peaks and Gasherbrum Twin peaks (6912m and 6877m). Some sources include Broad Peak (8051m) in the Gasherbrum

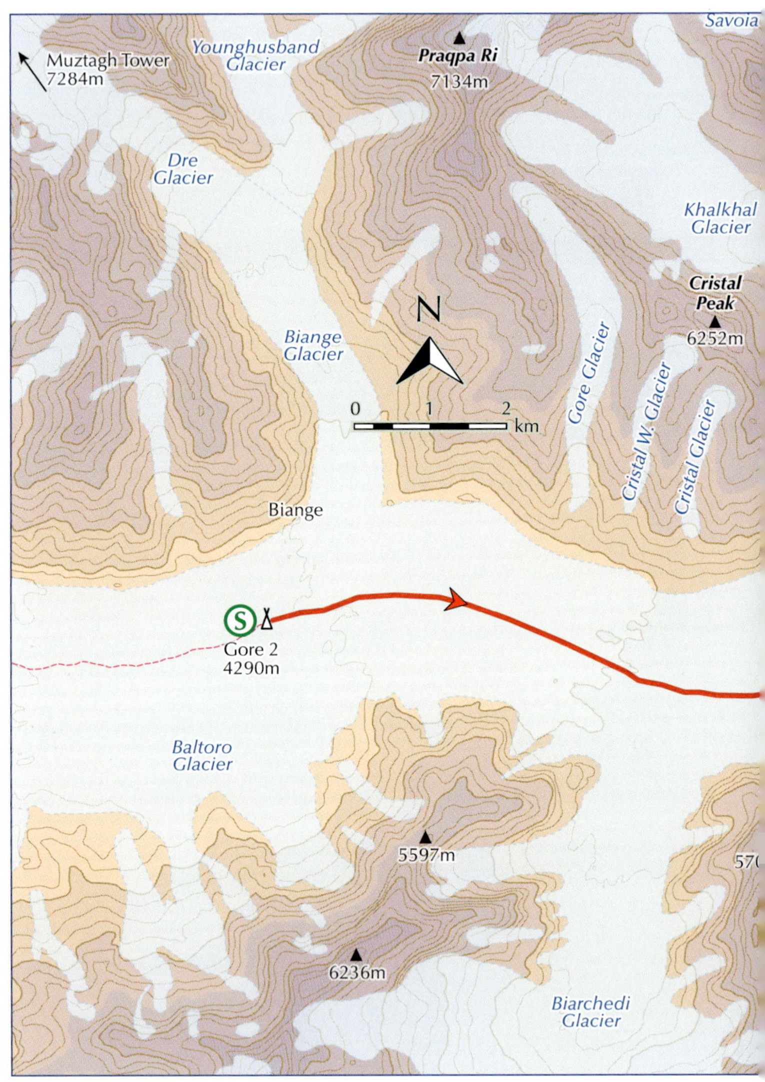

Savoia
Muztagh Tower
7284m
Younghusband
Glacier
Praqpa Ri
7134m
Dre
Glacier
Khalkhal
Glacier
Cristal
Peak
6252m
N
Biange
Glacier
0
1
2
km
Gore Glacier
Cristal W. Glacier
Cristal Glacier
Biange
S
Gore 2
4290m
Baltoro
Glacier
5597m
6236m
Biarchedi
Glacier

Broad Peak
8051m
To K2
S. Falchan Pass
6571m
Flat Peak
6657m
arble Peak
256m
Marble Glacier
m) Glacier
Falchan or Broad Peak Glacier
6215m
Sharp Peak
6215m
Godwin Austen Glacier
West-Gasherbrum Glacier
Twins
6882m
6446m
Concordia
4575m
Upper Baltoro Glacier
Mitre Peak
6030m
uating r Mitre lacier
To Gondogoro La
5585m
Vigne Glacier

group, making it seven Gasherbrum peaks. Gasherbrum means 'beautiful mountain' (*gasha* means 'beautiful').

To the left side, Cristal Peak (6252m) and Marble Peak (6256m) block the view towards K2. In 1892 Conway climbed Cristal Peak (named by Conway and Negrotto) hoping to get a view of K2, but the view was blocked by a narrow pyramid of rock. 'We remained an hour and a quarter on the summit in perfect comfort, eating our biscuits, and, by no disagreeable sensation whatever, feeling, so long as we sat quite still, that we were a foot above sea level. We smoked our pipes without labour.'On the right of Cristal Peak is the Fan Glacier. Conway also climbed up Fan Pass (around 5450m) in his quest to view K2. All these efforts were rewarded with grand views towards Broad Peak and others, but only a tiny glimpse of K2.

Luckily, there is plenty of time to enjoy the scenery en route to Concordia and, in this trek, the same route is followed in reverse – in case you missed anything first time round.

Gasherbrum IV

In 1936, Ardito Desio detailed his first sighting of Gasherbrum IV (or K3): 'The whole of this range, centred round the slim, pyramidal peak of Gasherbrum, is one of the most rugged in the entire Baltoro. Soaring, gleaming walls which appear to give ice no chance of a proper grip; sharp edges of singular outline; and a series of jagged teeth – these are the dominant features. We freely confess that we were unable to find any likely looking route by which Gasherbrum and the surrounding peaks might one day be climbed' (*La Spedizione Geografica Italiana nel Karakoram*, Milan-Rome 1936).

The Italian Alpine Club's 1958 expedition to Gasherbrum IV (or K3) hauled eleven tons of equipment on 450 shoulders to base camp. It is the 17th highest mountain in the world. Walter Bonatti and Carlo Mauri climbed Gasherbrum IV from the east side, the side not visible on this trek. It is an extremely demanding technical climb, from all sides. Some climbers say it is harder than K2.

In 2023 the southeast ridge was attempted by two Russian climbers in one of the most remarkable and ambitious expeditions of the year. Unfortunately, their bid was unsucessful and 250m below the summit Dmitry Golovchenko was sadly swept away in their tent.

www.summitpost.org/gasherbrum-iv/154584

There are some military camps along the trail which move position and/or are abandoned. One is roughly 1hr 15min before Concordia. Another, which is a distribution camp, is about 30min before.

After about 4–5hr, the route rounds the corner of Marble Peak (6256m) and K2 (8611m) will suddenly appear on the left (still 12km away). It's a soul-stirring experience, and followed by only a short hike to **Concordia** camp at 4575m.

Filippo de Filippi in 1909 described his first view of K2: 'Down at the end, alone, detached from all the other mountains, soared up K2, the indisputable sovereign of the region, gigantic and solitary, hidden from human sight by innumerable ranges, jealously defended by a vast throng of vassal peaks, protected from invasion by miles and miles of glaciers. Even to get within sight of it demands so much contrivance, so much marching, such a sum of labours'.

Or consider the words of **Fosco Maraini**: 'But now comes the supreme moment of all: after a breathless wait, behold at last the very Patriarch of the Mountains, regal, serene; a mountain conceived on a giant scale, given the space and setting that are meet and right for a giant. In the mighty mass of the whole, each single part seems so finely wrought, each one a telling note in a mighty chord; and in patterning of ridge, couloir, rock-face and ice-fall, thrusting inexorably upwards to the peak, there is the logic of a Bach fugue'.

K2 from Concordia

K2

K2 (8611m), climbed for first time by an Italian team in July 1954, also goes by a multitude of titles: Chogo-ri or Chhogori (which means 'big mountain' in Balti) or Lamba pahar (with a similar meaning in Urdu). In 1892, Eckenstein learned two other names for K2 from a local from Chongo: Skinmang and Dapsang. Though only slightly lower than Everest in height (237m), K2 constitutes the greater challenge.

Concordia (or Junction camp), the joining point of five glaciers, is an enormous glacial area with several campsite options. The landscape at Concordia feels like nature has abandoned it, and all you are left with is ice, rocks and the weather. Be aware of the polluted water here.

Broad Peak (8051m) (12th highest peak) (Phalchan-Kangri in Balti) was first climbed in 1957 by an Austrian team, after only one attempt in 1954 by the Germans under Herrligkoffer, who reached a height of 7130m.

Broad Peak from Broad Peak Base Camp

DAY 7

Excursion from Concordia

Start/finish	Concordia 4575m
Distance	24.4km
Ascent/descent	410m
Time	9–13hr return (K2 Base Camp)

What a place to wake up, **Concordia**. Sir Martin Conway gave the name to this place, recalling Concorde in the Bernese Oberland in Switzerland and the Place de la Concorde in Paris. A meeting place of giant glaciers, or roads in Paris, a vast plain in which two main rivers of ice join up forming the grand Baltoro Glacier. Looking south-east the Upper Baltoro leads to some impressive mountains like Chogolisa (7668m) (and subsidiary peak Bride Peak 7654m, named by Conway) and Baltoro Kangri (7300m) (or Golden Throne, or K8). Looking the other way, to the north, the supreme monarch K2 fills the skyline with Broad Peak (8051m) and Marble Peak (6256m) framing K2 (8611m).

A rest day could mean a lot. Stay in camp and relax, maybe do some laundry, read and write, or go for a hike exploring the area north of Concordia, towards Gasherbrum IV or the long hike to **Broad Peak Base Camp** (4820m) and **K2 Base Camp** (4965m). Or, crazy but true, hook up to Wi-Fi thanks to a 4G cell tower in Concordia. Battery recharge and a coffee-to-go – well, maybe not quite yet!

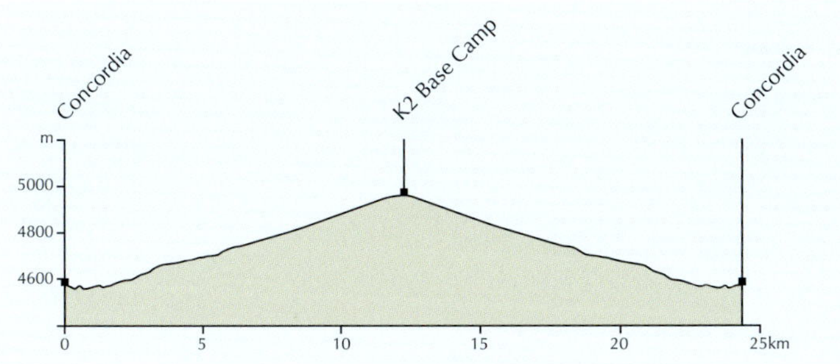

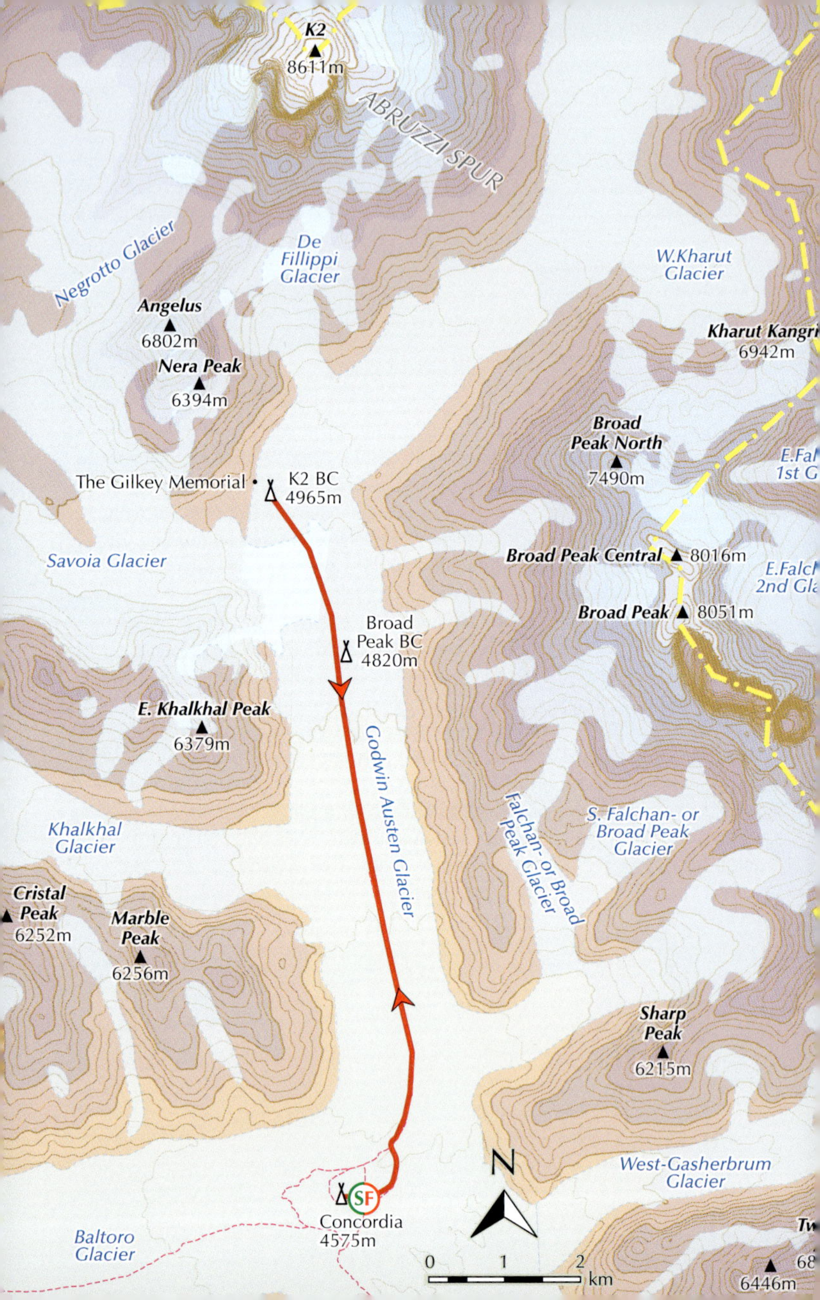

K2
8611m
ABRUZZI SPUR
Negrotto Glacier
De Fillippi Glacier
W.Kharut Glacier
Angelus
6802m
Nera Peak
6394m
Kharut Kangri
6942m
Broad Peak North
7490m
The Gilkey Memorial
K2 BC
4965m
Savoia Glacier
Broad Peak Central
8016m
Broad Peak
8051m
Broad Peak BC
4820m
E. Khalkhal Peak
6379m
Godwin Austen Glacier
Falchan- or Broad Peak Glacier
S. Falchan- or Broad Peak Glacier
Khalkhal Glacier
Cristal Peak
6252m
Marble Peak
6256m
Sharp Peak
6215m
West-Gasherbrum Glacier
N
Concordia
4575m
Baltoro Glacier
0
1
2
km
6446m

K2 Base Camp

For many people, reaching the Base Camp of K2, the second highest and reputedly toughest mountain in the world is the achievement of a lifetime. For those who are traversing the Gondogoro La, the K2 Base Camp trek offers some additional and valuable acclimatisation before crossing the pass. From Concordia it is a long tough day though. The trail, such as it is, is busiest during the climbing season as porters supply the base camps for ascents on both K2 and Broad Peak. You will need to take warm and weatherproof clothing, food and drink for a long day and a headlight for a possible return after dark.

For the K2 Base Camp trip leave early: for most people it is a long hard day, anything between 9–13hr of trekking. The beginning and the end of this trip are the hard parts. Near camp, there are some difficult crevasses and glacial rivers must be crossed: finding your way can be tricky. It would be recommended to have a guide or porter accompanying you.

Leave Concordia at first light and descend to the stream at the north edge of the camp area. From here, the route changes every year and every season due to glacier movements, usually making it a more difficult trip every time. After crossing the hard part (1hr), the trail gets easier on flatter moraine covered with loose stones of all sizes. Bring micro spikes. The crew should carry one ice axe to make steps in an ice passage, if neccesary. In 2023 we used an ice screw and some rope to secure a passage near Concordia.

There is a mobile mast and military camp on the way to Broad Peak BC. From Concordia most parties take about 3–4hr to reach **Broad Peak Base Camp**, also located on the crest of the moraine. Rest, food, and drink should be taken here and thought given to the potential of a further 3–4hr trek to K2 Base Camp and back, followed by another 5–6hr to return to Concordia.

A base camp is typically a small-tented village full of life and a communication centre. In the old days mail runners would have been the only communication for many expeditions – very different compared to now, with everything possible.

It's an appealing idea to visit either of the Base Camps for tea. The reality, however, is that the climbers and staff might not be very keen or hospitable. They might not want colds or other infections brought in or they might want to preserve the rations that they have hauled in at great expense for the duration of their expedition. On the other hand, they might like some new company. If you are lucky and are invited in, always show appropriate appreciation.

Getting closer to K2 Base Camp the mountain becomes overwhelming and totally fills up the whole camera viewfinder.

Further on, beyond Broad Peak Base Camp, the moraine and trail continue towards K2 which looms ahead. After about 45min the ridge disappears into steeper, broader slopes. Small cairns usually mark the route ahead. Take a diagonal route over the rocky ridge on the right and descend to another small stream. Cross the stream to the opposite bank (it gets more difficult to do so higher up) and follow the trail upstream. Soon the first tents of K2 Base Camp (4965m) will come into view. Usually in the season a makeshift crossing has been constructed near the first tents. The camp itself, called The Strip (a pop-up township), is spread over several hundred metres.

THE GILKEY MEMORIAL

The Gilkey Memorial near K2 Base Camp, honouring the fallen

On K2, aka The Killer Mountain, there has been a memorial since 1953, called the Gilkey Memorial, which is located about 20min north of K2 Base Camp on a rocky promontory. For every four summiteers, one person will die: this was standard up until the very successful 2022 season. The trekking here is difficult and unmarked with both rock and ice obstacles to negotiate. It can be difficult and dangerous to attempt to reach the Gilkey Memorial. The area in the vicinity of it has changed during recent years and there is a high risk of rock fall. Keep a safe distance and approach with care, or even better, just concentrate on reaching the Base Camp.The Gilkey Memorial was named after Art Gilkey, a member of the 1953 US K2 expedition: an epic effort was underway to rescue the team from a high camp, but while this was in progress Art was unfortunately swept away by an avalanche before he could be reached. K2 is located further north than Everest and is therefore more exposed to bad (and cold) weather.

In the words of Günther Dyhrenfurth: 'The man who, on such a dangerous enterprise, seeks the assurance of a safe retreat will not deserve to draw near to the Throne of the Gods'.

Return following the same route. Walking back the same way is just as amazing as the way in. Chogolisa (7668m) (and Bride Peak 7654m) and Baltoro Kangri

(7300m) (or Golden Throne) make up the views underlined by huge rivers of ice disappearing around the corner of Concordia. Chogolisa means 'big hunting area'.

Other excursions from Concordia

Before starting on the return journey to Askole, consider spending some more time up here. For example, one night at Broad Peak Base Camp followed by a more relaxed day at K2 Base Camp; or trek to Gasherbrum Base Camp (5150m) and see Gasherbrum I and II (two – three days extra). The 'Line of Control' between Pakistan and India is close here.

Alternatively, it is possible to cross the not-so-technical Gondogoro La pass (5595m) via Vigne Glacier into Hushe Valley and onwards to Skardu, an option described in Trek 3 in this guidebook. Nowadays most expeditions use this pass after finishing their climb to Skardu.

Famous French paraglider and altitude record holder Antoine Girard hopes to one day offer commercial tandem paragliding flights taking off from Concordia. Keep an eye to the sky when trekking on the Baltoro – you might be able to catch a ride. (Concordia to Paiju 1½–2 hours + 1 extra hour to get to Askole)

Trekking back to Joila Camp (see Trek 2, Days 7–10) takes four days – but with the ongoing road construction this trip could become shorter.

Antoine enjoying views towards K2 and the triple peak of Broad Peak, with Skyang Kangri or Staircase in between (photo: Antoine Girard)

DAY 8

Concordia to Gore 1

Start	Concordia 4575m
Finish	Gore 1 4175m
Distance	15.2km
Ascent	Negligible
Descent	400m
Time	8hr
Altitude loss	400m

Walking back the same route gives great satisfaction as the route is known, but the views are totally different, refreshing and even surprisingly new sometimes.

On the way down lunch is normally taken at **Gore 2** and camp at **Gore 1**. Muztagh Tower and Masherbrum are today's highlights. At Gore 1 there are no toilet facilities. A toilet tent would be convenient.

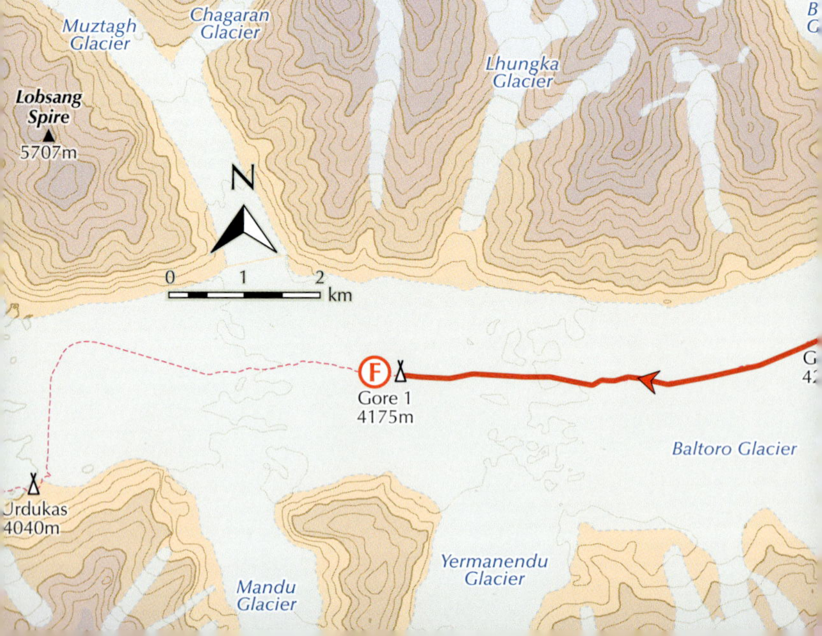

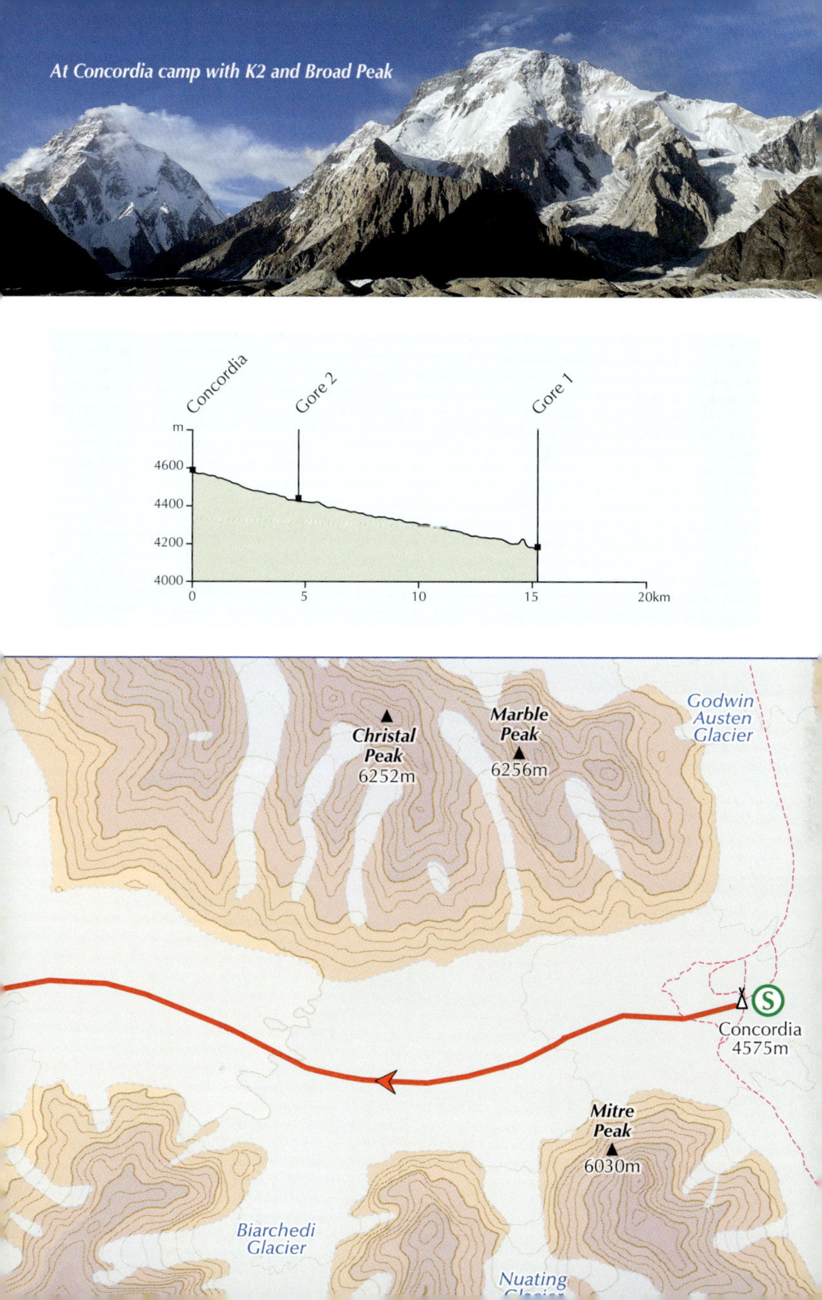
At Concordia camp with K2 and Broad Peak
Concordia
Gore 2
Gore 1
m
4600
4400
4200
4000
0
5
10
15
20km
Godwin
Austen
Glacier
Christal
Peak
6252m
Marble
Peak
6256m
Concordia
4575m
Mitre
Peak
6030m
Biarchedi
Glacier
Nuating

DAY 9

Gore 1 to Hoborse

Start	Gore 1 4175m
Finish	Hoborse 3825m
Distance	12.4km
Ascent	45m
Descent	395m
Time	7–8hr
Altitude loss	350m

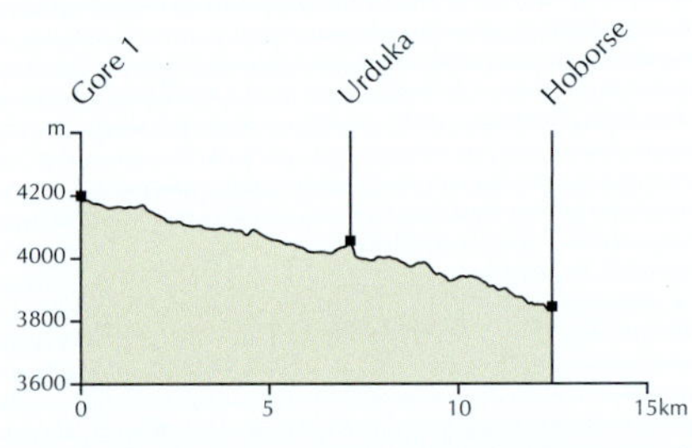

Some hard glacier travel, for about 3hr pounding along up and down over the endless stones, to the military camp at **Urdukas**, followed by a steep descent to the moraine and two side glaciers to cross to get to **Hoborse** to camp for the night.

Enjoy the Lobsang Spires, Cathedral Spire and the Trango Towers.

Ice movements on the Baltoro Glacier

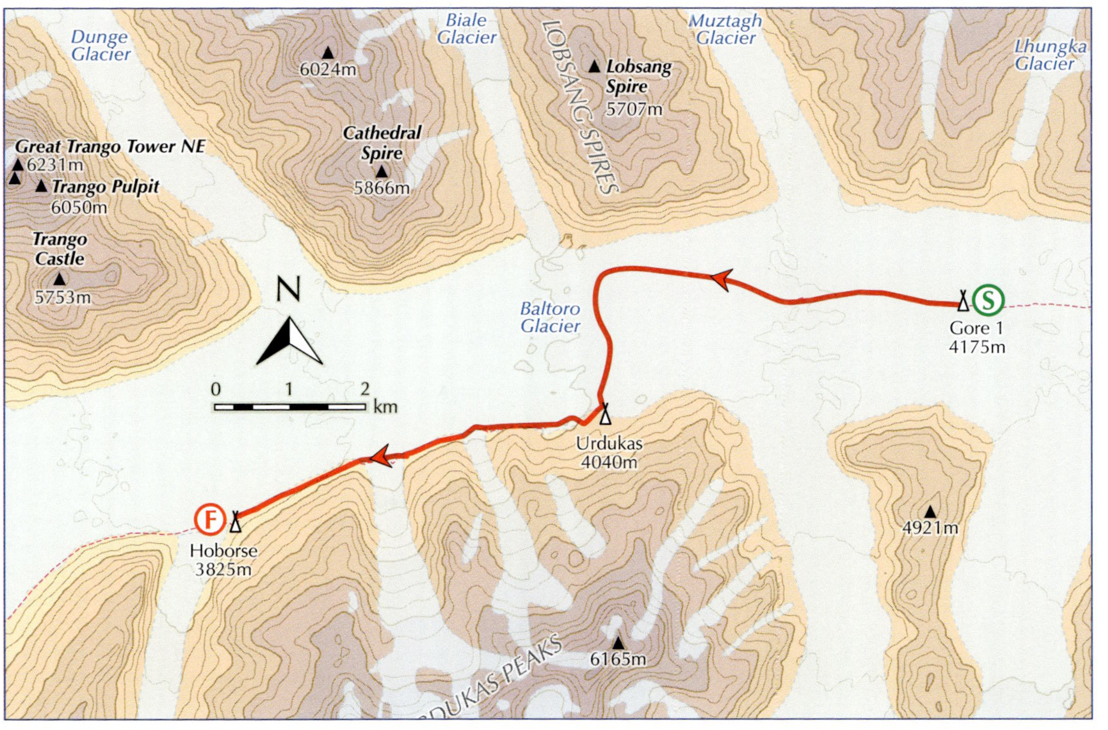
Dunge Glacier
6024m
Biale Glacier
LOBSANG SPIRES
Lobsang Spire
5707m
Muztagh Glacier
Lhungka Glacier
Great Trango Tower NE
6231m
Trango Pulpit
6050m
Cathedral Spire
5866m
Trango Castle
5753m
N
0
1
2
km
Baltoro Glacier
S
Gore 1
4175m
Urdukas
4040m
F
Hoborse
3825m
4921m
6165m
DUKAS PEAKS

DAY 10

Hoborse to Paiju

Start	Hoborse 3825m
Finish	Paiju 3395m
Distance	11.7km
Ascent	55m
Descent	485m
Time	6–7hr
Altitude loss	430m

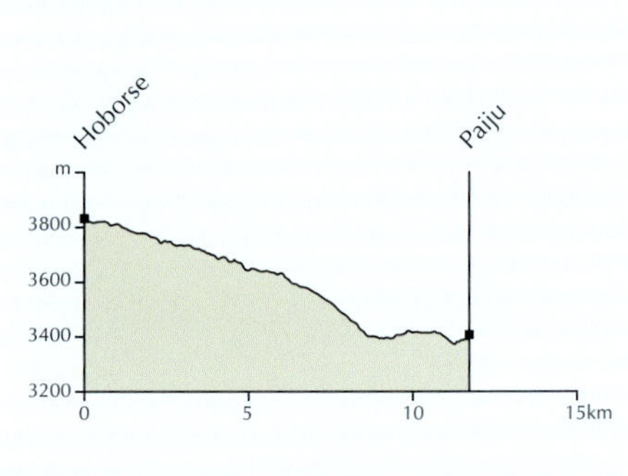

A bridge should be in place crossing the outlet from Liligo glacier, otherwise a river crossing or a detour of around 30min on the Baltoro Glacier is required.

After some time, join a good trail on top of the moraine, but the major job for today still lies ahead: crossing the Baltoro Glacier snout. This is the last section on ice for this trek, but it can be tricky to find the right exit route off the glacier. Just imagine how it must feel for expeditions who have spent weeks and weeks on ice, finally leaving it behind – a glorious moment!

> **Conway** writes in his book *Climbing in the Himalayas* (1894): 'McCormick and I had good reason for not wanting Zurbriggen [guide] out of our sight, for we were again short of tobacco and depended upon him for an occasional smoke'!

Paiju camp is finally reached at the end of a long 6–7hr day and 'shower cabins' are in high demand! Here the kitchen crew will collect any equipment they might have left behind in storage on the way up.

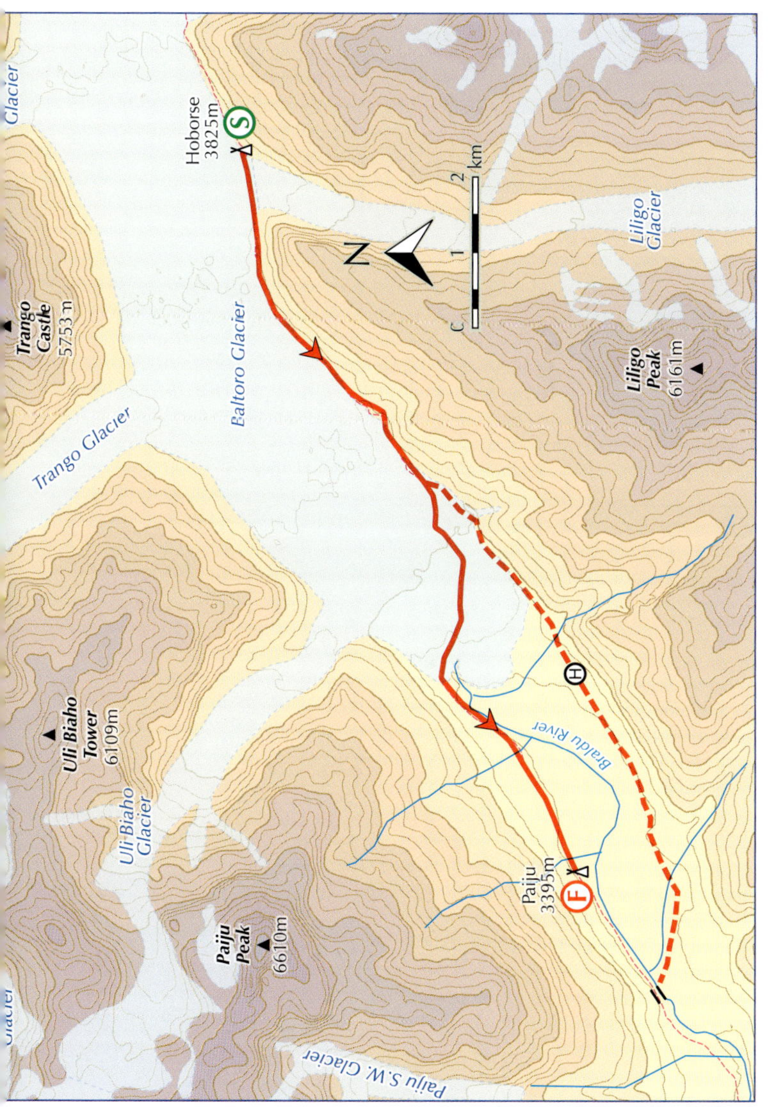
Hoborse
3825m
Baltoro Glacier
Trango Glacier
Trango Castle
5753 m
Uli Biaho Tower
6109m
Uli Biaho Glacier
Paiju Peak
6610m
Paiju
3395m
Braldu River
Paiju S.W. Glacier
Liligo Glacier
Liligo Peak
6161m
N
0
1
2
km

Some groups stop in Paiju for an extended lunchbreak, for around 3–4hr, and continue afterwards for 2–2½hr to Camp Bardumal, making the next day easier reaching Korophon or Askole.

DAY 11

Paiju to Joila

Start	Paiju 3395m
Finish	Joila Camp 3150m
Distance	19km
Ascent	280m
Descent	525m
Time	4–6hr
Altitude loss	245m

Map continues on page 181

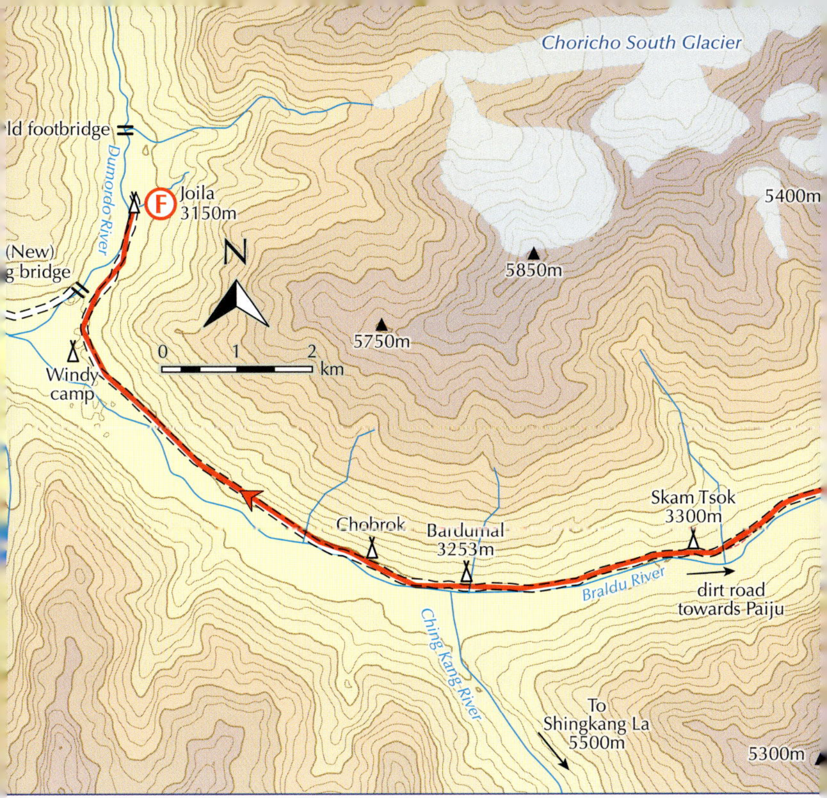

Choricho South Glacier
ld footbridge
Dumordo River
Joila
3150m
(New)
g bridge
Windy camp
N
0 1 2 km
5750m
5850m
5400m
Chobrok
Bardumal
3253m
Skam Tsok
3300m
Braldu River
dirt road towards Paiju
Ching Kang River
To Shingkang La 5500m
5300m

Paiju
Bardumal
Joila
m
3400
3200
3000
0
5
10
15
20km

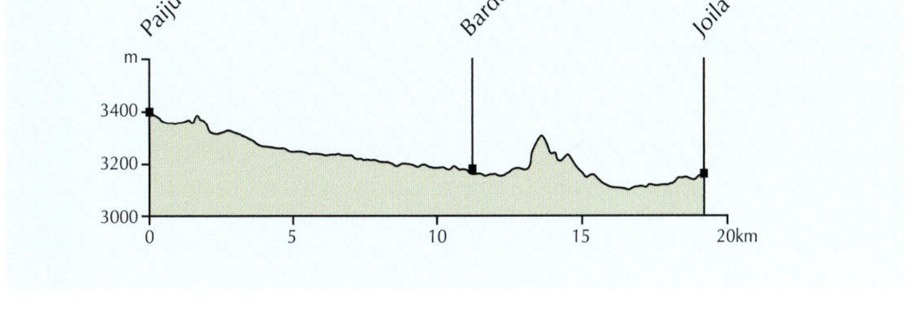

Today we say farewell to the impressive rocky peaks and high mountains. Again, a long day of 4–6hr of walking on a known trail, often close to the wild Braldu River.

DAY 12

Joila to Askole

Start	Joila Camp 3150m
Finish	Askole 3045m
Distance	17km
Ascent	Negligible
Descent	105m
Time	5hr
Altitude loss	105m
Note	For map, see Day 1

Depending on road developments part of today's walk could be by jeep. Next day pre-arranged jeeps will tackle the Braldu Gorge again and finally deliver dirty trekkers to the hotels in Skardu where showers might function!!

In 1892, **Conway** needed four days to get from Askole to Skardu, crossing the Skore La pass (5073m) and a trip on a raft made of blown-up goat skins and a framework of poles. His guide, Mattias Zurbriggen describes the approach to Askole: 'Three days' march brought us to Askole where the inhabitants came out to greet us with drums and horns – a curious confusion of sounds – till my patron [Conway] presented them with baksheesh, when they gratefully withdrew'.

FAREWELLS

The arrival at Askole is also the time to say thank you and farewell to the porters and staff. A speech of appreciation followed by the handing out of tips and any useful trekking items, finishing off with maybe a song or two makes a nice ceremony. At the end of each journey as we clamber aboard jeeps to ferry us back to a world of hotels, the porters have become our friends and the farewells are heartfelt.

TREK 3

Gondogoro La via Concordia

Start	Askole 3045m
Finish	Hushe 3155m
Distance	121.8km (including visit to K2 Base Camp: 146.2km)
Ascent	3105m (including visit to K2 Base Camp: 3515m)
Descent	3000m (including visit to K2 Base Camp: 3410m)
Grade	Difficult, technical and strenuous
Days	11 or 12 + 2 rest/acclimatisation days
Highest point	5595m
Permits	A restricted trek, needing a permit

At 5595m, the Gondogoro La pass is usually crossed as part of the K2 trek as a more adventurous, but quicker, alternative to retracing the route back down the Baltoro Glacier. It is a stunning excursion with grand views in both directions and a bonus of seeing Hidden Peak or Gasherbrum I (8080m) from the top. The pass is rarely crossed from the Hushe side because, although the most objectively dangerous side would be crossed earlier in the day and the risk of rockfall would therefore be reduced by the overnight freeze, if bad weather or poor snow conditions prevented the crossing, nobody would reach Concordia or K2 Base Camp. Many climbing expeditions use this route after climbing their peak as a faster route out to Skardu via Hushe.

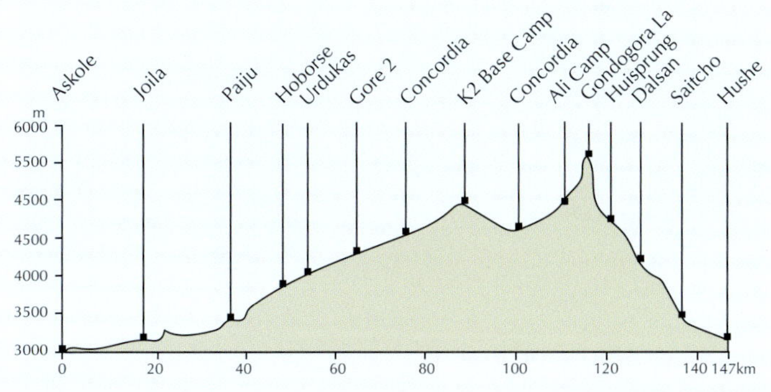

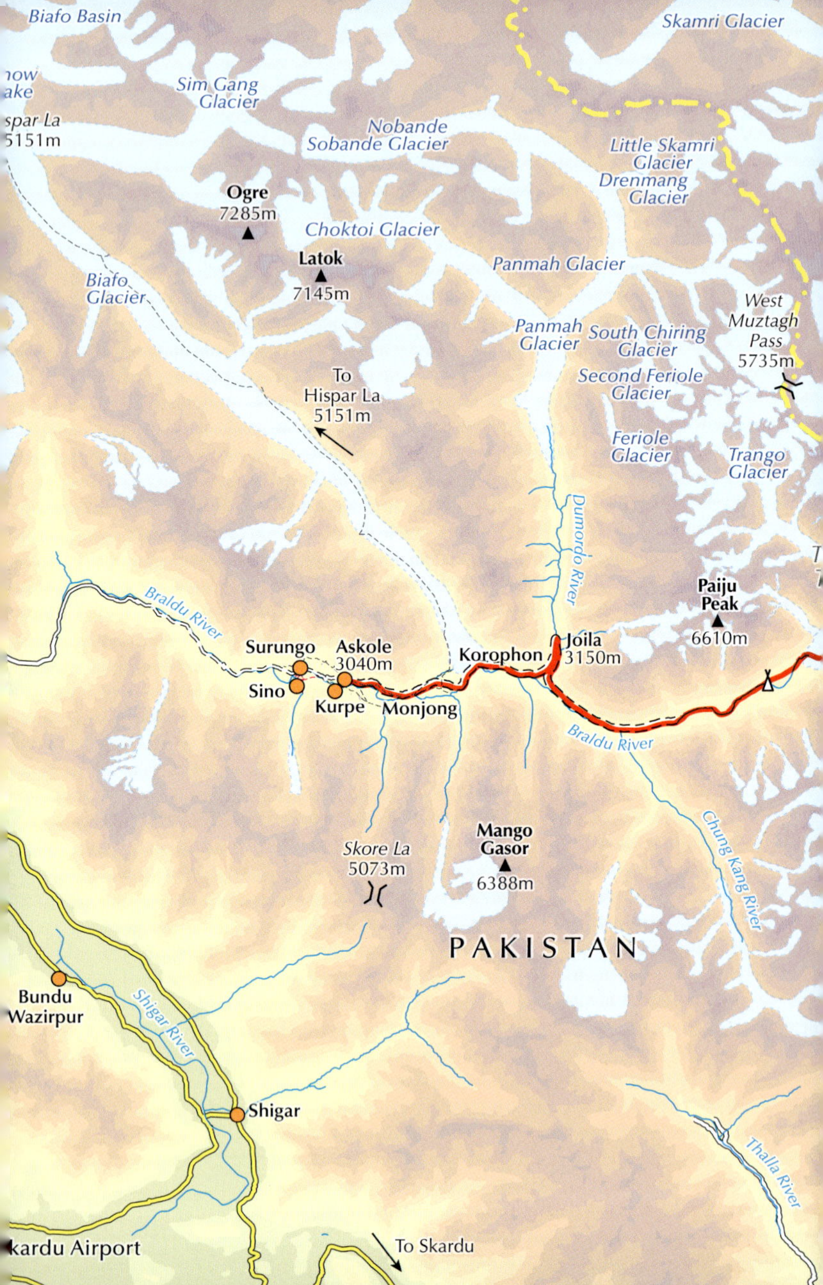

Biafo Basin
Skamri Glacier
now
ake
Sim Gang
Glacier
spar La
5151m
Nobande
Sobande Glacier
Little Skamri
Glacier
Drenmang
Glacier
Ogre
7285m
Choktoi Glacier
Latok
7145m
Panmah Glacier
Biafo
Glacier
West
Muztagh
Pass
5735m
Panmah
Glacier
South Chiring
Glacier
Second Feriole
Glacier
To
Hispar La
5151m
Feriole
Glacier
Trango
Glacier
Dumordo River
Paiju
Peak
6610m
Braldu River
Surungo
Askole
3040m
Korophon
Joila
3150m
Sino
Kurpe
Monjong
Braldu River
Chung Kang River
Skore La
5073m
Mango
Gasor
6388m
PAKISTAN
Bundu
Wazirpur
Shigar River
Shigar
Thalla River
kardu Airport
To Skardu

N
0
5
10
km
CHINA
K2 Glacier
Skyang Glacier
K2
8611m
Godwin Austen Glacier
Gasherbrum Glacier
Savoia Glacier
K2 BC
4965m
Broad Peak
8051m
Chagarlung
Muztagh Tower
7284m
Lhungka Glacier
Biange Glacier
CATHEDRALS
Gasherbrum II
8035m
Concordia
4575m
Gasherbrum I
8068m
8080m
Urdok
Urdukas
4040m
Baltoro Glacier
Upper Baltoro Glacier
Gasherbrum BC
5150m
Gondogoro Glacier
Abruzzi Glacier
Masherbrum La
5364m
Gondogoro La
5595m
Golden Throne or Baltoro Kangri
7300m
Sia Kangri or Queen Mary Peak
7381m
Masherbrum
7821m
Liligo Glacier
Gondogoro Glacier
Vigne Glacier
Chogolisa
7668m
Kondus Glacier
Chogolisa Glacier
uble Peak
6481m
Ghent
7401m
Kaberi Glacier
Charakusa Glacier
Link Sar
7041m
nboro
59m
Hushe
3155m
Hushe River
K6 or Baltistan Peak
7282m
Link Glacier
K6 Glacier
Sherpi Gang Glacier
Apo Brok
Hushe River
Khorkondus

Nearing Gondogoro La with a view to, from left to right, K2, Broad Peak, Gasherbrum IV, GII and GI (photo: Tom Richardson)

It should not be undertaken lightly, however, as a crossing includes dealing with altitude and cold, using crampons and helmets, and jumaring up and descending fixed ropes on steep, snowy and rocky terrain. During the main season, the Hushe Rescue Team put in fixed ropes. They can be used for a fee and if the ropes are in place, you will be able to make arrangements with a member of the Hushe Rescue Team at Concordia. Previous experience with the equipment (or at the very least practice in a safe area around Concordia or Ali Camp) is essential before attempting the crossing.

A very early start just before midnight the day before is essential for the crossing to both avoid stone fall triggered by sunshine on the snow and rocks (particularly on the Hushe side) and to also get the best views.

Follow the itinerary for the K2 Base Camp Trek to Concordia from where the route starts to Gondogoro La (Day 1–7 trekking from Askole to Concordia and K2 Base Camp + rest/acclimatisation days).

On the Hushe side of the pass there are fixed tents, meaning that tents being used to reach Ali Camp could be sent back down the Baltoro Glacier.

DAY 8

Concordia to Ali Camp

Start	Concordia 4575m
Finish	Ali Camp 4940m
Distance	10.2km
Ascent	395m
Descent	30m
Time	4–5hr
Altitude gain	365m

Whether you have spent the previous day trekking up the moraine to get to either or both Broad Peak and K2 Base Camps, or if you have relaxed and marvelled at the magnificent views in all directions from your camp in Concordia (4575m), the days approaching and crossing the Gondogoro La (5595m) will be a highlight of the trek.

The trail is far less well used than the Broad Peak and K2 Base Camp trail. Initially take the moraine on the south side of Concordia and follow the **Upper Baltoro Glacier** on its southern side below Mitre Peak (6030m) crossing several streams.

In 1892 Conway camped at the bottom of one of Mitre's buttresses on their return from climbing Pioneer Peak where the party was fed by fresh goat meat, naming the campsite **Goat's Delight** (4600m).

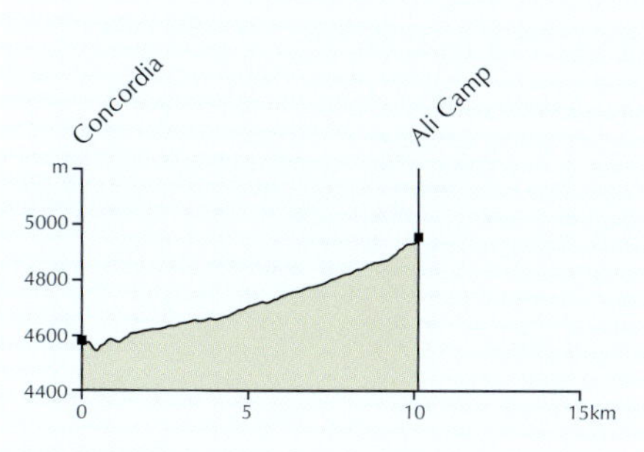

After some time, the terrain becomes less complex and, if walking in good conditions, it is mostly on grit-covered ice with visible and easily avoided crevasses. In deep

To Gasherbrum IV
7932m
Concordia
4575m
S
West-Gasherbrum
Glacier
To Askole
Baltoro
Glacier
6446m
Mitre
Peak
6030m
5700m
(Upper)
Baltoro Glacier
Nuating or Mitre
Glacier
5571m
N
0
1
2
km
Lhakora
6172m
5943m
6350m
VIGNE PEAKS OR KHUMUL GRI PEAKS
Vigne
Glacier
W. Vigne
Glacier
F
Ali Camp
4940m
Peak
c5900m
6674m
Gondogoro La
5595m
Khumil
Gri
6840m
6716m
Trinity- or
Tasa Peak
6700m
Vigne Col
c5950m
Chogolisa
7668m
Trinity Cwm or
Chogolisa Glacier

snow conditions however, parties might need to both use crampons and be roped up for safety.

Turn right and follow the **Vigne Glacier** (named after British explorer Godfrey Vigne 1801–1863). Eventually the angle reduces further, and the glacier forms a wide-open area with the West Vigne Glacier. On the west bank of the glacier is a flat area called **Ali Camp**. Care is needed when approaching Ali Camp due to some big open crevasses. One hour from Ali Camp there is still mobile network coverage.

Ali Camp is named after Ali Mohammed, a man from Hushe village who, in 1985, discovered the Gondogoro La as a short-cut home after working on an expedition to Chogolisa (7668m).

DAY 9

Ali Camp crossing the Gondogoro La to Huisprung

Start	Ali Camp 4940m
Finish	Huispring 4675m
Distance	10km
Ascent	735m
Descent	1000m
Time	6–7hr climb + 4–5hr descent
Altitude loss	265m

It is vital for safety to cross the Gondogoro La (5595m) early in the morning before frozen rocks, ice and snow thaw and create a serious hazard. The main risk is on the descent into the Hushe Valley. Between 11pm and midnight is the chosen departure time by most parties. The safest crossing is to have completed the whole thing before sunlight hits the Hushe side and melts ice that might be holding loose rocks.

Initially follow the moraine out from Ali Camp, then attach crampons and rope up to cross the West Vigne Glacier to the foot of the **Gondogoro La** in a SW direction. Helmets should be worn on the crossing of the pass. In the main season local climbers from Hushe village, known as the Hushe Rescue Team, helpfully fix lines up and down the pass for a reasonable charge.

Baltoro Glacier
Biarchedi Glacier
Biarchedi Peak
6781m
Gondogoro Ri
6810m
Gondogoro Glacier
6610m
Yermanendu Glacier
Masherbrum La
5364m
6273 m
5800m
Yermanendu Kangri
7163m
N
Huisprung
4675m
0
1
2
km
E. Gondogoro Glacier
N. Gondogoro Glacier
Laila Peak
6096m

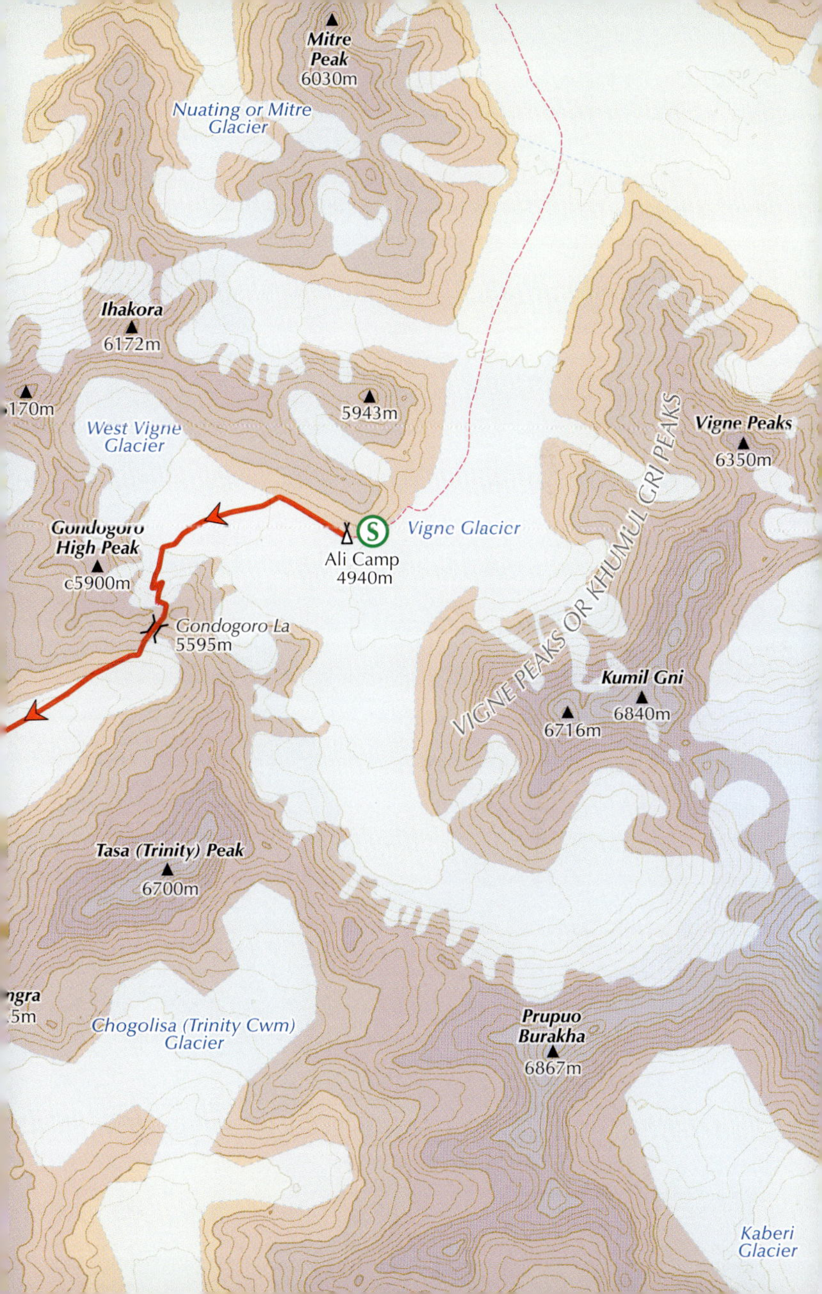
Mitre Peak
6030m
Nuating or Mitre Glacier
Ihakora
6172m
170m
5943m
West Vigne Glacier
Vigne Peaks
6350m
VIGNE PEAKS OR KHUMUL GRI PEAKS
Gondogoro High Peak
c5900m
Vigne Glacier
Ali Camp
4940m
Gondogoro La
5595m
Kumil Gni
6840m
6716m
Tasa (Trinity) Peak
6700m
ngra
5m
Chogolisa (Trinity Cwm) Glacier
Prupuo Burakha
6867m
Kaberi Glacier

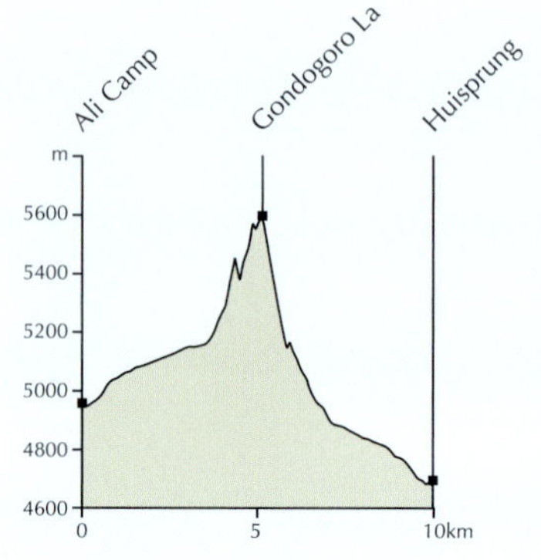

From the pass summit pause long enough to savour the fantastic **views** in both directions. K2, Broad Peak, Gasherbrum I and II, four of only fourteen 8000m plus peaks in the world in one direction and in the other direction, the Gondogoro Valley with the elegant Laila Peak (6096m) and Masherbrum II (or Masherbrum Far West; c7200m; climbed in 1988 by an Italian team).

Just below Gondogoro La, with K2 and Broad Peak in the background (photo: Tom Richardson)

Steep descent into the Gondogoro Valley (photo: Tom Richardson)

At the end of the fixed ropes section, the angle eases and it is usually possible to trek down the valley quite easily to a beautiful campsite by a lake, over-looked by Laila Peak, also called **Huisprung** (or Xhuspang).

Laila Peak (6096m) (or quite a bit higher according to some sources, 6986m) has had several ascents and ski descents. However, rumour has it that the first ascent was illegal.

Looking down the valley leading to Hushe, with lofty Laila Peak on the left (photo: Tom Richardson)

DAY 10

Huisprung to Dalsan

Start	Huisprung 4675m
Finish	Dalsan 4175m
Distance	7km
Ascent	Negligible
Descent	500m
Time	3–4hr
Altitude loss	500m

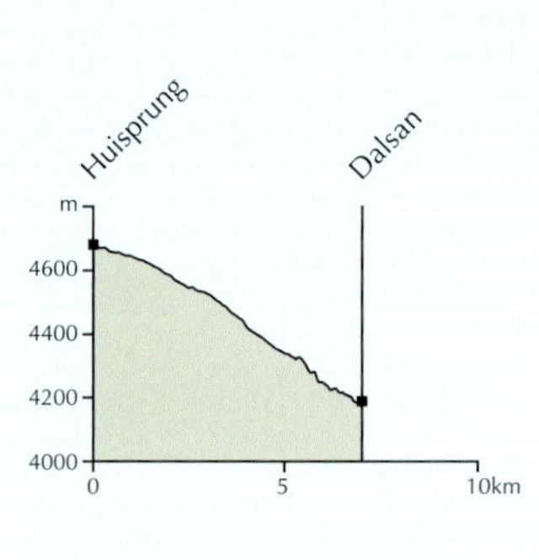

This shorter trekking day descends the ice of the East Gondogoro Glacier on easy angles, passing right under the dramatic summit of Laila Peak and many huge stones perched on plinths of slowly melting ice. Ahead emerges the tumbling mass of the West Gondogoro Glacier before which the route turns gently left following the trail on a moraine ridge to the grassy valley and lake at **Dalsan** (4175m) (Dalsampa). Yet another dramatic campsite. For those with extra energy, Gondogoro Peak 5650m could be climbed today! Gondogoro Peak is a straight forward non-technical climb, but rope, ice axes and crampons are needed in case of possible crevasses.

In 1911 the American explorer couple, the **Workman Bullocks** spent time in this area. From Hushe they went up the Aling Glacier, up the Masherbrum Glacier to a summit called Quartzite Peak (5132m) (called Crown Peak these days), up the Gondogoro Glacier all the way to height of c4900m, and up the Chogolisa Glacier. They had heard of another pass from locals, but could not find it.

In 1938 a **British Masherbrum** expedition of five climbers was defeated at a height of nearly 7600m due to bad weather. Their epic efforts are well described by James Waller in *The Everlasting Hills*.

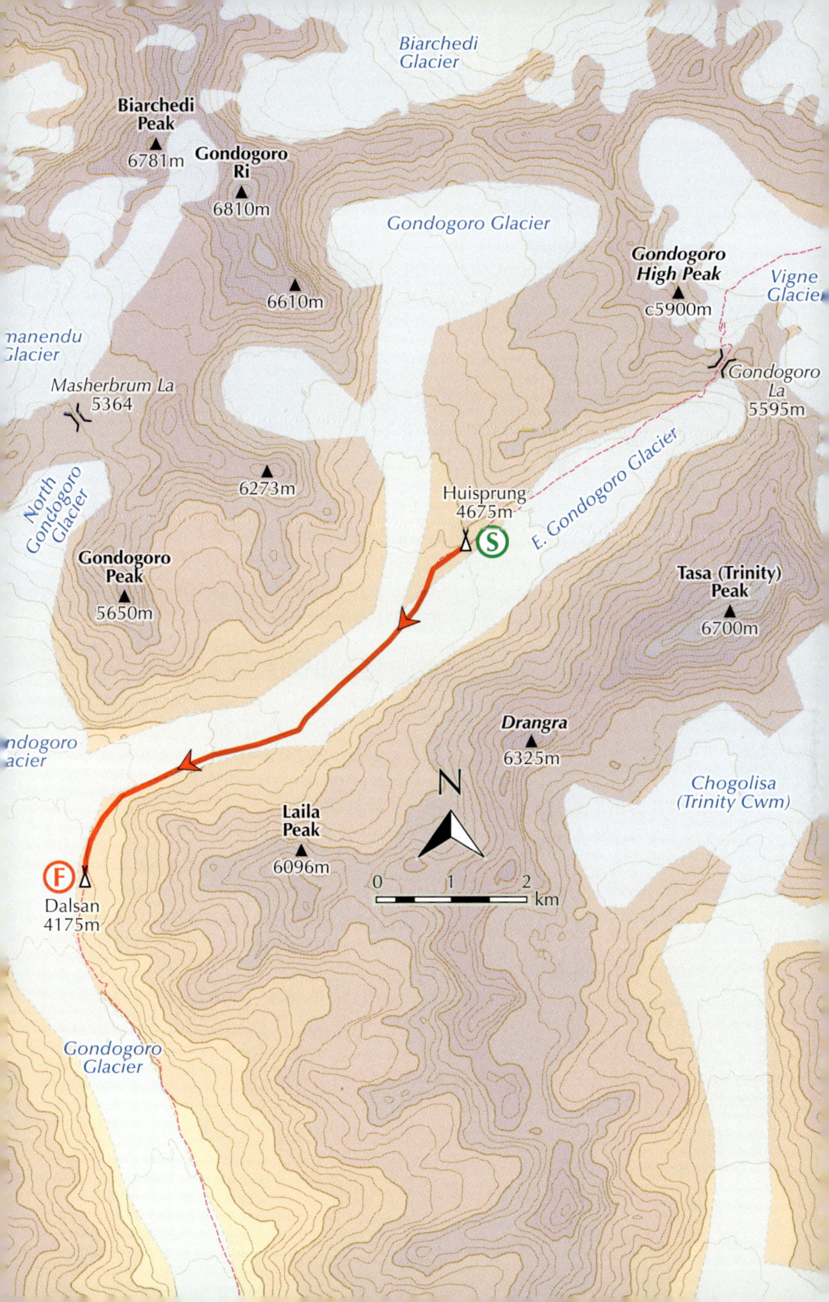
Biarchedi Glacier
Biarchedi Peak
6781m
Gondogoro Ri
6810m
Gondogoro Glacier
Gondogoro High Peak
c5900m
Vigne Glacier
6610m
Masherbrum La
5364
Gondogoro La
5595m
6273m
North Gondogoro Glacier
Huisprung
4675m
E. Gondogoro Glacier
S
Gondogoro Peak
5650m
Tasa (Trinity) Peak
6700m
Drangra
6325m
Chogolisa (Trinity Cwm)
Laila Peak
6096m
N
0
1
2
km
F
Dalsan
4175m
Gondogoro Glacier

DAY 11

Dalsan to Saitcho

Start	Dalsan 4175m
Finish	Saitcho 3395m
Distance	8.9km
Ascent	30m
Descent	810m
Time	3–4hr
Altitude loss	780m

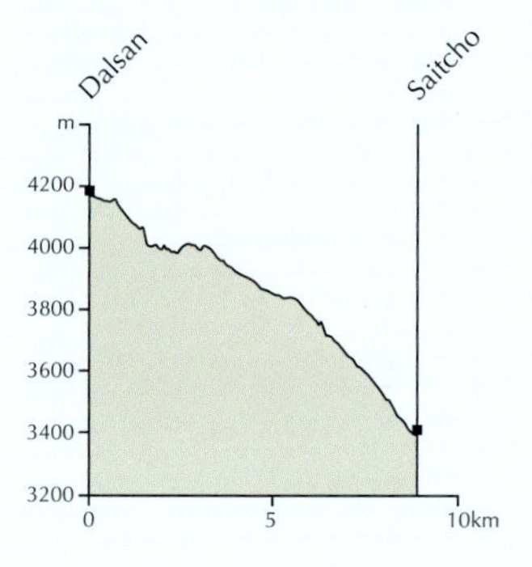

This day's trekking begins on straightforward terrain down the trail on the moraine near the camp. After a short distance an intruding cliff requires a narrow, exposed traverse on a ledge before easier ground is met. Care needs to be taken here and for some a rope is necessary. Later again several small rivers must be crossed before herders' seasonal shelters are reached at a place known (rather optimistically) as Gondogoro 'village'. Keeping left, the trail enters vegetation and eventually reaches the tree-enclosed camp at **Saitcho**. Here a permanent camp can be found with a shop and toilets.

Optional excursions from Saitcho

From Saitcho an interesting short trek could start following the Charakusa Glacier visiting the Base Camp for K6 (7282m) (or Baltistan Peak), K7 (6858m) and Link Sar (7041m). Videos from several expeditions can be found online via YouTube. Recommended is *Link Sar – The Last Great Unclimbed Mountain* by Graham Zimmerman and others, showing the first ascent of this extremely difficult mountain in August 2019, which needed a three-day descent, indicating just how difficult this mountain is.

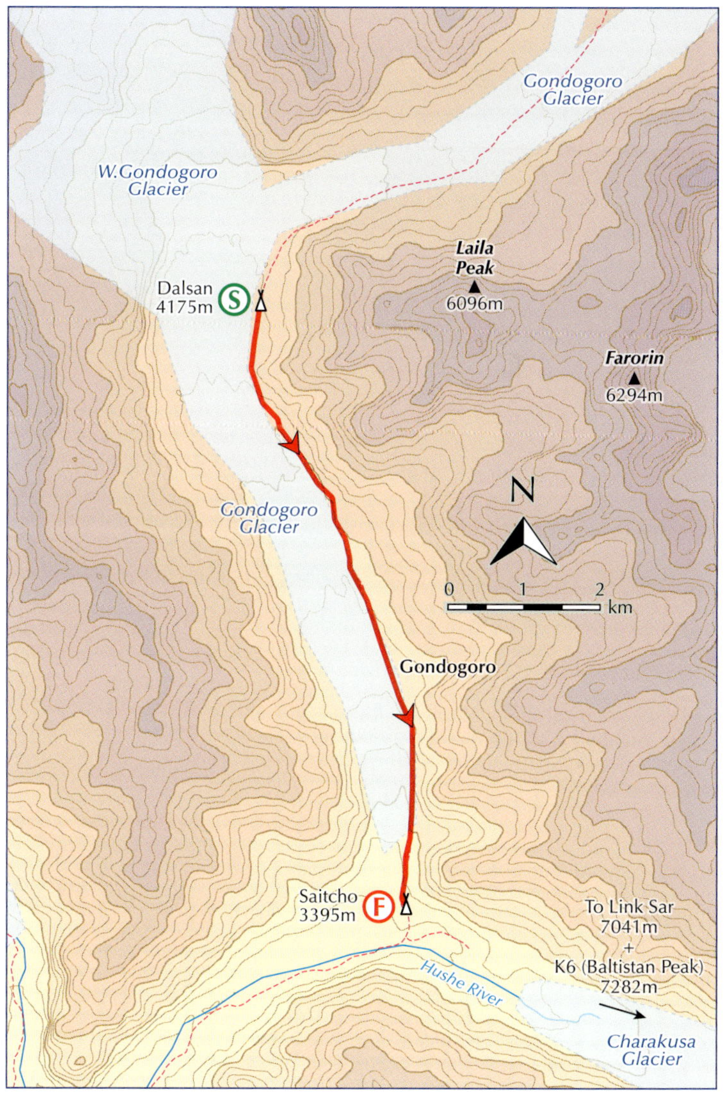
Gondogoro Glacier
W.Gondogoro Glacier
Laila Peak
6096m
Dalsan
4175m
S
Farorin
6294m
N
Gondogoro Glacier
0
1
2
km
Gondogoro
Saitcho
3395m
F
To Link Sar
7041m
+
K6 (Baltistan Peak)
7282m
Hushe River
Charakusa Glacier

DAY 12

Saitcho to Hushe

Start	Saitcho 3395m
Finish	Hushe 3155m
Distance	10.3km
Ascent	35m
Descent	275m
Time	6–7hr
Altitude loss	240m

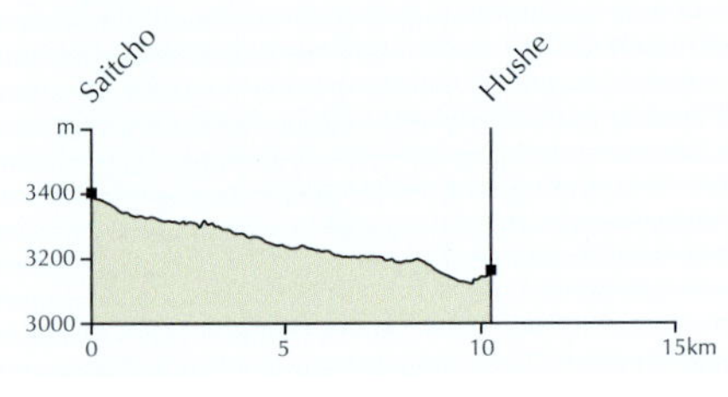

Again, it is worth an early start as the valley heats up dramatically during the day. Otherwise, it is 3–4hr of pleasant trail following the Hushe River to the village of the same name (also known as Hushey). The first building on arrival is the newly constructed National Park Office where it is necessary to officially check out.

Driving to Skardu and hotels is possible (roughly 6hr) but a last camp at Hushe village is recommended to absorb the village atmosphere and to enjoy a proper farewell party for the staff. **Hushe** has a refuge/campsite where you can overnight. From Hushe the trekking peak Besahul Peak (5600m) could be ascended, catching a last glimpse on K2. Besahul Peak (or Humbrok) is a non-technical climb gaining more than 1500m altitude. Attempting this peak it is best to be acclimatised.

An overnight is also possible at Khapalu, once the second largest kingdom in old Baltistan with a beautiful 700-year-old mosque, an old Raja Palace, and the ruins of an old fort, the Thorsikar Fort. These days, the Raja Palace houses a Serena Hotel.

The **Chak Chang Mosque** (Chaqchan) is the oldest mosque in Baltistan. Buddhist and Tibetan influences can be recognised in the building style.

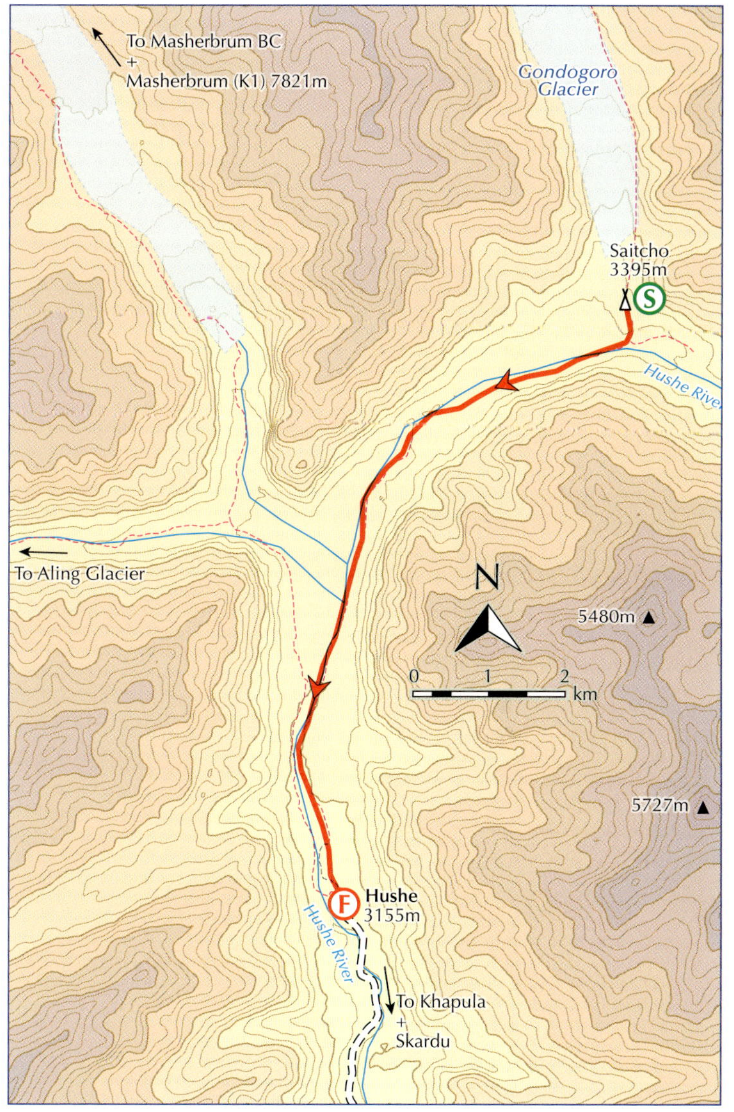
To Masherbrum BC
+
Masherbrum (K1) 7821m
Gondogoro
Glacier
Saitcho
3395m
S
Hushe River
To Aling Glacier
N
5480m
0
1
2
km
5727m
F
Hushe
3155m
Hushe River
To Khapula
+
Skardu

Nanga Parbat seen from the flight to Skardu

AP-BLC

NANGA PARBAT TREKS

Fairy Meadows (Trek 4; photo: Piotr Zycki)

Standing above the great bend of the Indus River at a height of 8126m, Nanga Parbat is the world's ninth-highest summit and the most westerly bastion of the 2400km-long Himalayan chain.

This tremendous mountain is a huge massif of rock and ice whose several sky-high peaks rise almost 7000m above the river. It has three major flanks: the North Face above the Rakhiot Glacier; the West-Northwest Face above the Diamir Glacier; and on the south side, the magnificent Rupal Face.

Nanga Parbat is among the most difficult of the 8000m peaks, and its climbing history is both long and tragic. By contrast, the trekker has several short and easy routes that can be made to the various base camp areas, while a longer and more challenging trek makes a partial tour of the mountain. The easiest of these itineraries leads to the Fairy Meadows and the foot of the Rakhiot Face, another one heads for the Diamir flank, while a third goes to the Rupal (or South) flank. The most difficult is the Mazeno Circuit (not described here).

The name Nanga Parbat is a derivation of the Sanskrit, *nanga parvata*, which means 'naked mountain', but it's also known as Diamir ('king of the mountains'), or Dardi meaning 'the dwelling place of the fairies', or Diarmul. First sketched and painted in 1856 by the German Adolf Schlagintweit, it was also described by Martin Conway in 1892 as 'a great white throne set in heaven'.

THE KILLER MOUNTAIN

Diamir Base Camp at Nanga Parbat (Trek 5; photo: Jasmine Star)

Once it became a focus for mountaineers, Nanga Parbat earned the title of Killer Mountain because of its many deadly accidents and avalanches (other monikers included the Fateful Peak, or the Mountain of Terror). Nanga Parbat has the dubious honour of ranking in the three deadliest 8000m mountains: 1 Annapurna; 2 K2; 3 Nanga Parbat.

The well-known Victorian alpinist, AF Mummery, was lost during a reconnaissance of the Diamir Face in 1895, along with two of his Gurkha companions. (Mummery's attempt was the first ever on any 8000m mountain and he managed to get up to around 6400m on the Diamir Face.) It was 58 years before the summit was achieved, by which time Nanga Parbat had claimed the lives of 28 other climbers and porters.

Nanga Parbat is often referred to as the German Mountain of Destiny. Six German mountaineering expeditions visited the mountain between 1932 and 1953, some in a period where the climbing efforts were mixed with domestic political issues, putting extra pressure on the climbers to succeed.

Nanga Parbat has seen climbing rivalry on both a national and international scale, as has been the case for most of the 8000m peaks, with intense competition within climbing communities to the claim the first ascent.

The Mazeno Circuit
Trek 4 Fairy Meadows and Rakhiot Base Camp Trek
Trek 5 Trek to Diamir Face or West Face of Nanga Parbat
PAKISTAN
S-1
N-35
Barmas
Jaglot
Daro
Bunji
To Gilgit
4669m
Rakhiot Bridge 1179m
Doya
Drang
Jalipur
To Islamabad 428km (from Chilas)
Chilas
Karakoram Highway
N-35
Indus
Bunar Das 1180m
Gunar Farm
Gunar Gah
Patro Gah
Tato 2585m
Tato Gah
Trek 4
Fairy Meadows 3295m
Juliper Pass
Rakhiot BC
Dimroi 1625m
Serre 2440m
Ganalo Glacier
Rakhiot Glacier
Trek 5
Diamir BC 4210m
Diamir Glacier
Nanga Parbat 8126m
N
0
5
10
km
Bazhin Glacier
Ru
Tap
Airl Glacier
Shaigiri
Mazeno Pass 5377m
The Mazeno Circuit
Rupal Glacier
Jalhari Glacier
Shaigiri Glacier
Dodhar Glacier
Shonthar Glacier
Ghughuel Glacier
Chhichi Gah

Nanga Parbat has also suffered some group causalities in the past, which means that there are multiple deaths in one climbing season. In 1934, for example, there were 10 deaths, and 16 in 1937. More recently, in 2013, 11 climbers of different nationalities were killed by Taliban fighters at Diamir Base Camp.

On 3 July 1953, Nanga Parbat was finally summited by the Austrian climber Hermann Buhl, just five weeks after Everest (8848m) had been climbed. In Buhl's book, *Nanga Parbat Pilgrimage*, he describes the mountain '... that pitiless domain demanding its holocaust and giving nothing in return, luring men into its thrall, never to set them free again'.

The inhabitants of the Nanga Parbat valleys don't always conform to central government rules from Islamabad. As John Keay noted:

> Chilas itself is on the Indus below Bunji and below Gor. Its inhabitants had, in common with their neighbours along the river, an unusual form of government; they were republicans. Indeed, each village was a self-governing entity with its own council of state to which even women might be elected.
>
> *The Gilgit Game, 1979*

Be prepared for some surprises like extra demands as I experienced in 1990 on my way to the Diamir Face (read 'Personal Recollections of the Diarmir Face' in Trek 5).

APPROACH

In the olden days, the approach to the mountain was on foot from Srinagar, 125km to the south in Kashmir. The trek took up to two weeks, including two pass crossings, and there would be as many as 600 porters required to bring an expedition to its base. But today – weather permitting – a one hour flight from the capital Islamabad

SOME CLIMBING ROUTES ON NANGA PARBAT

- Rakhiot Face on the north side: Buhl Route 1953; Japanese Route 1995
- Diamir Face on the north-west side: Mummery 1895; Kinshofer Route 1962; Messner solo 1978
- Rupal Face on the south side, with four famous 'shorter' climbing routes to get to the summit: Schell Route 1976; Reinhold and Günther Messner 1970; House-Anderson Route 2005; Polish Mexican Route 1985.

carries trekkers to the mountain town of Gilgit at 1500m, on the way passing very close to Nanga Parbat itself. Pakistan International Airways (PIA) flies at least once a day (weather permitting) to Gilgit. Prices in 2022 were around £39/€45 one-way and £78/€91 for a return. It is an amazing flight during which you are transferred from the hot lowlands into the glistening kingdom of the world's highest peaks, while a slower and much more time-consuming approach by road follows the Indus River all way from Islamabad via the Karakoram Highway (KKH).

To get to Gilgit by road, NATCO is a leading transport company that connects northern Pakistan with the rest of the country. Count on 12 hours' drive to Gilgit from Islamabad, or 10–11 hours to Nanga Parbat. There are three departures every day in the morning from Islamabad to Gilgit, though the 9am departure is specifically for tourists for safety reasons. (Chilas is on the whole a more unsafe town than Gilgit, and there is one area in particular that the government has warned is unsafe for tourists travelling at night.) The bus terminal can be found in the I-11/4 sector of Islamabad, next to a petrol station and just outside the main city area.

Before going on trek spend some time in and around Gilgit, where you can visit the bazaar, watch a game of polo, and stock up with the delicious local apricots. For more information on Gilgit, see the introduction.

From Gilgit you need transport to drive two hours/80km to Rakhiot Bridge at the foot of Nanga Parbat. Use a local bus or rent some transport (with driver included).

Remember...

The main trekking season extends from May until September; there are currently no restrictions but please double check before departure.

Remember to take 10 copies of your passport along to hand out at all the police check points! Bring snacks and water and ear plugs (and Imodium). Overland from Islamabad to

The better section of the road to Fairy Meadows (photo: Jasmine Star)

Gilgit is a beautiful trip but hard work and could take anything from 10–14 hours (or more depending on the road conditions and surprises!). Road improvements are an ongoing process, which will hopefully make the journey shorter and shorter. As of 2022, from Islamabad to Besham it takes three and a half hours, onwards to Dassu two hours, and from Dassu to Chilas three hours, and two more hours to Gilgit (10 and a half hours in total).

TREKKING ROUTES

The most challenging trek is the circuit route crossing the Mazeno Pass (5377m), completed for the first time by the Brit Edmund Candler in 1913 but before that used by men from Chilas when raiding Tarshing, Rupal and other villages. It is not described here but is shown on the map.

All other treks are reasonably straight forward, not too difficult and follow the same way in and out to the different Base Camps of Nanga Parbat.

Nanga Parbat has three faces which can be visited, all of them of course rather impressive; two have been selected for this guidebook.

At the time of writing there are no restrictions visiting any Base Camp on Nanga Parbat.

OTHER TREKS NOT DESCRIBED

Trek to the Rupal Face or South Face

Starts from Gilgit, driving to Astor (2345m) and Tarshing (2911m) and trekking to Rupal village (3155m), camping at the highest spot either Tap (Bazhin) (3550m) or Shaigiri (3750m). Explore the area by going up to Mazeno Base Camp. Count on one- or two-days return trekking to the road head.

The Mazeno Circuit

This trek should keep you busy for 12 to 16 days. It is a demanding trek, mainly because crossing the Mazeno Pass (5377m) on its northern side, involves a 200–300 metre steep icy stretch where climbing equipment is needed. The day of crossing the pass itself normally takes seven hours, with a 600m climb and 1150m descent. In 1895 Mummery and his party crossed this pass after admitting the Rupal Face as being too difficult to climb Nanga Parbat.

After a day of acclimatisation at Tarshing village (2911m) start the trek to Herligkoffer Base Camp. Follow the Rupal Face trek and onwards trail via the following possible stages and include some rest days: Shaigiri (3750m), Mazeno BC (4150m), Mazeno High Camp (4800m), cross the pass (5377m) and descend to Upper Loiba or Edelweiss Camp (4390m), Jut Village, Serre Village where the Diamir trek is joined.

Diamir Face of Nanga Parbat (photo: Jasmine Star)

TREK 4

Fairy Meadows and Rakhiot Base Camp trek

Start/finish	Tato (2585m)
Distance	24.5km
Ascent/descent	1390m
Grade	Easy – moderate
Days	3 + 1 day rest/acclimatisation
Highest point	3965m
Note	This trek could be made longer – read the text for suggestions. Resorts/cottages can be found at Rakhiot Bridge (located on the Karakoram Highway) and Fairy Meadows.

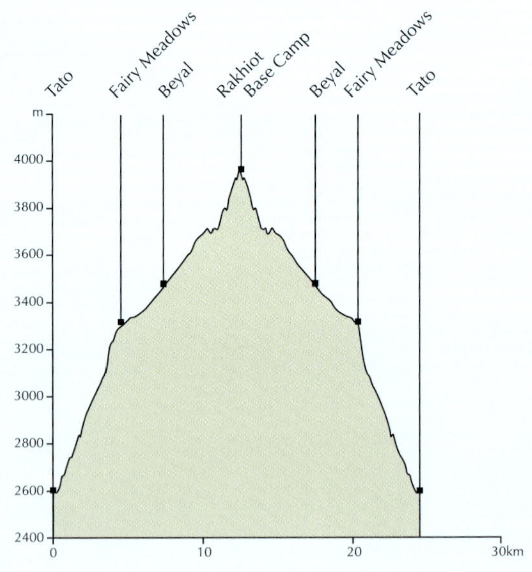

To Rakhiot Bridge
Tato Gah
Tato
2585m
N
0
1
2
km
Jabardar Peak
4513m
Juliper Gah
Fairy Meadows
3295m
Beyal
3530m
N. Juliper Peak
5215m
Juliper Pass
4837m
Rakhiot Glacier
Rakhiot BC
3965m
Ganalo Glacier
S. Juliper Peak
5206m
Camp 1
4468m
Ganalo Peak
6608m

DAY 1

Tato to Fairy Meadows

Start	Tato (2585m)
Finish	Fairy Meadows (3295m)
Distance	4.4km
Ascent	710m
Descent	Negligible
Time	2–4hr
Altitude gain	710m
Warning	Driving/trekking from Gilgit (1500m) to Fairy Meadows (3295m) in one day can result in altitude sickness. Be aware. Make sure to start with an extra day of acclimatisation at Fairy Meadows before exploring onwards.

From Gilgit, the hot, 2hr approach to the start of this trek is made by vehicle along the Karakoram Highway, which was opened in 1978 – an open jeep will reward you with some cooling air in the stifling heat.

As you travel southward on the **Karakoram Highway**, note the intricately decorated trucks and busses passing by: this is a busy road, a lifeline, not only for the northern regions, but also for carrying trade between Pakistan and China. In the barren wasteland of the Indus Valley, the highway suffers from dramatic landslides; sometimes trucks run out of road and tumble down into the river – but as you progress, so Nanga Parbat grows in stature ahead.

Along the Indus River, and elsewhere in Pakistan, there are still some remains to be found from the once-Buddhist culture, with several **rock paintings** on today's stretch. Often, they are indicated by signposts along the highway.

At Rakhiot Bridge (1179m) (sometimes spelled Raikot) you transfer to local jeeps that use a private dirt road leading to the village of **Tato** (2585m) in a little under 1hr. From there it is a walk of 2hr or more to **Fairy Meadows** (3295m), during which the landscape undergoes a total change from hot, arid desert to a dense forest and meadows full of edelweiss and wild roses, all at pleasant temperatures. It is almost like being in the Swiss Alps, with farmhouses and hay barns, and should you arrive without a tent, there's accommodation similar to that offered in a Nepalese teahouse, with showers and even a full meal service available. From here the view of the Rakhiot Face is overwhelming.

RECOMMENDED REST DAY AT FAIRY MEADOWS

To safely acclimatise, a rest day is strongly advised here.

DAY 2

Fairy Meadows to Beyal via Base Camp

Start	Fairy Meadows 3295m
Finish	Beyal 3530m – via Base Camp 3965m
Distance	12.4 km (3.9km to Beyal and 8.5km return trip to Base Camp)
Ascent	680m
Descent	445m
Time	To Beyal 1hr 30min–2hr; return trip to BC 3–4hr
Altitude gain	235m

Walking from Fairy Meadows to Beyal with Nanga Parbat (photo: Jasmine Star)

After Fairy Meadows, the next hamlet is **Beyal**, at 3530m. This can be reached in 1hr 30min on an easy trail, and on arrival the same kind of facilities as at Fairy Meadows can be found.

It then takes another 4–5hr to reach the **Rakhiot Base Camp** area, set at the moraine end of a gigantic river of ice at 3965m, where a muted version of the groaning sounds of the glacier can be heard.

While this may still be a place fit for human habitation, above the moraine the Rakhiot Face seems ready to collapse onto Base Camp. High up, hanging glaciers with delicately chiselled snow ridges, vertical snow ribs and ice runnels, can produce a deadly bombardment of huge **avalanches**. At this camp there are memorials to several mountaineers killed by such avalanches or other disasters.

Side-trips from Base Camp

As well as the short trek to base camp, you could make side-trips to the summer alps at Susarboin (4200m), with grand views towards the massive North Face, or even more challenging, try climbing either the non-technical Southern Juliper Peak (5206m) from Beyal, or technical Buldar Peak (5602m) to gain even better views towards Nanga Parbat.

Southern Juliper Peak (Jiliper) (5206m): although the climb is not technical, it is best to tackle this mountain with climbing experience and the right gear. Start from Beyal (3530m) to the Jiliper (or Khusto) Pass (at 4837m) in a westerly direction parallel to a stream. A camp is advised on the west side of the pass from where Juliper Peak can be climbed in 3–4hr.

Buldar Peak (5602m): two or three days extra would be needed. The peak could be climbed with an extra camp at around 4200m or 4500m, which could be reached in about 4–5hr from Beyal, with some steep sections. From high camp count on 6–7hr for a return climb, equipped with crampons, ice axe, harness, climbing rope for a technical climb on the snowy ridge north to Buldar Peak.

Visit Camp 1: if you want to walk onwards to Camp 1 (4468m), this will take 2hr and involves a 500-metre climb. To enjoy this best, you would need one extra overnight at Base Camp.

DAY 3

Beyal to Tato and transport to Rakhiot Bridge

Start	Beyal 3530m
Finish	Tato 2585m
Distance	7.7km
Ascent	Negligible
Descent	945m
Time	3–4hr
Altitude loss	945m

After having spent several days exploring the area, should you wish to walk, rather than take the jeep, back to Rakhiot Bridge, follow the old route on the opposite side of the river at **Tato** and enjoy views towards the Rakaposhi (7788m) and Haramosh (7397m) ranges in the distance, with the Indus River swirling below.

From Rakhiot Bridge there are several options: drive to Islamabad, Gilgit or Skardu.

Petroglyphs on rocks near Chilas in the Indus valley dating from 200 *BCE* ***(photo: Kenneth Hanson)***

Nanga Parbat Rupal or South Face (photo: Michael Beek)

TREK 5

Trek to Diamir Face or West Face of Nanga Parbat

Start/finish	Bunar Das 1280m
Distance	54.6km (including visit to Diamir Base Camp: 69km)
Ascent/descent	3410m (including visit to Diamir Base Camp: 4080m)
Grade	Strenuous
Days	5 or 6
Highest point	3540m (optional visit to Diamir Base Camp 4210m)
Warning	Daily major altitude gains can be expected. Visiting the Diamir district/Face can be hazardous. The local tribesmen have a reputation for rather ferocious haggling and unreasonable demands on funds and equipment. Be warned. A locally-respected guide or spokesperson is a good precaution.

Leave the Karakoram Highway behind and climb/drive up a valley starting from Bunar Das (1280m) (near Jalipur). Bunar Das has just some basic shops. Drive or trek for about 13km (2hr) on a narrow road into a desolate and arid valley and the village of **Dimroi** (or Diamaroi) (1625m) becomes visible. To reach the village, a cable way must be used to cross the river (or drive with the jeep onwards to the village Halai and backtrack to Dimroi). Walking from Bunar Das to Dimroi takes 3–4hr.

PERSONAL RECOLLECTIONS OF THE DIAMIR FACE

Some years ago (1990), I guided a BBC film team to the Diamir Face where climbers Chris Bonington, Jim Curran, Sigi Hupfauer and Charles Houston were to make a documentary about Nanga Parbat. On our flight to Gilgit, the overloaded Fokker Friendship struggled through a major monsoon storm that denied us the hoped-for close views of the mountain, but once our stranded luggage finally caught up with us a day later, we tackled the summer heat of the Karakoram Highway on open jeeps for two and a half hours, heading for Rakhiot Bridge towards Chilas, the principal town in this part of the Indus Valley. Before reaching Chilas an old jeep track led away to the south, climbing steeply into the Bunar Valley. The trip was not going to be easy since the local staff were giving us nonstop challenges with new demands and changes. When our trip was finished and we had to pay our porters their final wages – after they had already been increased several times, and I had been in Chilas two days earlier to exchange foreign currency since we had run out of rupees – we still ended up with trouble. Thinking it was a smart move, I had invited a policeman along with me from Chilas to the end of the road leading into the Diamir Valley. However, the payment still had a dramatic finale as we ended up having to escape from armed locals demanding even more. The policeman was the only unarmed local at the scene!

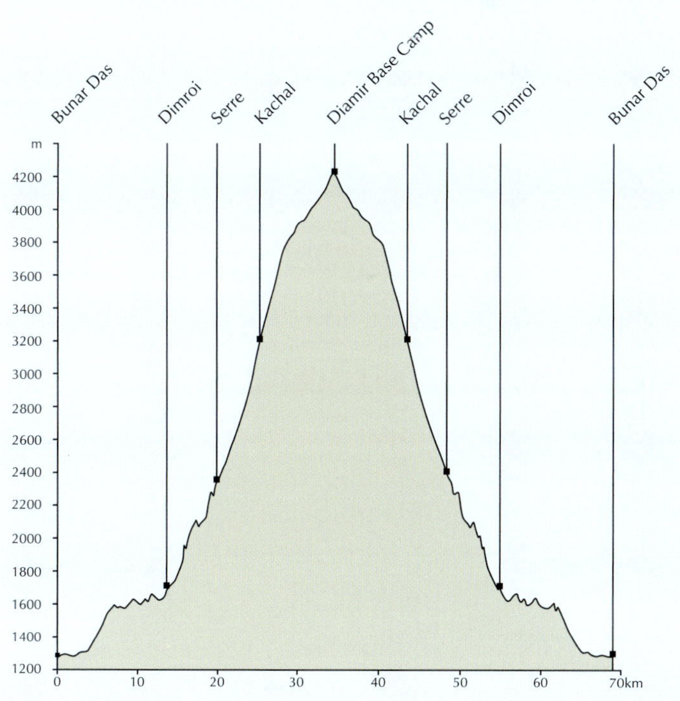

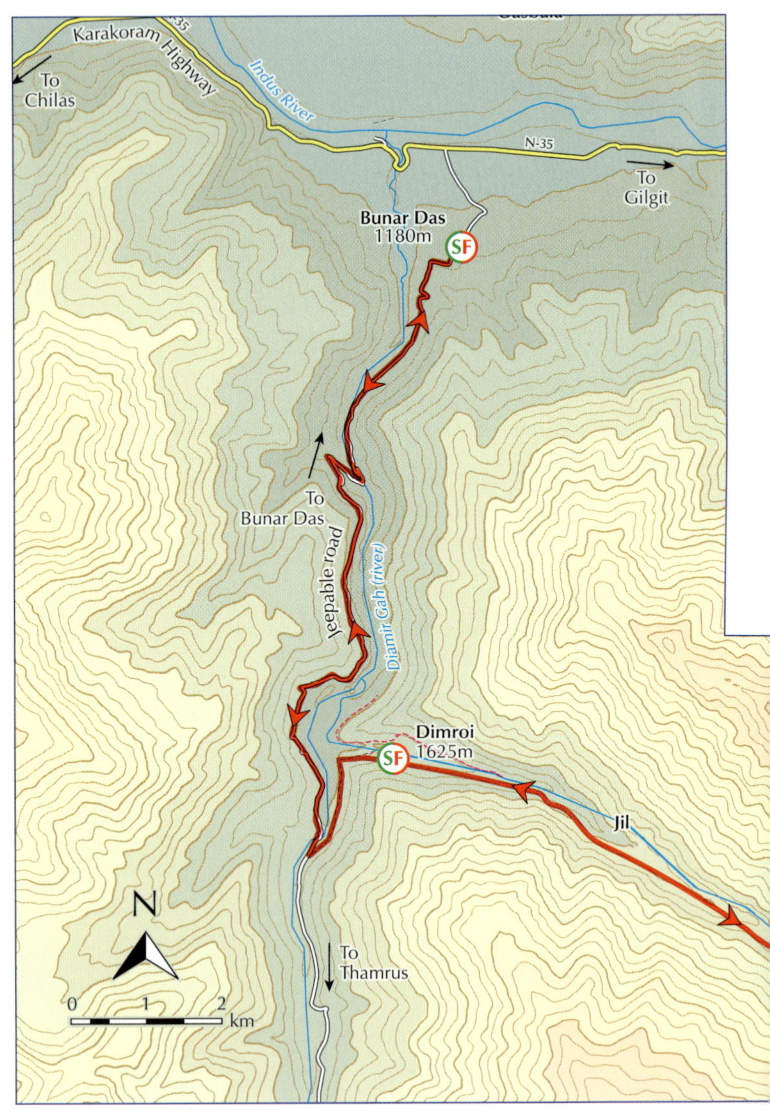
Karakoram Highway
To
Chilas
Indus River
N-35
To
Gilgit
Bunar Das
1180m
SF
To
Bunar Das
Jeepable road
Diamir Gah (river)
Dimroi
1625m
SF
Jil
N
To
Thamrus
0
1
2
km

Diamir Face of Nanga Parbat (photo: Jasmine Star)

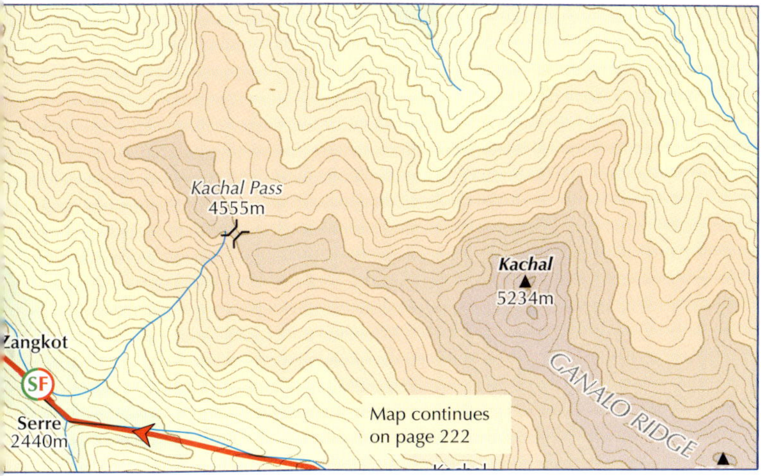

Kachal Pass
4555m

Kachal
5234m

Zangkot

Serre
2440m

GANALO RIDGE

Map continues
on page 222

Kachal Pass
4555m
Kachal
5234m
Zangkot
SF
Serre
2440m
GANALO RIDGE
5542m
Kachal
3540m
SF
Airl Gah
N
0
1
2
km
Diamir Glacier
Airl Gah
5227m
Diamiral Peak
5570m
Loiba
Glacier
Mazeno Pass
5358m
Mamu
Choti
5730m
Mazeno
High camp
4750m
Airl
Glacier

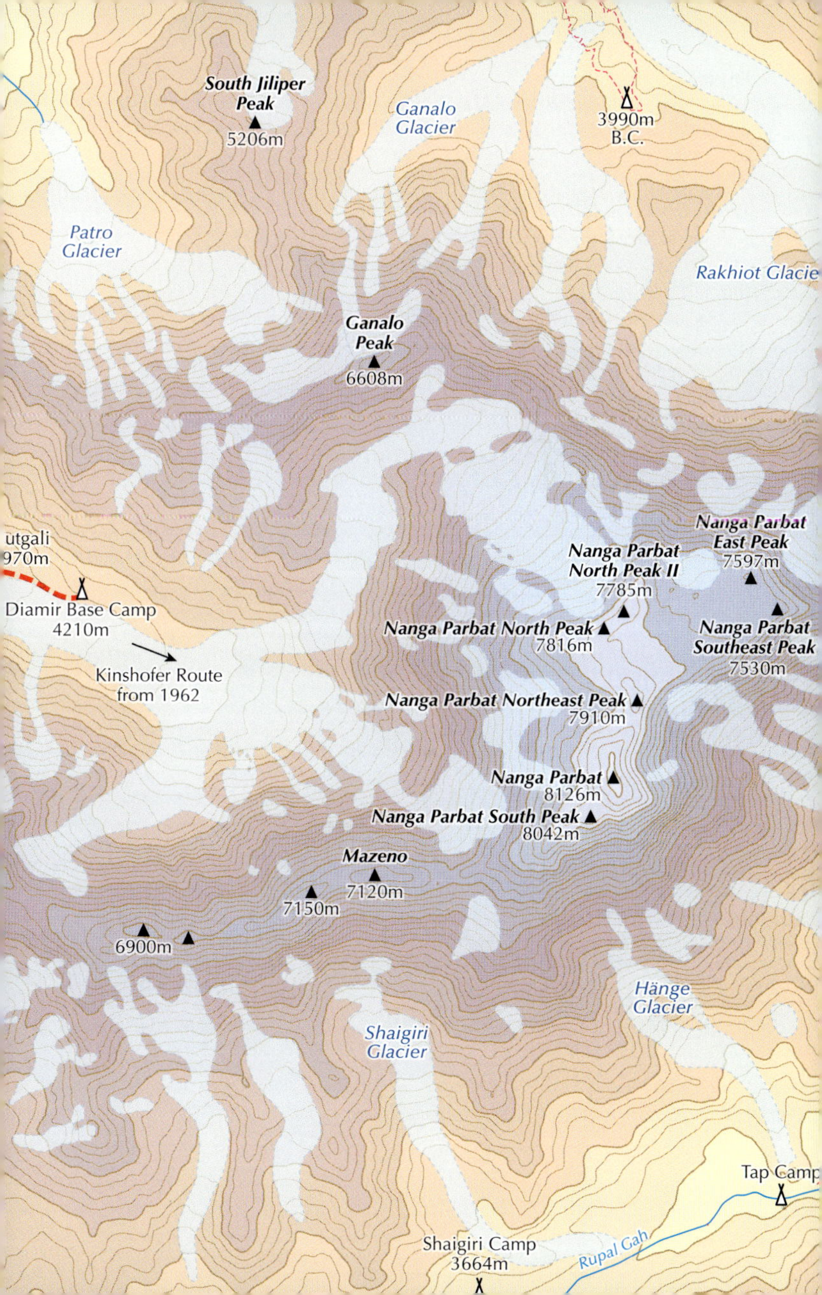
South Jiliper Peak
5206m
Ganalo Glacier
3990m B.C.
Patro Glacier
Rakhiot Glacie
Ganalo Peak
6608m
utgali
970m
Diamir Base Camp
4210m
Kinshofer Route from 1962
Nanga Parbat East Peak
7597m
Nanga Parbat North Peak II
7785m
Nanga Parbat North Peak
7816m
Nanga Parbat Southeast Peak
7530m
Nanga Parbat Northeast Peak
7910m
Nanga Parbat
8126m
Nanga Parbat South Peak
8042m
Mazeno
7120m
7150m
6900m
Hänge Glacier
Shaigiri Glacier
Tap Camp
Rupal Gah
Shaigiri Camp
3664m

Next day is a long one of 5–6hr and a nearly 1000m climb through the Rudiamir Pal Valley to the hamlet of **Serre** (2440m) (or Sejel, or Serregoloboundo), passing hamlets of **Jil** and **Zangot** with terraced fields hugging the hillsides and livestock grazing on the pastures high above; a route involving several exposed and questionable portions of trail and narrow gorge sections.

The last day up will lead to the hamlet of **Kachal** (3540m) (or Kajul) (a 1100m climb of 5–6hr).

As a day trip, or if there is enough time, move to the end of the trail at Gutgali (3970m), camp here and visit **Diamir Base Camp** (4210m) (or Lathobow Alpine Meadow) (4hr up and 2hr 30min down).

Base Camp nestles in an alpine meadow at the side of a glacier, a little grassy sanctuary with the huge Diamir Face looming over it: a scene rich in climbing history, and the likely resting place of Mummery, who died in 1895.

It normally takes two days to walk back to Dimroi via one night at Serre village.

If you decide to drive to Chilas and Islamabad then just before Chilas near the Talpan Bridge several **rock paintings** can be found showing the meditating Buddha, Buddhist stupas and wheels of life, the ibex, and some soldiers.

Charles Houston, Sigi Hupfauer and Chris Bonington in Diamir valley

APPENDIX A

Useful contacts

Tourist visas
https://visa.nadra.gov.pk

Before departure note your relevant embassy address in Pakistan.

Outdoor associations

Alpine Club of Pakistan
www.alpineclub.org.pk

Adventure Foundation of Pakistan (AFP)
www.adventurefoundation.org.pk

PTDC – Pakistan Tourism Development Corporation (1970)
http://www.tourism.gov.pk

Transport

NATCO bus services
www.natco.gov.pk

Baltistan Tours
(my choice since 1989)
www.baltistantours.com

APPENDIX B

Agents in Pakistan and abroad

Pakistan

The tour operators are organised in PATO (Pakistan Association of Tour Operators, www.pato.org.pk). On the PATO website, a list of more than 150 members can be found; try some companies and find out different approaches and prices (in 2019, 350 tour operators existed in Skardu alone).

UK

KE Adventure Travel
(KE stands for Karakoram Experience – this company, established in 1984, have unequalled knowledge of the region)
www.keadventure.com

Mountain Kingdoms
www.mountainkingdoms.com

Exodus Travels
www.exodus.co.uk

The Mountain Company
www.themountaincompany.co.uk

Germany

Michael Beek
www.beek-pakistan.de

DAV Summit Club
www.dav-summit-club.de

Talhammer
(offering overnight at K2 and Gasherbrum BC; or Lukpa La pass)
www.talhammer.de

Schulz Aktiv Reisen
www.schulz-aktiv-reisen.de

Denmark

Kipling Travel
www.kiplingtravel.dk

The Netherlands

Snowleopard Adventures
www.snowleopard.nl

France

Allibert Trekking
www.allibert-trekking.com

Terres d'Aventure
www.terdav.com

Tamera
www.tamera.fr

Routard
www.routard.com

US

GeoEx
(sometimes offers K2)
www.geoex.com

Epic Backpackers Tour
www.epicbackpackertours.com

APPENDIX C

English to Urdu glossary

English	Urdu
one	ek
two	doh
three	teen
four	char
five	paanch
Peace be on you (greeting)	Salaam alay kum
And onto you peace (reply)	Waalay kum as Salaam
What is your name?	Aapka naam kya heh?
I don't understand	Moojhay sumej naheen a-reha
Thank you	Shukria
Good bye	Khoodha haafis
yes	jihaan
no	naheen
Hoorah!	Zindabad!
Bravo!	Shabash!

English	Urdu
wonderful/fantastic/ awesome	zabardast
bridge	puli
mountain	pahar
path	rasta
river	daria
road	sarak
village	gaon
firewood	lakhri
today	aaj
tomorrow	kal
morning	subah
evening	shaam
day	din
hour	ghantay
Which way to Askole?	Askole kiss taraf heh?

APPENDIX D

Further reading

For a good book shop in Pakistan visit Saeed Book Bank in Blue Sector, Islamabad.

Books on the mountainous areas of northern Pakistan

Allan, Sandy, *In Some Lost Place: The first ascent of Nanga Parbat's Mazeno Ridge* (2015 UK)
Bauer, Paul, *Himalayan Quest: The German expeditions to Siniolchum and Nanga Parbat* (1938 London)
Bonington, Chris, *Mountaineer* (1989 London)
Brown, Joe, *The Hard Years* (1967 London)
Buhl, Hermann, *Nanga Parbat Pilgrimage* (1956 London)
Cassin, Ricardo, *50 Years of Alpinism* (1981 Leicester)
Cave, Andy, *Learning to Breathe* (2005 London)
Child, Greg, *Thin Air: Encounters in the Himalayas* (1988 Somerset, UK)
Clinch, Nicholas, *A Walk in the Sky* (Hidden Peak) (1982 Seattle)
Conway, Martin, *Climbing in The Himalayas: Climbing and Exploration in the Karakoram- Himalayas* (1894 London)
Curran, Jim, *Trango: the Nameless Tower* (1978 Sheffield)
Curran, Jim, *K2, Triumph and Tragedy* (1987 London)
Desio, Prof. Ardito, *Ascent of K2* (1955 London)
Desio, Prof. Ardito, *La Spedizione Geografica Italiana nel Karakoram* (1936 Milan-Rome)
Diemberger, Kurt, *Summits and Secrets* (1971 London)
Dyhrenfurth, G.O., *To the Third Pole – The History of the High Himalaya* (1955 London)
Fanshawe, Andy and Stephen Venables, *Himalaya Alpine-Style* (1996 London)
Filippi, Filippo de, *Karakoram and Western Himalaya 1909: An account of the expedition of H.R.H. Prince Luigi Amadeo of Savoy, Duke of the Abruzzi* (1912 New York)
Filippi, Filippo de, *The Italian Expedition to the Himalaya, Karakoram and Eastern Turkestan 1913–1914* (1932 London)
Girard, Antoine, *En vol vers les 8000* (2018 France)
Haberl, Jim, *K2 Dreams and Reality* (1994 Canada)
Herrligkoffer, Karl M., *Nanga Parbat* (1954 London)
Hinkes, Alan, *8000 meters: Climbing The World's Highest Mountains* (2013 Cicerone, UK)
Houston, Charles Snead and Robert Bates, *K2 the savage mountain* (1955 London)
Keay, John, *When Men and Mountains Meet* (1983 London)
Keay, John, *The Gilgit Game* (1979 London)
Keay, John, *Himalaya: Exploring the Roof of the World* (2022 London)
Knight, E.F., *Where Three Empires Meet* (1978 Karachi)

Kukuczka, Jerzy, *My Vertical World* (1992 London)
Longstaff, Tom, *This My Voyage* (1950 London)
Maraini, Fosco, *The Ascent of Gasherbrum IV* (1961 London)
Maraini, Fosco, *Where Four Worlds Meet* (1964 London)
Mazel, David, *Mountaineering Women: Stories by Early Climbers* (1994 Texas, USA)
Messner, Reinhold, *The Naked Mountain: Nanga Parbat, Brother, Death and Solitude* (2003 Marlborough/UK)
Prior, Colin, *The Karakoram: Ice Mountains of Pakistan* (2021 London/New York) – impressive photo book
Razzetti, Steve, *Top Treks of the World* (2001 London)
Ridgeway, Rick, *The Last Step: the American ascent of K2* (1980 Seattle)
Rowell, Galen, *In the Throne Room of the Mountain Gods* (1986 San Francisco)
Saunders, Victor, *Elusive Summits: Four Expeditions in the Karakoram* (1990 London)
Saunders, Victor, *No Place to Fall: Superalpinism in the High Himalaya* (1994 London)
Searle, Mike, *Colliding Continents: A Geological Exploration of the Himalaya, Karakoram, and Tibet* (2013 UK)
Scott, Doug, *The Ogre: Biography of a mountain and the dramatic story of the first ascent* (2017 Sheffield)
Shipton, Eric, *Blank on the Map* (1938 London)
Shirahata, Shiro, *The Karakoram: Mountains of Pakistan* (1990 Seattle)
Tullis, Julie, *Clouds from Both Sides* (1986 London)
Viesturs, Ed and David Roberts, *K2: Life and Death on the World's Most Dangerous Mountain* (2009 New York)
Waller, James, *The Everlasting Hills* (1939 Edinburgh)
Workman, Fanny and William, *In the Ice World of Himálaya* (1901 London)
Workman, Fanny and William, *Ice-Bound Heights of the Mustagh* (1908 London)
Workman, Fanny and William, *The Call of the Snowy Hispar* (1910 London)
Younghusband, Sir Francis, *The Heart of a Continent* (1896 London)

Trekking and climbing guidebooks

Shaw, Isobel and Ben, *Pakistan Trekking Guide: Himalaya, Karakoram and Hindu Kush* (2011 2nd edition) – covering just about everything; excellent guidebook
Beek, Michael, *Pakistan: Land, Geschichte, Kultur, Trekking* (2019 Germany) – excellent guidebook in German
Kielkowski, Jan, *K2 and Northern Baltoro* (Mustagh 1997)
Kielkowski, Jan, *Nanga Parbat Group* (2015)

Birdwatchers' books

Grimmett, Richard and Inskipp, Tim, *Birds of Pakistan* (2008 Helm Field Guides)
Mirza, Prof. Z. B. *A Field Guide to Birds of Pakistan* (2014 Lahore/Rawalpindi WWF Pakistan)
Roberts, T. J., *The Birds of Pakistan* (1991 Oxford University Press, two volumes)
An interesting Pakistani website describing 362 birds is www.birdsofgilgit.com/region.html

Maps

Sheet maps

In the UK, Stanfords (shops in London and Bristol or www.stanfords.co.uk) and the Map Shop (www.themapshop.co.uk) stock a range of maps.

- **CKNP Trekking map (SEED: Social Economic Environmental Development):** a project funded by the Governments of Italy and Pakistan (1:400,000) – handy small map with routes and camps indicated.
- **Trekking map Karakoram** – K2, Gasherbrum, Broad Peak, Hispar Trek, Hunza – by Terra Quest (1:175,000) 2016 – laminated map; very handy map with routes and camps indicated
- **K2 and Baltoro Glacier in the Karakorum** – Satellite Image Map 1:80,000 – 2004, 2013 – a detailed satellite map with an enormous number of names and heights info on it – printed in Poland
- **Leomann Maps** printed in the UK – four sheets covering the Karakoram 1:200,000. Sheet 1 Gilgit, Hunza, Rakaposhi, Batura Area. Sheet 2 Skardu, Hispar, Biafo area. Sheet 3 K2, Baltoro, Gasherbrum, Masherbrum, Saltoro groups. Sheet 4 Siachen, Rimo, Saser groups. Some trekking information printed on the reverse.
- **US Army map**. India and Pakistan. Jammu and Kashmir: Mundik 1:250,000 covering Haramosh Range, Masherbrum Range, Ladakh Range, Great Karakoram, Baltoro Muztagh (2nd edition 1962; later edition possible)
- **Baltoro Glacier K2**. Central Karakoram 1:100,000 – K2, Masherbrum, Broad Peak, Chogolisa, Golden Throne, Gasherbrum. Surveyed by the 1929 and 1954 Italian Expeditions. Beautiful map originally from 1969, published in Italy by 'Dai tipi dell'Istuto Geografico Militare'
- **The Baltoro Glacier 1:100,000 inserted folded map for** *The Mountaineering Annual '88*. Published by Yama-Kei Publishers Co., Ltd. Survey of Tsuneo Miyamori/JAPAN-PAKISTAN K2 Expedition 1977 – good map with detailed height of mountains on reverse.
- **The Eight Thousand Metre Peaks of the Karakoram**. Orographical Sketch Map Scale 1:50,000 – prepared by Jerzy Wala, Krakow, Poland 1993 (1st edition); revised 1994. Produced by The Climbing Company Ltd. in the UK. Distributed by Cordee
- **Karakoram Sheet 1 and 2**. Orographical Sketch Map. Published by the Swiss Foundation for Alpine Research Zurich, Switzerland – Initiator Anders Bolinder. Prepared by Jerzy Wala, Kraków, Poland. 1990 Sheet 1: Chilinji, Gilgit, Karakoram Highway, Hispar-Biafo, Shimshal, Skardu. Sheet 2: Baltoro Glacier, K2, Hushe, Khapalu, Siachen Glaicer, Rimo Mountains, Rimo Muztagh, Sasser Muztagh, Leh

- **Nanga Parbat – Alpenvereinskarte 1:50,000 (Nr.0/7) Deutsche Himalaya-Expedition 1934**. First print 1936. Reprint 1980 – excellent map.
- **Karakorum 1:600,000 Servei General d'Informació de Muntanya, Sabadell 1995**

Maps in books

- **G.O.Dyhrenfurth – Baltoro 1939**
- **Fanny Workman Bullock and William Hunter Workman** – The Call of the Snowy Hispar 1910 – The Hispar Glacier and Tributaries in the Karakoram Range. Explored by the Bullock-Workman Expedition 1908. By Dr Cesare Calciati and Dr Mathias Koncza. 1:100,000 Excellent detailed map. The couple wrote several books with some excellent maps.
- **Filippo de Filippi – Karakoram and Western Himalaya 1909**
- **Eric Shipton – Blank on the Map 1938**
- **Himalayan Journals**

Other

When back from a visit to the Karakoram, check out this web site to discover peak names: www.himalaya-info.org/index.htm

Acknowledgements

In 1989 I was lucky enough to be introduced to the mountains of Pakistan by Glenn Rowley and Tim Greening, of Karakoram Experience (called 'KE Adventure Travel' nowadays), and Mohammed Iqbal, from Baltistan Tours. My learning process was only possible with the help of so many local staff and KE colleagues, and writing this book has only been possible as a result of the many trips I have been able to guide in Pakistan, and the support from the people mentioned above.

Originally, this book was planned to be co-written by KE colleague and climber Tom Richardson from the UK. For several reasons he had to leave the project at an early stage, but not before he had managed to start on some of the chapters. Thanks, Tom, for your valuable input.

A heartfelt apology for any names I have unwittingly omitted from this list, but I would like to say: *shukriya* to guides like Mohammed Khan, Karim, Little Nabi, Big Nabi, Javed, Shakoor Ali, climber Mohammed Iqbal and kitchen staff Mohammed Ali, Mohammed Amin, Jousuf and Ghafoor in Pakistan. Thanks also Glenn and Tim, especially the mighty Rex Munro from Australia who showed me the ropes in Pakistan; Steve Razzetti, Pete Royall, Kit Wilkinson, Val Pitkethly, Victor Saunders, Pam Andrews, Kate Harper, Terry Ralphs, Dave Wilson, Amos Doron, Karl Farkas, Tom Gilchrist, Graham Moss, Mark van Alstine, Andy Criscone and Tom Richardson.

Mohammed Khan

Karim (with the author)

Not forgetting the 'joila-man', Haji Hussain Chopa from Askole, making it possible to cross the Panmah River.

All our work in the field was made possible by endless support from people in offices in the UK and Pakistan, like Yousuf Wazir and Musa Khan from Baltistan Tours. Baltistan Tours is now in the capable hands of Mohammed's son, Zafar, who is doing an excellent job (just as good as his father).

My thanks also to all the trekkers who have joined me on many Pakistan treks and adventures – and lived to tell the tale! To Dave Deisley for some proof reading. To trekker Prof. Dr Khaleeq-Uz-Zaman for the inside information on Pakistan.

Zafar Iqbal from Baltistan Tours helped me to write this book, collecting facts, interviewing people, answering my questions, all of which proved to be extremely helpful. Without Zafar's contribution the book would be half as accurate. Thanks Zafar.

The website from Baltistan Tours also provided some useful information for this book.

To all authors of numerous old and recent books on Pakistan, which I have had the pleasure of reading over many years reading, learning from their stories (see Appendix D 'Further Reading').

Some of the more recent guidebooks have given me some inspiration. I have to say thank you to the authors of excellent trekking guidebooks: Isobel Shaw and Ben Shaw; Michael Beek; Moritz Steinhilber.

Grateful thanks to Mike Searle – Professor of Earth Sciences at Oxford – who contributed with a paper on geology. To well-known British author John Keay, for his permission to use some quotes out of his books.

To Professor David Butz from Canada. Mr Muhammad Ali Nawaz from the Snowleopard organisation in Islamabad. Information on and sketches of birds by Prof. Z.B. Mirza and Huma Wasiq and WWF Islamabad assistance from Hammad Naqi Khan and Rabia Tahir.

To the 1990 BBC team, with whom I travelled to Nanga Parbat B.C., making a documentary with the most inspiring team of climbers I have ever had around me: Chris Bonington, Jim Curran, Charles Houston from the US, and Sigi Hupfauer from Germany.

For Jasmine Star's input on the Biafo–Hispar trek.

For photos throughout the book by the author and by the following people: Jasmine Star, Tom Richardson, Muhammad Ashar, Dave Morgan, Antoine Girard, Colin Prior, Kenneth Hanson, Michael Beek and Piotr Zycky (see his excellent photos at https://pbase.com/ptz/pakistan).

To His Excellency Ambassador Ahmad Farooq to Pakistan in Copenhagen.

To the Cicerone team in the UK for their endless patience dealing with all my requests, polishing my English (special thanks here to copyeditor Helen Johnson, who is now pretty good at Dutch), cartographer/designer, editor, printer – all of whom have contributed to make this a book of true value. Special thanks to Natalie Simpson for replying to hundreds of emails. Great job, everybody!

To my parents for taking me just about every summer to the Alps and for allowing me to explore the Dutch Alps for the rest of the year. And finally, to my own children, Laura and Max, for letting me leave on my adventures.

NOTES

NOTES

DOWNLOAD THE GPX FILES

All the routes in this guide are available for download from:

www.cicerone.co.uk/1056/GPX

as standard format GPX files. You should be able to load them into most online GPX systems and mobile devices, whether GPS or smartphone. You may need to convert the file into your preferred format using a conversion programme such as gpsvisualizer.com or one of the many other such websites and programmes.

When you follow this link, you will be asked for your email address and where you purchased the guidebook, and have the option to subscribe to the Cicerone e-newsletter.

www.cicerone.co.uk

LISTING OF CICERONE GUIDES

BRITISH ISLES CHALLENGES, COLLECTIONS AND ACTIVITIES

Cycling Land's End to John o' Groats
Great Walks on the England Coast Path
The Big Rounds
The Book of the Bivvy
The Book of the Bothy
The Mountains of England and Wales: Vol 1 Wales
The Mountains of England and Wales: Vol 2 England
The National Trails
Walking the End to End Trail

SHORT WALKS SERIES

Short Walks Hadrian's Wall
Short Walks in Arnside and Silverdale
Short Walks in Cornwall: Falmouth and the Lizard
Short Walks in Dumfries and Galloway
Short Walks in Nidderdale
Short Walks in Pembrokeshire: Tenby and the south
Short Walks in the South Downs: Brighton, Eastbourne and Arundel
Short Walks in the Surrey Hills
Short Walks Lake District – Coniston and Langdale
Short Walks Lake District: Keswick, Borrowdale and Buttermere
Short Walks Lake District: Windermere Ambleside and Grasmere
Short Walks on the Malvern Hills
Short Walks Winchester

SCOTLAND

Ben Nevis and Glen Coe
Cycling in the Hebrides
Cycling the North Coast 500
Great Mountain Days in Scotland
Mountain Biking in Southern and Central Scotland
Mountain Biking in West and North West Scotland
Not the West Highland Way
Scotland
Scotland's Best Small Mountains
Scotland's Mountain Ridges
Scottish Wild Country Backpacking
Skye's Cuillin Ridge Traverse
The Borders Abbeys Way
The Great Glen Way
The Great Glen Way Map Booklet
The Hebridean Way
The Hebrides
The Isle of Mull
The Isle of Skye
The Skye Trail
The Southern Upland Way
The West Highland Way
The West Highland Way Map Booklet
Walking Ben Lawers, Rannoch and Atholl
Walking in the Cairngorms
Walking in the Pentland Hills
Walking in the Scottish Borders
Walking in the Southern Uplands
Walking in Torridon, Fisherfield, Fannichs and An Teallach
Walking Loch Lomond and the Trossachs
Walking on Arran
Walking on Harris and Lewis
Walking on Jura, Islay and Colonsay
Walking on Rum and the Small Isles
Walking on the Orkney and Shetland Isles
Walking on Uist and Barra
Walking the Cape Wrath Trail
Walking the Corbetts
Vol 1 South of the Great Glen
Vol 2 North of the Great Glen
Walking the Galloway Hills
Walking the John o' Groats Trail
Walking the Munros
Vol 1 – Southern, Central and Western Highlands
Vol 2 – Northern Highlands and the Cairngorms
Winter Climbs in the Cairngorms
Winter Climbs: Ben Nevis and Glen Coe

NORTHERN ENGLAND ROUTES

Cycling the Reivers Route
Cycling the Way of the Roses
Hadrian's Cycleway
Hadrian's Wall Path
Hadrian's Wall Path Map Booklet
The Coast to Coast Cycle Route
The Coast to Coast Walk
The Coast to Coast Walk Map Booklet
The Pennine Way
The Pennine Way Map Booklet
Walking the Dales Way
Walking the Dales Way Map Booklet

NORTH-EAST ENGLAND, YORKSHIRE DALES AND PENNINES

Cycling in the Yorkshire Dales
Great Mountain Days in the Pennines
Mountain Biking in the Yorkshire Dales
The Cleveland Way and the Yorkshire Wolds Way
The North York Moors
Trail and Fell Running in the Yorkshire Dales
Walking in County Durham
Walking in Northumberland
Walking in the North Pennines
Walking in the Yorkshire Dales:
North and East
South and West
Walking St Cuthbert's Way
Walking St Oswald's Way and Northumberland Coast Path

NORTH-WEST ENGLAND AND THE ISLE OF MAN

Cycling the Pennine Bridleway
Isle of Man Coastal Path
The Lancashire Cycleway
The Lune Valley and Howgills
Walking in Cumbria's Eden Valley
Walking in Lancashire
Walking in the Forest of Bowland and Pendle
Walking on the Isle of Man
Walking on the West Pennine Moors
Walking the Ribble Way
Walks in Silverdale and Arnside

LAKE DISTRICT

Bikepacking in the Lake District
Cycling in the Lake District
Great Mountain Days in the Lake District
Joss Naylor's Lakes, Meres and Waters of the Lake District
Lake District Winter Climbs
Lake District:
High Level and Fell Walks
Low Level and Lake Walks
Mountain Biking in the Lake District
Outdoor Adventures with Children – Lake District
Scrambles in the Lake District –
North
South
Trail and Fell Running in the Lake District
Walking The Cumbria Way
Walking the Lake District Fells –
Borrowdale
Buttermere
Coniston
Keswick
Langdale
Mardale and the Far East
Patterdale
Wasdale
Walking the Tour of the Lake District

DERBYSHIRE, PEAK DISTRICT AND MIDLANDS

Cycling in the Peak District
Dark Peak Walks
Scrambles in the Dark Peak

Walking in Derbyshire
Walking in the Peak District –
White Peak East
White Peak West

SOUTHERN ENGLAND

20 Classic Sportive Rides in
South East England
South West England
Cycling in the Cotswolds
Mountain Biking on the
North Downs
South Downs
Suffolk Coast and Heath Walks
The Cotswold Way
The Cotswold Way Map Booklet
The Kennet and Avon Canal
The Lea Valley Walk
The North Downs Way
The North Downs Way Map Booklet
The Peddars Way and Norfolk
Coast Path
The Pilgrims' Way
The Ridgeway National Trail
The Ridgeway National Trail
Map Booklet
The South Downs Way
The South Downs Way Map Booklet
The Thames Path
The Thames Path Map Booklet
The Two Moors Way
The Two Moors Way Map Booklet
Walking Hampshire's Test Way
Walking in Cornwall
Walking in Essex
Walking in Kent
Walking in London
Walking in Norfolk
Walking in the Chilterns
Walking in the Cotswolds
Walking in the Isles of Scilly
Walking in the New Forest
Walking in the North Wessex Downs
Walking on Dartmoor
Walking on Guernsey
Walking on Jersey
Walking on the Isle of Wight
Walking the Dartmoor Way
Walking the Jurassic Coast
Walking the South West Coast Path
Walking the South West Coast Path
Map Booklets
– Vol 1: Minehead to St Ives
– Vol 2: St Ives to Plymouth
– Vol 3: Plymouth to Poole
Walks in the South Downs
National Park

WALES AND WELSH BORDERS

Cycle Touring in Wales
Cycling Lon Las Cymru
Great Mountain Days in Snowdonia
Hillwalking in Shropshire
Mountain Walking in Snowdonia
Offa's Dyke Path
Offa's Dyke Path Map Booklet
Ridges of Snowdonia
Scrambles in Snowdonia
Snowdonia: 30 Low-level and
Easy Walks
– North
– South
The Cambrian Way
The Pembrokeshire Coast Path
The Pembrokeshire Coast Path
Map Booklet
The Snowdonia Way
Walking Glyndwr's Way
Walking in Carmarthenshire
Walking in Pembrokeshire
Walking in the Brecon Beacons
Walking in the Forest of Dean
Walking in the Wye Valley
Walking on Gower
Walking the Severn Way
Walking the Shropshire Way
Walking the Wales Coast Path

INTERNATIONAL CHALLENGES, COLLECTIONS AND ACTIVITIES

Europe's High Points
Walking the Via Francigena
Pilgrim Route – Part 1

AFRICA

Kilimanjaro
Walking in the Drakensberg
Walks and Scrambles in the
Moroccan Anti-Atlas

ALPS CROSS-BORDER ROUTES

100 Hut Walks in the Alps
Alpine Ski Mountaineering
Vol 1 – Western Alps
The Karnischer Hohenweg
The Tour of the Bernina
Trail Running – Chamonix and the
Mont Blanc region
Trekking Chamonix to Zermatt
Trekking in the Alps
Trekking in the Silvretta and
Ratikon Alps
Trekking Munich to Venice
Trekking the Tour du Mont Blanc
Trekking the Tour du Mont Blanc
Map Booklet
Walking in the Alps

PYRENEES AND FRANCE/SPAIN CROSS-BORDER ROUTES

Shorter Treks in the Pyrenees
The Pyrenean Haute Route
The Pyrenees
Trekking the GR11 Trail
Walks and Climbs in the Pyrenees

AUSTRIA

Innsbruck Mountain Adventures
Trekking Austria's Adlerweg
Trekking in Austria's Hohe Tauern
Trekking in Austria's Zillertal Alps
Trekking in the Stubai Alps
Walking in Austria
Walking in the Salzkammergut:
the Austrian Lake District

EASTERN EUROPE

The Danube Cycleway Vol 2
The High Tatras
The Mountains of Romania
Walking in Hungary

FRANCE, BELGIUM AND LUXEMBOURG

Camino de Santiago – Via Podiensis
Chamonix Mountain Adventures
Cycle Touring in France
Cycling London to Paris
Cycling the Canal de la Garonne
Cycling the Canal du Midi
Cycling the Route des Grandes Alpes
Mont Blanc Walks
Mountain Adventures in
the Maurienne
Short Treks on Corsica
The Elbe Cycle Route
The GR5 Trail
The GR5 Trail – Benelux and
Lorraine
The GR5 Trail – Vosges and Jura
The Grand Traverse of the
Massif Central
The Moselle Cycle Route
The River Loire Cycle Route
The River Rhone Cycle Route
Trekking in the Vanoise
Trekking the Cathar Way
Trekking the GR10
Trekking the GR20 Corsica
Trekking the Robert Louis
Stevenson Trail
Via Ferratas of the French Alps
Walking in Provence – East
Walking in Provence – West
Walking in the Ardennes
Walking in the Auvergne
Walking in the Brianconnais
Walking in the Dordogne
Walking in the Haute Savoie: North
Walking in the Haute Savoie: South
Walking on Corsica
Walking the Brittany Coast Path

GERMANY

Hiking and Cycling in the
Black Forest
The Danube Cycleway Vol 1
The Rhine Cycle Route

The Westweg
Walking in the Bavarian Alps

IRELAND

The Wild Atlantic Way and Western Ireland
Walking the Wicklow Way

ITALY

Alta Via – Trekking in the Dolomites – Vols 1&2
Day Walks in the Dolomites
Italy's Grande Traversata delle Alpi
Italy's Sibillini National Park
Ski Touring and Snowshoeing in the Dolomites
The Way of St Francis
Trekking in the Apennines
Trekking the Giants' Trail: Alta Via 1 through the Italian Pennine Alps
Via Ferratas of the Italian Dolomites – Vols 1&2
Walking in Abruzzo
Walking in Italy's Cinque Terre
Walking in Italy's Stelvio National Park
Walking in Sicily
Walking in the Aosta Valley
Walking in the Dolomites
Walking in Tuscany
Walking in Umbria
Walking Lake Como and Maggiore
Walking Lake Garda and Iseo
Walking on the Amalfi Coast
Walking the Via Francigena Pilgrim Route – Parts 2&3
Walks and Treks in the Maritime Alps

MEDITERRANEAN

The High Mountains of Crete
Trekking in Greece
Walking and Trekking in Zagori
Walking and Trekking on Corfu
Walking in Cyprus
Walking on Malta
Walking on the Greek Islands – the Cyclades

NEW ZEALAND AND AUSTRALIA

Hiking the Overland Track

NORTH AMERICA

Hiking and Cycling the California Missions Trail
The John Muir Trail
The Pacific Crest Trail

SOUTH AMERICA

Aconcagua and the Southern Andes
Hiking and Biking Peru's Inca Trails
Trekking in Torres del Paine

SCANDINAVIA, ICELAND AND GREENLAND

Hiking in Norway – South
Trekking in Greenland – The Arctic Circle Trail
Trekking the Kungsleden
Walking and Trekking in Iceland

SLOVENIA, CROATIA, SERBIA, MONTENEGRO AND ALBANIA

Hiking Slovenia's Juliana Trail
Mountain Biking in Slovenia
The Islands of Croatia
The Julian Alps of Slovenia
The Mountains of Montenegro
The Peaks of the Balkans Trail
The Slovene Mountain Trail
Walking in Slovenia: The Karavanke
Walks and Treks in Croatia

SPAIN AND PORTUGAL

Camino de Santiago: Camino Frances
Coastal Walks in Andalucia
Costa Blanca Mountain Adventures
Cycling the Camino de Santiago
Cycling the Ruta Via de la Plata
Mountain Walking in Mallorca
Mountain Walking in Southern Catalunya
Portugal's Rota Vicentina
Spain's Sendero Historico: The GR1
The Andalucian Coast to Coast Walk
The Camino del Norte and Camino Primitivo
The Camino Ingles and Ruta do Mar
The Camino Portugues
The Mountains Around Nerja
The Mountains of Ronda and Grazalema
The Sierras of Extremadura
Trekking in Mallorca
Trekking in the Canary Islands
Trekking the GR7 in Andalucia
Walking and Trekking in the Sierra Nevada
Walking in Andalucia
Walking in Catalunya – Barcelona
Walking in Catalunya – Girona Pyrenees
Walking in Portugal
Walking in the Algarve
Walking in the Picos de Europa
Walking La Via de la Plata and Camino Sanabres
Walking on Gran Canaria
Walking on La Gomera and El Hierro
Walking on La Palma
Walking on Lanzarote and Fuerteventura
Walking on Madeira
Walking on Tenerife
Walking on the Azores
Walking on the Costa Blanca
Walking the Camino dos Faros

SWITZERLAND

Switzerland's Jura Crest Trail
The Swiss Alps
Tour of the Jungfrau Region
Trekking the Swiss Via Alpina
Walking in the Bernese Oberland – Jungfrau region
Walking in the Engadine – Switzerland
Walking in the Valais
Walking in Ticino
Walking in Zermatt and Saas-Fee

CHINA, JAPAN AND ASIA

Hiking and Trekking in the Japan Alps and Mount Fuji
Hiking in Hong Kong
Japan's Kumano Kodo Pilgrimage
Trekking in Tajikistan

HIMALAYA

Annapurna
8000 metres
Everest: A Trekker's Guide
Trekking in Bhutan
Trekking in Ladakh
Trekking in the Himalaya
Trekking in the Karakoram

MOUNTAIN LITERATURE

A Walk in the Clouds
Abode of the Gods
Fifty Years of Adventure
The Pennine Way – the Path, the People, the Journey
Unjustifiable Risk?
Unjustifiable Risk?

TECHNIQUES

Fastpacking
Geocaching in the UK
Map and Compass
Outdoor Photography
The Mountain Hut Book

MINI GUIDES

Alpine Flowers
Navigation
Pocket First Aid and Wilderness Medicine
Snow

For full information on all our guides, books and eBooks, visit our website:
www.cicerone.co.uk